SCRIPT DOCTOR

The Inside Story of Doctor Who 1986-1989

SCRIPT DOCTOR

The Inside Story of **Doctor Who** 1986-1989

ANDREW CARTMEL

TEN ACRE FILMS

Script Doctor: The Inside Story of **Doctor Who** 1986-89

Originally published October 2015 by Miwk Publishing Ltd.
Miwk Publishing, 45a Bell Street, Reigate, Surrey RH2 7AQ.

This edition published in January 2021 by Ten Acre Films Ltd,
by arrangement with Miwk Publishing Ltd.

ISBN 978-1-908630-68-1

A CIP catalogue record for this book is available from the British Library.

Book design by Robert Hammond.

Every attempt has been made to contact and credit the copyright holders of
the photographs used in this book. Any errors or omissions will be corrected
in future printings. No infringement is intended.

Typeset in Dante MT and Futura.

CONTENTS

Acknowledgements   9

Introduction by Steven Moffat   11

Foreword by Sylvester McCoy   15

Prologue   17

1. The Search for Sylvester   19

2. *Time and the Rani* I   29

3. *Time and the Rani* II   41

4. *Paradise Towers*   51

5. *Delta and the Bannermen*   73

6. *Dragonfire*   89

7. *Remembrance of the Daleks* I   103

8. *Remembrance of the Daleks* II   117

9. *The Greatest Show in the Galaxy*   131

10. *Silver Nemesis*   145

11. *The Happiness Patrol*   159

12. *Battlefield*   171

13. *The Curse of Fenric*   183

14. *Ghost Light*   193

15. *Survival*   203

Afterword by Sophie Aldred   212

Epilogue   214

Coda   216

Doctor Who Audition Piece #1   218

Doctor Who Audition Piece #2   220

For my brother James.

ACKNOWLEDGEMENTS

I'd like to thank the following:

Ben Aaronovitch, for living through it with me and for reading the manuscript, chuckling all the way.

Matthew West and Robert Hammond, for bringing out this sumptuous new edition.

Steve Moffat for providing a groovy new introduction.

Ian Briggs, Kevin Clarke, Graeme Curry, Malcolm Kohll, Rona Munro, Marc Platt and Stephen Wyatt, for being there at the time and forming, along with Ben Aaronovitch, one of the finest writing teams in television.

Steve Cook for a fantastic cover photo — and many others.

Sophie Aldred, Mark Ayres, Ian Briggs, Kevin Davies, Kate Druce, Peri Godbold, Simon Harries, Marcus Hearn, John Kelly, Marc Platt, Mike Tucker, Mark Wyman and Stephen Wyatt for helping to source photos.

Steve Roberts, Ed Stradling and Richard Bignell for helping in our quest for the original audition scripts.

Mark McGeechan for posing for the hardback cover.

Richard Marson for making the crucial initial introductions which led to this new edition.

And Sylvester McCoy and Sophie Aldred for providing an Introduction and Afterword, for the pleasure of their company, and for bringing our scripts to life.

INTRODUCTION
by Steven Moffat

As I'm fond of telling people, running **Doctor Who** is a bit like being strapped to the front of train, yelling directions to the driver.

At this point, people usually say "You don't have to yell directions to a train driver, there are tracks. It goes the same way whatever you shout!"

And I say, "Yep."

Back in the old days, when I was first being strapped to the front of the **Doctor Who** train – no, let's abandon that metaphor, I'm far too prone to that sort of thing – when I first took this job, a scary thing happened. Russell T Davies, my far cleverer predecessor, wrote a book with Ben Cook. In it, he recorded, in heart-stopping, gut-lurching detail the day to day rollercoaster (metaphor alert) of making **Doctor Who**. As I said to Russell at the time, reading it, for me, was like taking possession of a big scary mansion, and finding the tearstained diary of the previous occupant (whereabouts unknown). I read page after page of writer/producer terror and sucked the corner of my Dalek duvet, wondering if the same nightmares would befall me.

Reader, I wonder no more. Yes, they did. All those nightmares, day after day, were mine to cherish. I do love this job, more than anything else I've ever done – but I'd like you to remind me of that when I'm stretchered past you.

However, there is more to read than Russell's wonderful book. Oh, we're not done yet. In the darker recesses of the **Doctor Who** mansion (which is strapped, you will remember, to the front of the **Doctor Who** train, on top of the **Doctor Who** rollercoaster) there is another *Document of Fear*. I speak of the volume you hold in your hands; the equally wonderful diary of Andrew Cartmel, the last of the classic series script editors; the man who saw in Sylvester McCoy and saw out the eighties.

Ah, now there's a subject - eighties **Doctor Who**. There is a fair amount of nonsense talked about this era. While the general audience has many fond memories of this time, among the fans, there is a different story. Despite many of John Nathan-Turner's productions topping the fan polls there is ... shall we say, controversy; a received idea that the show was past its best. I remember reading in some scif-fi mag a deeply stupid review of *The Caves of Androzani* (now hailed as the greatest story ever) complaining that it was all set in Portakabins! Not sure why this should be, but I can theorise.

I went to see the terrific Alan Partridge movie recently, and shortly afterwards got stuck in a conversation where I was being told, very firmly, that Alan hadn't been really good since the original radio series. And this bloke would know, apparently, because he was a fan 'from the very beginning.' But that's being a fan, isn't it? Telling people who aren't watching the show properly that it isn't any good any more!

I should know. That's exactly what I'm like. Frankly, I probably wrote that Portakabin review. So let's set the record straight.

In the last few years of classic **Doctor Who**, the show caught fire again. John Nathan-Turner took a mad but brilliant gamble and cast Andrew Cartmel as the Script Editor, and gave that fine old show a mighty kick up the backside. It took a moment to settle in (as you're about to read) but before you know it, there are shows like *Remembrance of the Daleks*, *Ghostlight*, *The Curse of Fenric*, *The Greatest Show in the Galaxy* – some of my favourite stories ever – and in every episode a new, punky sensibility that made the tired old Doctor brand new and dangerous again.

Reading the story of how those shows came about, the arguments are familiar (sorry, Andrew, JN-T was completely right about the rocket launcher) but there is something very different from the **Doctor Who** I'm used to making. And no, I'm not talking about the budget - **Doctor Who** will never have enough money, and if it did, I'd still want more. No, I regret to say (for the sake of my much-compromised personal cool) I'm talking about love.

These days, **Doctor Who** is a jewel in the crown of the BBC. That's not new – it always was. What's new is that it is acknowledged. **Doctor Who** is loved and helped at every level of the BBC, just as it should be, and just as it needs. But in the late eighties, the Beeb's senior management were stupid enough to be embarrassed by what was once, and would be again, a flagship drama: they were happy to ignore it, to starve it, to let it die. Beyond stupid and beneath contempt – decades later, it still makes me cross. I'm so glad it's not the good old days any more. You are about to read about how some great shows were made – it is remarkable that they were made in the circumstances they were.

One more thing. While we're on the subject of fan myths (we weren't, but let's pretend) there is also an idea floating about, that the old series and the new are somehow very different. Well, let's deal with that one right now. Go and watch *Survival*, the very last show of the classic series, back to back with *Rose*, the very first show of the revival. Both beautifully written and directed, and both indisputably the same show. As it always has been. As, I hope, it always will be. The seeds of everything the show became, were right back there in 1989. So thank you Andrew Cartmel, and good for you, John Nathan-Turner.

Enough about the past, and even the present – because one of the peculiarities of **Doctor Who** is that in all likelihood, its future creative leader is reading these words. Hello! Where have you been? Read on, my lucky friend, but with courage! And the very best of luck to you. And don't worry, I'll be along in a few years to tell you the show isn't as good as it used to be, and cut it out with the Portakabins.

Steven Moffat
October 2013

FOREWORD
by Sylvester McCoy

I remember John Nathan-Turner telling me the story of how Andrew Cartmel got the job script editing **Doctor Who**. John was currently the producer of the show and had the final, and indeed the only, say on who was hired for this critical post. He interviewed Andrew and they were getting along well and then he sprang the crucial question. 'If you could achieve one thing with **Doctor Who**, what would it be?'

Andrew, without an instant's hesitation, replied 'Overthrow the government.'

John grinned, his eyes twinkling as he remembered the moment. 'I decided to hire Andrew on the spot,' he said. He went on to tell Andrew that he wouldn't *actually* be able to overthrow the government, that the most he could do on a show like **Doctor Who** was get a message across about how black people and white people and green people and purple people were all equal. But he liked Andrew's passion and conviction — and his sense of humour — and he knew he'd found the right man for the job.

I attended my own job interview with John in that same red office of his, full of **Doctor Who** paraphernalia. Normally when you go up for a job the meeting takes at most half an hour, and I only had enough charm for about half an hour. But the meeting went on for two hours, so I had to start recycling my charm. I got the job, though, and that was the first time I met Andrew.

We hit it off immediately because we were of like mind. Andrew was against the establishment and in favour of a healthy measure of anarchy. We also agreed on the way the Doctor's character should develop — darker and more mysterious. It was like peeling an onion, stripping away the previous interpretations to reveal a new and more interesting layer to the character.

It was fun working with Andrew and he always involved the writers fully, bringing them along to meet me and discuss ideas. I always enjoyed these meetings, having a drink and chatting away. However, I seem to remember that most of the writers preferred hanging out with Sophie — and who can blame them?

We didn't fully realise it at the time, but it was a golden age. Andrew got on with the scripts, John sat benignly in the captain's cabin and Kate Easteal made sure that the office ran smoothly in the midst of all the madness that goes with making **Doctor Who**. I just tried to learn my lines and not bump into the monsters.

I always had the impression that Andrew was having a great time, enjoying what he was doing (either that or he was a very good actor). I also felt he was always attuned to what I wanted to do with the Doctor and this gave me the courage to go further. Andrew was my ally.

During the years when we were making the show I remember Andrew was constantly writing things down in a notebook. I didn't realise he was keeping a diary — I thought he was being inspired. But reading this book, I'm very glad he did keep a diary, because he's succeeded in bringing a whole lost era vividly back to life. Now I wish I'd kept a diary myself. But I thought we were just making a TV programme. I didn't realise we were making history.

We never managed to overthrow the government. But we made some memorable televsion. And we did have a lot of fun.

Sylvester McCoy
Richmond, London, 31 January 2005

PROLOGUE

The Daleks come through here. Ace jumps through this window.

Wednesday 2 March 1988. A cool sunny day in West London. We were preparing to make *Remembrance of the Daleks*. In the morning we went out to look at a proposed location for the school in Ben Aaronovitch's story. Ben and I sat in Andrew Morgan's car. Driving through the bright London morning traffic. Coffee smell in the back of the white Volvo – Ben had a cup and so did Andrew. The school was on a side street just off Kings Road in Hammersmith. 'Macbeth Street,' said Lynn Grant, our assistant floor manager. 'And I have a theatrical background!'

'So have I,' said Andrew. They were talking about the old stage superstition about the Scottish Play. It's said to betoken disaster. Well, we would see. Personally, I had no fears. I knew this one was going to be a classic. I glanced over at Ben, a big bloke – all right, a fat bloke – with unruly black hair. He was wearing jeans, a T-shirt, a battered old leather jacket. Meeting him in the street, you'd think 'heavy metal slob'… until you started to talk to him.

It was clear from the amused eyes behind Ben's thick glasses that the big Aaronovitch brain was buzzing away productively on something. Ben is unique in that he's a natural born screenwriter but also understands science fiction. His script for the Dalek show was terrific and I couldn't wait to see it shot.

John Nathan-Turner was waiting outside the school, breath fogging on the cool air between puffs of smoke from one of his perennial cigarettes. John was a solid imposing man of middle height, whose stance suggested suppressed energy, or maybe coffee nerves. He had a fondness for cheerfully vulgar Hawaiian shirts, but if he was wearing one then it was buried under his winter sheepskin coat. He was called John Nathan-Turner, he told me, because there was already a John Turner on the Equity books. An actor then, he became a floor manager at the BBC and worked his way up, becoming the producer of **Doctor Who**, the most famous science fiction television series these isles had yet spawned. Hell, the most famous television series.

John was a former athlete (rugby player) with a cherub's face battered by booze, and a mass of curly black hair. His eyes gleamed with mischief.

We walked into the playground, Andrew Morgan showing us around.

Andrew was the director of the Dalek story. Lynn was his assistant, a foxy little chick. 'You see,' said Andrew as we walked across the empty winter playground, 'You can have camera platforms all around here.'

Into the deserted school. Warm sleepy smell of the gymnasium. Up a low-ceilinged stone stairwell. 'This takes me back,' said John. 'This takes *me* back,' said Ben, who would have been in a school like this himself only four or five years earlier. He was the youngest writer on the team and one of the youngest to work at the BBC.

Upstairs, there was a chemistry lab exactly as I'd imagined the one in the script. Andrew Morgan strode around proudly. 'The Daleks come through here. Ace jumps through this window.' Sunlight striking across the pale wood floorboards. There was a peaceful, gentle vibe to the place. 'It's a nice school, isn't it?' said Ben. And he smiled and fumbled for a cigarette. John offered him one and they lit up as we stepped outside, back into the cool March air and the empty playground.

I stared up at the sky over Hammersmith. I was feeling a mounting sense of excitement as my second season of **Doctor Who** began to move into production. I was halfway through my sojourn on the show and it was going to be one hell of a ride.

CHAPTER 1
The Search for Sylvester

This man is corpsing me wild.

'Problems at work?' asked Sandy, the personnel officer. My heart was warmed by her protective manner. If anyone was giving me a problem at work – she seemed to be saying – she'd sort it out. What other reason could there be for me to wanting to quit my lucrative job at one of Cambridge's cutting-edge software firms?

In fact, I wanted to leave because I'd just been recruited as the new script editor on **Doctor Who**.

I had walked to work that morning, my senses sharpened with apprehension, breathing the sweet smell of the grass on Parker's Piece. I felt like I was marching to the showdown at the OK Corral. Or is it **High Noon**? When I had talked to my agent, Richard Wakeley, about quitting this job and how I should handle it, he had said, 'Let's face it, whatever you do, they aren't going to be best pleased.'

After my final interview with the personnel officer, I sat down at my computer and there was a beeping at all the computers around me as a message on the VAX – a primitive precursor of email – circulated to say that I was leaving the company. Every terminal beeped except mine. The message began, 'Believe it or not, after just three months…'

I started clearing out my desk. I rolled my chair across the office carpet to throw away some papers in my workmate Mark's wastepaper basket. He looked up wistfully and said, 'You never did get your own bin, did you?'

That night I said goodbye to Cambridge, leaving footsteps in the frost on Parker's Piece after a final drink in the Free Press. Coals smoked in the old pub's fireplace. I drank too much. I couldn't finish my Glenfiddich. They gave me a huge going away card in a bright yellow envelope. Outside, fog hung in the evening sky over Cambridge railway station. My mind had already left this place, moving ahead to **Doctor Who**.

On the train home I read **Tiger, Tiger** by Alfred Bester. I loved it, which isn't surprising since it's a science fiction classic. I lent the book to my little brother and he loved it, too. 'It made my blood boil,' said Chuck, adding though that he thought the ending was a bit 'simperingly existential'.

My love of science fiction began when I was five years old: I was standing in the Fort Garry Public Library and my Mum reached down **Have Space Suit Will Travel** for me because the 'H' shelf was too high to reach. H for Heinlein, Robert A Heinlein, a name I'd get to know well. Once I'd read **Have Spacesuit…** I read everything else the library had by him. And then I swiftly made the acquaintance of Lester Del Rey (the awe-inspiring **Day of** the Giants, in which the gods of ancient Norse mythology fight against nuclear weapons), Murray Leinster, and Andre Norton – **Storm Over Warlock** blew my young mind, I even got over my disappointment when I learned Andre Norton was a woman. As was Podkayne, in **Podkayne of Mars**. Another shocker.

Some hip cousins, heading south on the hippie trail to Mexico, turned me on to Isaac Asimov, Arthur C. Clarke and, best of all, Ray Bradbury. I remember reading **Frost and Fire** and **There Will Come Soft Rains** in my Manitoba basement on a rainy day and my life changing.

One day I wandered into the grown-up section of the library and borrowed **Dangerous Visions**, Harlan Ellison's landmark SF anthology. Once again, everything took a quantum leap forward. These were stories written by, and for, adult minds.

At the movies, I was astonished by Kubrick's **2001: A Space Odyssey** but it didn't have the emotional impact of **Planet of the Apes** ('Take your hands off me, you damned dirty ape'), which I saw sitting in the front seat of my Dad's Chevrolet at the Pembina Drive-In Cinema. I also saw **Soylent Green** and **Silent Running**, but the stand-out from that period was **The Omega Man** with Charlton Heston (again) gunning down mutants. When I later read Richard Matheson's novel I realised they'd bowdlerised it. The movie was supposed to be about *vampires*. More memorable still was **Fantastic Voyage** with Raquel Welch in her skin-tight scuba gear swimming gracefully through giant lymph nodes. I wanted to be one of the guys that peeled the antibodies off Raquel when the immune system attacked her.

Meanwhile, of course, I was also soaking up cathode rays, devotedly watching our big old black and white television set.

There was **Star Trek**, for which Ellison wrote the classic episode *The City on the Edge of Forever* and Theodore Sturgeon wrote *Amok Time*. And the magnificent **Twilight Zone** which introduced me to the writing of Richard Matheson and Charles Beaumont and Rod Serling himself (who would go on to write the script of **Planet of the Apes**). And of course there was **The Outer Limits**, scaring the life out of me with *Demon With a Glass Hand* and marking my mind forever with *Soldier* (I never forgot the scene where the soldier from the war-torn future looks in astonishment at the kitchen refuse of the 1960s family: they were throwing away *food!*). Both stories, incidentally, that were also the work of Harlan Ellison.

And, finally, there was this odd British import, which appeared erratically in the schedules of CJAY-TV, Channel 7, broadcasting out of Winnipeg, in the frozen wilds of Canada. It was called **Doctor Who** and starred a sinister gentlemen called William Hartnell and some extraordinary robots called Daleks. The eerie keening of its music and the menacing swirling of its titles must have both terrified and captivated us. But, to tell the truth, all I really remember of that handful of black and white episodes was that indelible moment when they manage to get one of the Daleks open *and this squishy black thing crawled out.*

Memories to treasure.

Fast forward almost a quarter of a century to me walking nervously into an office at the BBC in West London to meet Jonathan Powell, the Head of Drama at the BBC and the man who ultimately had the say over whether or not I got hired to script edit **Doctor Who**.

Jonathan was suave and well dressed, tall and thin, with curly pale hair, and glasses. He gave the impression of a smooth, intelligent operator, and he had a quiet voice which unnerved people. At least, it unnerved me. You had to strain to hear what he said. Jonathan was a games player par excellence so this was quite possibly a deliberate tactic. Basically, Jonathan Powell was an enigma to me. Later I met an old friend of his, and mentioned this. 'It's too bad,' said the friend. 'The job makes such poker players of these people. Jonathan used to be a great fun-merchant.'

But Powell was pleasant enough and put me at my ease. He asked me if I had any story ideas for the show and, of course, I had one ready. I don't remember the details but it was a neat little eco-parable, and he smiled politely and nodded as I finished. Then we talked about science fiction. He mentioned Robert Heinlein, which to me was a very good sign.

Finally, Powell asked me, 'Who do you think **Doctor Who** is for?' I gave a politician's answer: '**Doctor Who** is for everyone.' Jonathan shook his head vigorously and contradicted me. '**Doctor Who** is for children,' he said very firmly.

I said that I agreed, but I was lying through my teeth. I already believed, with equal firmness, that it was an adult show with adult possibilities. Kids should be able to watch it and enjoy it too, preferably from behind the sofa, but we weren't catering to them. It had to be as intelligent and serious as any piece of adult drama.

It had to be *good.*

There was snow on the rooftops of Shepherd's Bush. As I made my way to my first day of **Doctor Who**, I reflected that it would be strange to be able to say, 'I started work at the BBC in the big freeze of 1986, the worst winter in umpteen years, with snow everywhere and everything ground to a halt and the office they gave me was unheated.' But I was going to have more serious problems than the weather and unheated offices.

I took a strike leaflet from a frozen guy on the picket line outside Centre House and went up to see a personnel lady called Tanya, who was wearing green boots. Then off to Union House on Shepherd's Bush Green. There the uniformed commissionaires, Nick and Mick, were reading Stephen Bach's **Final Cut**, a scathing description of Michael Cimino's debacle, offering theories on the cinematic value of **Heaven's Gate**. The reception area was packed with little kids auditioning for **EastEnders**. My Doc Martens echoed along the third-floor corridor of Union House where I was to have my office, U312, a small room of my own just down from the **Doctor Who** office. U312 sounds like a submarine. It was still full of debris from the previous script editor, Eric Saward, who had reportedly stormed out after an argument. The key had been snapped off in the desk drawer so I couldn't open it. When, eventually, the official BBC carpenter opened it, the drawer was revealed to contain some pages of script and a glass rolling around on its side with the dried residue of red wine still in it. There was definitely a last-days-in-the-bunker feel to the place.

I went into the **Doctor Who** office to sit there and wait, all alone, for the producer and the secretary to come back from their stranded frozen weekends. The answering machine began mysteriously winding, rewinding, talking to itself. There was a message for Kate Easteal, the **Doctor Who** secretary, from some secretarial girlfriend. 'Hello Kate, you old tart.' There was also a nutcase actor ringing up to hassle John Nathan-Turner about the **Doctor Who** role. When John arrived, shedding snow, he addressed the latter, ringing the actor back. 'I think you made your point with your daily letter,' he said.

In total contrast we spent the rest of the morning watching VHS cassettes of an actor who was a very serious contender to play the new Doctor. We sat in the tiny machine-jammed video room which John called 'the Pyramid of Death'. I was choking with the heat and John's cigarette smoke in there, but the tapes were fascinating. The actor was a perky little Scottish elf called Sylvester McCoy. I kept wanting to call him Sylvester Malone. He was full of mischief and charm and anarchy. He had certainly charmed the ass off the young woman presenter of **Roustabout**, and even charmed the ass off the rabbit who was her co-star.

Sylvester was to be the next star of **Doctor Who**, if he could tone down his Scots accent for John – and if I had anything to say about it. His note accompanying the videotape said, 'Watch this one first. Love, Sylv.'

'How cheeky,' said John.

I pillaged the BBC stationery cupboards and typed a two-hander for the Doctor and Mel, his current companion, played by Bonnie Langford. The two-hander was to serve as an audition piece for actors being considered for the role of the Doctor. I typed the scene on a stone-age BBC manual typewriter, filched from the empty office next to mine. When I made a mistake I had to paint it out with a white paste called Tipp-Ex. Even in 1987 this was primitive stuff. The scene was shaping up nicely though.

While I was waiting for the Tipp-Ex to dry, I rejected a couple more unsolicited scripts from the intimidatingly large slush pile which dominated my office. I went through Eric Saward's desk, chucking all his stuff out. I wanted pristine new BBC stationery, not Eric's old paper clips and chewed pencils.

(Years later, I would be in a lift with Eric Saward and a cluster of other **Doctor Who** script editors from an earlier epoch. We were rising through a luxury hotel in London, on our way to give a talk at a convention. 'You're not a proper **Doctor Who** script editor, Andrew,' said Eric. There was immediate silence in the lift. My hackles instantly rose and I turned on him, ready for a full-scale blazing argument. Eric smiled contentedly at me and patted the comfortable girth of his paunch. He indicated the other script editors, all of them generously apportioned gentlemen with years of eating to their credit, and then indicated my own flat belly. I simmered down immediately and realised I'd been tricked by a master. It was then I began to realise what an agreeably smart guy Eric was.)

I went through the filing cabinets which stood beside the office door, and which contained every **Doctor Who** script ever written. I found the first appearance of the Daleks and read the scene, just out of historical fascination.

I delivered the two-hander. It was going to be read by John Nathan-Turner (as Mel) and Sylvester McCoy. I was now rooting for him as the new Doctor. Sylvester arrived with a Bugs Bunny briefcase and I showed him into John's office. Sylvester's politeness and utter attention to what I was saying was disconcerting; on the screen he is mischief incarnate and has no respect for anyone. I felt like saying don't waste time on me, I'm only the script editor.

As I headed home, cold flakes were still falling from the dark sky. A London schoolgirl looked up and said, 'Ah, flipping snow. Why don't you go to the other countries?'

Elsewhere, the casting of the Doctor for the new series was still an open question. Sylvester remained the front runner, but John was keeping his options open and 'seeing other people'. For instance, there was a very strange message on the **Doctor Who** answer-phone, talking about gouts of caribou blood and whales in the sky. We suspected Ken Campbell, who was coming in for an audition the next day.

Meanwhile, the Scottish nutcase (and, let's be clear here; I'm not talking about the estimable Sylvester, but rather a teenage nutcase who had been pestering the office daily for months) had actually got himself an audition. The great thing about John Nathan-Turner was that he had an open mind, and he was always willing to give new talent a chance. Of course, this could backfire. The Scottish nutcase came sweeping down the corridor past my office dressed in purple pantomime boots, purple breeches, purple velvet frock coat and a three-cornered hat with a long purple feather. One might have been inclined to admire his chutzpah, if one hadn't been acutely aware of his obsessive pestering and insistence that he *was* the new Doctor. Plus I believed his mother was waiting for him in reception.

He *wasn't* the new Doctor, as it turned out.

Afterwards, explaining why he didn't just laugh in the guy's face, John said, 'He had me spooked.' He was a little scary. He left thick blue folders full of papers. The first page said '*Doctor Who – the Peter White era*' (name changed to protect the guilty). It was followed by seven seasons broken down into episodes with cast lists and storylines for all of them.

Next up, Ken Campbell, who could only be a huge improvement. Ken is a famed British actor and founding member of the wonderful Science Fiction Theatre of Liverpool, whose staging of **The Illuminatus! Trilogy** and **The Hitchhiker's Guide to the Galaxy** have become legends. I was an admirer and I was dying to meet him. He came into John's office in a long coat, sleeveless cartoon T-shirt and a wide-brimmed hat. Nothing purple, thank God. He was surprisingly nervous and my heart went out to him.

He grinned when I mentioned the name of Charles Fort. Ken Campbell was a bald, pot-bellied, powerful-looking, bug-eyed man. He stalked the room as he read the audition script. 'Play it pottier,' said John. Ken stared at the shelf above the **Doctor Who** trophy cabinet. 'I'll look at the Ice Warrior for inspiration,' he said. The audition piece was the four-page two-hander for Mel and the Doctor which I wrote in about 15 minutes flat, and it wasn't bad. It was basically a lot of variations on the theme of time. I was thinking of Alan Moore's Doctor Manhattan when I wrote it. It plays with the notion of fragmented time. A confusion of arrivals and departures. It *is* a little weird. 'Is this right?' said Kate Easteal as she typed it. And then, 'Oh, it's sad.'

After the audition, Kate said that a friend of hers was in the pub and that Ken Campbell was there talking about how impressed he was with the new script editor of **Doctor Who**. 'He has to say things like that,' I said. 'He didn't know it was going to get back to you,' said Kate.

I had told Ken, truthfully, that I thought his play of H. P. Lovecraft's

The Case of Charles Dexter Ward was superb. But I wondered if he would still have been saying how impressed he was with me if he'd known he was unlikely to get the part. My impression of his performance was that he was too powerful and menacing. He would have been a uniquely scary Doctor. But the only opinion that counted was the producer's, and John Nathan-Turner just thought he was weird. Ken probably didn't substantially improve his cause by saying that half his face 'belongs to a spanking Colonel called Henry.'

When we weren't auditioning actors, I was busy in script conferences – rather too many script conferences it felt like – auditioning writers. Christopher Barlas came in. He was a cynical old hand; used to script edit **Emmerdale Farm**. I hadn't been particularly taken with the scripts I'd read of his, but in person he talked about things like the dangers of nuclear war and the fragmented-timeline brilliance of Pinter's **Betrayal** and a certain interest stirred in the air between us. 'Since you used to be a script editor yourself, I'll drop a certain amount of script editor bullshit,' I told him. Next up was Jeffrey Caine, who wore a pink sweater and wrote in a blue notebook and mentioned Frederick Pohl, a good name to drop. Both these writers were put forward by Diana Tyler, their agent (who was very nearly my agent). Both seemed rather tired television writers. I was feeling rather tired myself. By the time I'd finished seeing them, as well as the writers I was personally pushing for (Stephen Wyatt, Malcolm Kohll, Ian Briggs), my head was splitting open. I borrowed some paracetamol from the **Doctor Who** office and left the bottle on my desk, prominently available for instant use.

In the **Doctor Who** office we got a letter from a concerned mum begging for her little boy to be allowed to come and watch the filming of an episode. 'It would mean so much to him – particularly with the pressure of his coming A-levels,' she concluded. 'A-levels?' said Kate. 'He's no little boy. He's a fucking barker!'

'Barker' was John Nathan-Turner's expression for hardcore fans of the most annoying variety. Possibly because they reminded him of little dogs snapping at his heels, or possibly because they were barking mad.

We were gearing up to shoot screen tests. Ken Trew from the costume department said, apropos of John, 'I wonder if he wants frockage for them, and what frockage he wants?' John had taken the two-hander I'd written for the screen test home with him but that morning he forgot to bring it in again. In my heart of hearts I was secretly delighted. I had known it wasn't great and I was itching for the opportunity to rewrite it. I sat down at my desk, imagine the villainess as Maggie Thatcher, and that got some ideas going.

Wednesday 18 February 1987. I was sitting in Television Centre watching the snow fall, eating foul cold pasta in the BBC Club restaurant. Kate Easteal and John Nathan-Turner were out in the bar among the **Top of the Pops** nymphets. A band called *Curiosity Killed the Cat* were drinking at the bar, all in black suede shoes, white socks and turned-up trousers. We were there because we were shooting the screen tests for the new Doctor. Sylvester McCoy was waiting with his straw hat and a wicker basket and a huge wide US Air Force insignia tie.

'I almost walked into the Weather, and it was live,' said Andrew Morgan. We were in the control room of a tiny studio called Pres (for Presentation) B. There was a big glowing clock and a wall full of television-screens offering various views of the studio; one had the talk show **Wogan** playing on it. I nipped into the studio down below during a pause; it had white curved walls. Joanna Newbery, our assistant floor manager, was there wearing a head mike. I was feeling a stupendous rush of excitement inside me. Back in the control room I stared at all those screens. I wanted this. I could do things in this world.

Voice in the control room. 'Can we lose Network?' 'Disable the studio out.' 'Happy, Jo?' 'Happy on the floor.' 'It's coming out of my VHS input.' The sound guys were watching **M*A*S*H**, which they found considerably more interesting than the screen test.

Sylvester McCoy appeared. He came on like a cross between Bugs Bunny and Richard Burton. He blew the other candidates off the screen. Janet Fielding (who had played Tegan Jovanka, one of the earlier companions) was reading in for Mel. She was responding to Sylvester, rising to the occasion, working with him on bits of business, rehearsing with him at every pause in the recording. Their leave-taking scene put a lump in my throat.

In the confrontation scene, Janet played my character, the villainous Ms X, as if she was Maggie Thatcher. She knew! I was having flashbacks to my first stage play; feeling the occasional moments of guilt at having written all these words that people had to say. Janet *liked* Sylvester: 'This man is corpsing me wild.'

I loved seeing the cameras beavering around on the black and white monitors, the cables snaking. Andrew Morgan had an admirable bulldozing professionalism, getting things done. 'MCU of the Doctor instead of the two-shot.' Janet Fielding put one of the other candidates at his ease, talking about **Doctor Who**. 'It's not his name,' she explained.

7.35 Doctor Who

starring **Sylvester McCoy**
with **Bonnie Langford**
in *Strange Matter*
The first of a four-part
adventure by
PIP AND JANE BAKER
With the show in crisis,
Andrew arrives to some
disappointing scripts.

Melanie.....BONNIE LANGFORD
The Doctor.SYLVESTER MCCOY
Ikona......MARK GREENSTREET
Rani................KATE O'MARA
Urak......RICHARD GAUNTLETT
Sarn................KAREN CLEGG
Beyus........RONALD PICKERING

Theme music composed by
RON GRAINER
Theme arrangement and incidental music
KEFF MCCULLOCH
Costume designer KEN TREW
Script editor ANDREW CARTMEL
Designer GEOFF POWELL
Producer JOHN NATHAN-TURNER
Director ANDREW MORGAN

• BACK PAGES: 87 and
INFO: page 76

★ CEEFAX SUBTITLES

7.35 Doctor Who

starring **Sylvester McCoy**
with **Bonnie Langford**
in *Strange Matter*
The second of a four-part
adventure by
PIP AND JANE BAKER
Will Jane Baker find her
large envelope? And what's
with the giant brain?

Melanie.....BONNIE LANGFORD
Ikona......MARK GREENSTREET
The Doctor.SYLVESTER MCCOY
Rani................KATE O'MARA
Beyus........RONALD PICKERING
Urak......RICHARD GAUNTLETT
Faroon.......WANDA VENTHAM

Incidental music KEFF MCCULLOCH
Make-up designer LESLIE RAWSTORNE
Script editor ANDREW CARTMEL
Designer GEOFF POWELL
Producer JOHN NATHAN-TURNER
Director ANDREW MORGAN
Videos: The Seeds of Death,
BBCV 4072,
Pyramids of Mars, BBCV 4073 *and*
The Web of Fear, BBCV 4074
from retailers at £9.99 each

★ CEEFAX SUBTITLES

CHAPTER 2
Time and the Rani I

How are they going to unclip the people?

As the big freeze continued, there was hardly even a skeleton staff in place and the corridors of the BBC were haunted by the ringing of unattended telephones. I discovered that BBC toilet paper came in giant rolls in big flat metal drums and didn't have any perforations and the saw-teeth on the metal drums didn't work. My office was freezing. Pipes were bursting all over London. In the street, the crunching echoes of my footsteps followed me in the snow. The milk I poured on my cereal in the morning had been out on the windowsill overnight. It wasn't frozen, but it was so cold it hurt my teeth.

But, as I said, the weather wasn't going to be the problem.

I had this script for the first four-parter of the new **Doctor Who** season. It was by Pip and Jane Baker, seasoned pros who had written the stories which I didn't like in the previous season. They also created the Rani, a female Time Lord, which was an excellent idea.

However, I personally didn't like their new script and if I had had the power to do so I'd have had it completely rewritten or simply ditched it. The story was solid enough, but it didn't do anything for me. And I didn't like their characters or their dialogue. It was a script where characters say things like 'earthling' and 'radiation wave meter' (they go back to the TARDIS in search of the radiation wave meter, which is kept in the 'tool room'). They also say things like 'inaction is anathema' and 'egalitarian', 'inert', 'debilitating', 'indolent' (twice) and 'incompetent fool'.

I talked to John about the script and we decided we had to have the Baker twins (which is what John called them; they're actually a husband and wife team) come in to discuss changes. John told me to make the phone call. Jane Baker answered the phone. I came to learn that she always does this; her husband Pip would apparently only pick up the instrument in the event of a national emergency. Towards the end of our conversation, Jane said, 'But basically you like the script?' And I heard myself saying, 'Oh yes. Basically the shape of the script is fine.' I hung up, feeling like I'd just lost my virginity.

A couple of days later, I had my first meeting with Pip and Jane Baker. The meeting didn't go well. I couldn't begin to be honest with them about how hopeless I felt their script was and they seemed to me utterly intransigent about the few changes I did suggest.

After the meeting, I called goodbye to Pip Baker, who was hurrying off down the corridor in search of the loo. 'Pip! Andrew said goodbye to you!' called Jane Baker. This may well have been the highpoint of our relationship.

In the course of the meeting, I let slip that I was on a training course the following week and Jane Baker shrieked 'training' with what I took to be venomous pleasure – because I was just this upstart of a kid who didn't know anything. I was angry about this, but also about the script (*Strange Matter* was what it was initially called; it was later re-titled *Time and the Rani* in an homage to J B Priestley's **Time and the Conways**). To my mind it was all wrong. I personally felt their take on science fiction in general and **Doctor Who** in particular was old fashioned. On top of that, there was their dialogue and characters. I was depressed. How could I allow a script like that to go out in a series with my name on it?

The script involved a group of geniuses from history who have been kidnapped by the villainous female Time Lord, the Rani. I suggested that instead of Solomon, who was one of the historical geniuses Pip and Jane had chosen, they should substitute Albert Einstein. I thought we could make dramatic play of his part in developing the atom bomb and thereby give the whole thing some relevance and bite. But Pip and Jane wanted Solomon. Indeed, they had written an end-of-episode cliff-hanger around the old anecdote of Solomon passing judgement on who was the real mother of a child. If you don't know the story (surprisingly few people do), it goes something like this. Two women come to Solomon, each one claiming a certain baby belongs to her. Solomon offers to chop the baby in two so they can share it equally. Of course, the real mother reacts with horror at this suggestion and is thereby identified. Clever old Solomon.

In the Bakers' draft script we see Solomon just as he is being presented with the vexed question of the baby and the two mothers. Pip and Jane's notion was to stop the sequence just as the axe was being raised over the baby. *Voilà!* Cliff-hanger. To be continued next week. What would happen to that baby? The nation would be in suspense.

Never mind that this would all have been a bit expensive and involve building a special King Solomon set and costuming extras just for a brief sequence, I felt it would also be completely irrelevant, because the Doctor and his companion would have nothing to do with it. Fortunately the baby execution concept fell by the wayside when it turned out John was baffled by the whole sequence as written. I had to recount the Solomon anecdote to him – he'd never heard it before. When I explained, comprehension dawned, but not approval.

I was given the tricky duty of telling the Bakers that this sequence had to go. Jane Baker hurried to John's office, saying they couldn't possibly substitute Einstein for Solomon in the script, because nobody knew the story of Einstein and his letter to Roosevelt. 'But Jane, I didn't know the Solomon story,' said John Nathan-Turner softly, bless him.

It was a hollow victory, though. Einstein was instated in the script in a half-hearted way. Even now you might discern some faint subplot about him signing a fateful paper concerning the nuclear age and the fate of mankind. Or perhaps not.

Andrew Morgan came in to discuss the Pip and Jane Baker script which he'd be directing. 'It'll be good,' he kept saying.

I walked into West Ruislip tube station and there was a sign up saying 'Toilets are closed, all out of water. The telephones don't work. Beware of wet paint.' I'd just had lunch with Pip and Jane Baker.

This was John Nathan-Turner's idea. He wanted to create peace and harmony between his script editor and the writers of his first four-parter. Not a bad idea. John's heart was very much in the right place, and he was fond of Pip and Jane. 'Take them to lunch. Be nice to them. They just need some bollock-tickling.' He arranged some expenses and, with BBC money stuffed in my pocket, I boarded the train with trepidation, on my way to visit Pip and Jane and win them over.

I had lunch with them in a Spanish seafood restaurant. The wine was fantastic. 'Say when, Pip,' I said as I refilled his glass. 'When,' said Jane. She also said, 'Pip wants the salmon.'

To me the Bakers seemed strange, intractable. I despaired of ever reaching them. They were bursting with integrity and high principles, always fighting for the rights of the writer – principles which I felt were perhaps deserving of a better cause than the script currently under discussion. The wine was absolutely fantastic, though. Was it some kind of Rioja?

I had some scripts by Chris Russell in my bag in the boot of Pip and Jane's Opel Manta. Chris Russell was more like it. I had pretty much abandoned any hope of finding common ground with the Bakers. Despite lunch and the wine we never broke the ice. We were still very much at arm's length and I was reduced to asking Tetrap questions.

Pip and Jane went out of their way to drive me to the tube station, which was kind of them, and which I appreciated.

The following Monday, Jonathan Powell cornered me in the loo at Threshold House. 'Jeopardy,' he said. 'Jeopardy, jeopardy, jeopardy.' He was talking about Pip and Jane's script. 'Build up the Rani. Make clear why she needs the Doctor,' he said. I was amazed that he'd actually read the script. And he seemed to have a clear line on what it was lacking. 'Jeopardy.'

'No, it's great. It's going to be good,' said Andrew Morgan. He kept saying that.

Tuesday 17 February 1987. At the first production meeting, I was sitting with Ken Trew as he sorted through an overflowing ashtray, counting how many of the chain-smoked butts were his own. Sitting across the table from me, both fleshy and hunched forward, pink faces listening attentively, were John Nathan-Turner and Andrew Morgan. The producer and director looked like brothers.

Geoff Powell's designs for *Time and the Rani* were brilliant – this was more like **Dr Strangelove** than **Doctor Who**. Delicate green marbling on the cardboard walls of his model, crumpled paper to suggest the rock of a cliff, photocopy of a lake in a Welsh tourism ad with his drawing of a building stuck onto it. Andrew was saying 'Use a high-speed video camera for the dream sequence.' Ken suggested recycling sandals from the previous year. More technical talk concerning the Tetraps: 'We'll try little dummy figures hanging and CSOing the rest of it. We'll just have to sort out a harness for the actress.' (CSO means **c**olour **s**eparation **o**verlay. It's BBC terminology for what, elsewhere, is known as chroma key compositing.) Pip and Jane's script was offering a fair number of technical challenges, like the giant fluorescent tarantula and the web it spins. 'Tarantulas don't spin webs.' 'Fluorescent ones do.'

At the end of a long, inconclusive morning with a problematical script involving a lot of special effects, Andrew turned to the technical team and grinned and said, 'Great. I think it's great. Over to you boys.'

Pip and Jane came into the **Doctor Who** office for a story conference. We also had Andrew Morgan there and that was a great advantage. This made it three against two. It also offered a wonderful confusion whenever John said something like 'And Andrew thinks…'

Andrew opened by saying, 'Thanks for all the problems. No, no. I love it.'

Jane Baker kept on insisting on the reinstatement of lines that I'd cut. 'I don't know if it was a mistake in the typing,' she kept saying. There ensued a detailed argument, because she wanted the word 'earthling' back in one of their speeches. There were other gems, like 'It says here "You fool". It should be "You incompetent fool".' John slipped me the wink. 'Four and a half thousand to build that central console,' he said, referring to the set of the Rani's lab. He was slyly making the point that a lot of money would have to be spent to bring the Bakers' script to life. And so they should play nice.

My hostility towards the Bakers abated somewhat when I saw how disappointed Pip was about the puzzles he wanted to include in the story: 'What you're saying is that you don't want the puzzle gates at all.' I felt sorry for him. (In so far as they linger in my memory, these puzzle gates required one to solve a symbolic puzzle on the surface of the door to get them to open.)

I walked to lunch, floating on air. Andrew and John and I, with our three-pronged attack, seemed to be making progress. Would we actually get the sort of script I wanted out of this? Well, no.

Our Friday story conference resumed on Monday and I sat there swallowing my anger. I felt that Jane Baker had just been unbelievably rude to me. If I'd had a free hand as a script editor on this first story, I'd have let Pip and Jane Baker go at this stage. John had to keep talking, because I was speechless with rage.

This meeting was the exact opposite of Friday's. The Bakers weren't giving an inch. Indeed they were reclaiming lost ground. John kept talking. His story ideas were strong, clear and effective. I counted to ten, waiting for my anger to fade. Watching a cloud pass the window.

Outside the office, John told me, 'Don't rise to the bait.' But I was still smouldering with rage. At the end of the meeting, I just walked out without bothering to smile or say goodbye or shake hands. Later, John called me into his office and told me that this had been a strategic mistake. He said that the correct thing to have done would have been to see them off politely, then to shut the door of the office and go into conference with him and Andrew.

'Then they'd be shitting conkers,' said John.

One piece of good news, which ordinarily would have made the day. We'd got Sylvester McCoy. John got on the phone, haggling over Sylvester's contract. He explained about the lucrative side benefits of the US convention circuit. 'Mother Pertwee's out there now,' he said.

'It's like wrestling with smoke,' I said to Jo Newbery, in regard to some difficulty or other, and she cracked up. Of course, I'd forgotten – that was a line from the screen test I wrote and she must have heard it about 300 times while she had been floor managing that evening. Jo and Christopher Sandeman, the assistant floor managers from Andrew Morgan's crew, had popped into my office to hang out and were as excited as kids when I opened a filing cabinet and showed them the first **Doctor Who** script ever. 'See that name,' said Jo, going down the technical credits list, 'Barry Newbery? That's my dad.'

Kate Easteal laughed as she opened the **Doctor Who** fan mail. Someone had sent in a suggestion for the new Doctor's new companion. The letter read, 'Here's a piece of crumpet.' And they'd enclosed a fragment of breakfast crumpet, wrapped in tin foil.

Friday 27 February 1987. 'Don't send me up, please,' said John Nathan-Turner in an icy voice. 'I haven't come down from last time.' There was an awkward silence in the planning meeting. Geoff Powell, our immensely talented designer, insisted on cracking jokes and he had just cracked one too many. John just asked him a question in John's usual soft, somewhat effeminate voice and Geoff replied in an identical voice. He probably wasn't intending to deliberately take the piss out of John, but that's what it sounded like.

Andrew Morgan's face was reflected, expressionless, in the shiny table top. Jo sat opposite me, in a mauve shirt, with that fetching streak of premature silver in her lustrous dark hair.

Monday 2 March 1987. Sylvester McCoy was on **Blue Peter** in the afternoon, for about 45 seconds. The presenter was asking **Doctor Who** questions and Sylvester, poor bloke, didn't know the answers. Before he could get his balance back, the snippet was over. The next day he appeared on a Birmingham afternoon talk show with John-Nathan Turner. John had bright blue shoes on. Sylvester had got over **Blue Peter** debacle of the day before and was on brilliant form, wonderfully irreverent and insulting and anarchic.

Thursday 5 March 1987. I phoned up the Bakers to see if we could get their rewrites before the weekend. Pip on the phone was like a fish out of water. 'I'll put you on to Jane. She's just getting a large envelope.' Then there was a voice in the background on the phone. 'Is that the phone? I didn't hear it. I was just getting a large envelope.'

A week later, I took the final episode of Pip and Jane's script to Drama Typing at the Television Centre (past the ironing boards and turn right at the smell of fresh laundry from the costume department), but only after another early morning hour on the phone to Pip and Jane, although it was actually only Jane who spoke to me over the phone.

I was being pushed hard by Andrew Morgan to get the rewrites on Pip and Jane's scripts. I was pushing myself hard as well. Cigarette ash on my floor after a meeting with Andrew Morgan. Papers strewn everywhere. Andrew was showing the strain as much as I was, as we kept pushing at the script, trying to pull it all together. 'Yes, love,' he said into the phone. 'Sorry darling.' In fact, Andrew Morgan was a very beefy and un-camp, ex-rugby-playing sort of guy.

'Thought we were finished! Thought we were finished!' he screeched after a three-way phone conversation with me and Jane about the script. 'We don't want to prostitute the whole thing,' Jane had said.

'I'm sure that it will all be very happy and lovely,' said Andrew.

'Any scripties?' said John Nathan-Turner. We were waiting for various drafts from various writers. By now, Pip and Jane were not the only ones on board. There was a whole group of other writers at various stages of being commissioned. I was getting like the father of a large family when I addressed one of them. One morning, I called Robin Mukherjee 'Stephen-Ian-Malcolm-Robin'. I took him to lunch at Television Centre and almost choked to death on a roast potato.

I got a letter from Australia telling me how John had dragged **Doctor Who** down into the pit. But I could only go by my own experiences since I had joined the show and to me John Nathan-Turner seemed utterly a realist. He spotted flaws in scripts and his suggestions *worked*.

Monday 30 March 1987. Ian Fraser, who was production manager on *Paradise Towers*, appeared in my office doorway. He wanted to talk about Patrick Troughton, who had died that weekend. I met the Second Doctor once, shortly after I started on the programme. He was sitting on a filing cabinet in the **Doctor Who** office, swinging his legs, talking to Kate Easteal. Pat Troughton was a nice guy who seemed very young, much younger than his calendar years. It was a shock that he'd gone.

But, in a life-goes-on kind of way, the same day also saw rehearsals begin for *Time and the Rani*. Bonnie Langford turned up with a metallic briefcase with Mickey Mouse on it. Sylvester arrived with one with Sylvester and Tweety Pie. Sylvester looked at the briefcases and said, 'Let's mate them.'

'How are they going to unclip the people?' asked Bonnie, referring to the actors in the role of Tetraps who would be required to hang upside down.

During the rehearsal, Pip and Jane were as excited as kids, which I could understand, and which made me feel quite kindly disposed towards them. We had a read-through and Pip and Jane flipped madly through the scripts, muttering about the changes they weren't aware of. 'I couldn't look at them, I didn't dare,' said John Nathan-Turner afterwards.

It was strange how the story's heart began to beat during a read-through. The script began to come to life. 'Let me feel your purse – whoops, a Freudian slip – *pulse*,' said Sylvester, reading his lines.

After the rehearsal, I walked out into the car park with Sylvester and John. Sylvester asked if there was anything back at the office for him. 'Only fan mail,' said John, 'Nothing lovely.' Back at the office, the **Doctor Who** answer-phone had 21 messages on it, people ringing about Patrick Troughton.

Friday 3 April 1987. The location shooting for *Time and the Rani* was about to begin and I got a ride to Frome in Somerset with Chris Sandeman and Joy Sinclair, our production assistant. We passed a giant white chalk horse on a green hillside. We began shooting on a wet Saturday morning, in a quarry, naturally. I sat in the outside broadcast (OB) van, called a scanner, where I could see what was happening on various screens. Voices in the dark. 'The tape is running with bars on it.' 'Give us a guess on bars timing because it's getting wet up here.'

Out in the rain in the stone-strewn quarry BBC technicians were wandering around wearing helmets that said things like 'Gaffer'. Geoff Powell was wearing one that read 'Dickhead'.

Someone in the scanner took objection to Sylvester's tartan scarf. Presumably it was causing interference on the picture (I think they call it the 'herringbone effect'). Sylvester stood there, small and unhappy, as big burly technicians took his tartan scarf away. My maroon 100 per cent acrylic scarf was almost famous. I offered it as a substitute and it very nearly got the job.

I left the scanner and went and sat in the make-up caravan, looking at a basket on a shelf marked 'Spare ladders and genius wigs'. Sylvester McCoy was sitting here with me, his face slightly orange in the television make-up. We had picked our way across the orange mud together. I was glad to have the chance to chat and make friends with Sylvester.

Outside in the wet, Dave Chapman our talented, affable, long-haired video effects designer, was looking for fossils. We were now in Cloford Quarry, near Nunney, and it was raining heavily. One of the guys in a BBC hardhat was squeegee-ing the rainwater off the triangular mirrors on the face of the Rani's TARDIS. The Tetraps' eyes rolled in their masks under radio control. The Tetraps were the season's monsters. Four-eyed (hence Tetrap), pot-bellied, bat-winged. Not in the least scary, as far as I was concerned. But when the actor was standing near you in one of those costumes, at the edge of your vision, it was an eerie presence.

'You look ever so silly,' said John Nathan-Turner. I was wearing a white helmet over the khaki hood of my anorak (the anorak was not yet universally recognised as the badge of the geek, merely a useful waterproof garment). There were pissing sounds as the big red plastic tea and coffee containers were drained onto the ground. The production manager, Tony Redston, was calling for silence on his megaphone, calling for the builders to turn off their generator. 'Kill the genny, please.' 'They can't hear you,' said Jo, 'the genny's making too much noise.'

Back at the hotel that night, in the bar, we sat at a table covered with glasses containing the location drink, gin and tonic. I asked Andrew how he had got that brilliant shot in the **Zoo Vet** episode he directed where the lion looked like it had really died (sad majesty, light going out of the eyes).

'The lion really died,' said Andrew.

The hotel walls were thin and I was kept up half the night, first by the sound of somebody bonking frenziedly and then by the sound of somebody throwing up with equal violence. I told Andrew about this as we drove to the next day's location and he said, 'They were probably both Geoff.' We were now at Whatley Quarry near Murder Combe. The rain had stopped and the sun had just come out. 'Here's the old currant,' said one of the technicians. 'The old currant bun.' Rhyming slang. 'There's the continuity gone for a Burton.'

'Amazing place isn't it?' said Andrew Morgan. It was. We drove down the sloping road into this deep quarry and it looked like a miniature Grand Canyon in the morning sun. Cables were spooled in figures of eight on the mud. Ducks were swimming in the milky green water of the sump. Sylvester's powerful voice echoed across the quarry. He had a copy of the **Observer** rolled up in his pocket. Headless Tetraps wandered around. Bonnie Langford sat in a blue Land-Rover. She was wearing a blue satin **Peter Pan – The Musical** bomber jacket. A camera was standing on its tripod in the water. Tony Redston was on his megaphone. 'How are we doing chaps? Can we have Mark now please? Losing a lot of time here.'

The visual effects designer, Colin Mapson, rigged an explosive charge in the beautiful water of the sump. 'Anyone want any more ear defenders?' asked Jo. 'Oh yes, I enjoyed the last pair,' said Ken Trew. Then there was a stinging explosion, like a fist driven deep into the sump, raising a saucer of mud in the milky green water. I felt the explosion more than heard it, with my ears blocked. Felt it in my solar plexus. It made the inside of my body tingle.

We took a shot of the animatronic Tetrap head, poking its tongue out when the controls were squeezed. 'Yuck,' said Bonnie. 'That is vileness personified.'

'Once more with feeling,' said the cameraman.

The quarry had been dressed with stylised gargoyles designed by Geoff, beautiful menacing shapes that looked like they had come from the prow of a dragon ship. They made me want to ask Geoff for a production sketch, as a souvenir. I was helping wrap boulders in blue foil to pile up on the steps between the gargoyles. Sylvester was crouching behind a rock rolling his R's: 'The Rani's overriding priority.' A jet fighter thundered over the quarry in the thick cloud, bringing a momentary fear of nuclear war, a prehistoric monster in the fog. An extra scratched his nose with a Tetrap gun.

Karen Clegg, who played Sarn, had yellow and green reptile make-up with scales on her face. She was looking at the extras in their Tetrap outfits. They were like sort of furry, four-eyed, pot bellied vampire bats. 'They're like those things in **Return of the Jedi**,' said Karen. 'What are they called?' 'Wookiees.' She nodded. 'Wookiees. Or gremlins. I liked the gremlins. Not the nasty ones. The nice ones.' The wardrobe crew had all stuck Tetrap tufts on their hardhats.

On our fourth day on location, Chris Sandeman told me he'd never seen a script editor stay on location for more than an hour and a half before. When Bonnie yawned on six monitor screens, everyone in the scanner started to yawn. Walkie-talkie conversations buzzed around me in the dark. 'I've sprayed out the camera end cable Barry.' 'Punch up two, please.' Gargoyle heads hung grimly in the quarry in the rain. 'I don't like this fucking rain,' said Andrew. Karen was running through puddles. Hollow BBC plastic rocks could be seen wobbling on the monitor. A yellow cable box was in shot. 'We'll quigley that out.' 'Good morning Dickhead,' said Andrew's voice. Geoff must have arrived.

They set up a scene with Mark Greenstreet and Bonnie. 'Do you want any screaming?' asked Bonnie. After each take, the wardrobe people moved in with umbrellas to shield the actors from the rain. The wardrobe people's Tetrap tufts were looking a little wet and bedraggled. The actors' voices echoed in the quarry. Mark, who played Ikona, had to make himself cry for a scene. He began crying while everyone else standing around was still laughing at a joke. Wanda Ventham, as Faroon, had to cry too. I watched her on the monitor screen. A superb actress bringing every detail of emotion to the surface, the suffering showing on her face. It was a moment of genuine magic. Then the bastards made her do it again. Then they decided to use the first take after all.

I choked on smoke-gun smoke as I inspected the ridged skull of the reptilian skeleton Colin Mapson had built. Colin rigged another explosion. I put in my bright yellow ear defenders. There was a jagged low boom that hit me like a kick in the stomach. Smoke everywhere and that firecracker smell. Andrew said, 'Now we'll do the skeleton's point of view.'

We had almost finished. I wandered over to take one last admiring look at Geoff's gargoyles. The wind whipped through the quarry and on the steps blue foil was blowing free of the rocks. None of the rocks I had wrapped, though.

7.35 Doctor Who

starring **Sylvester McCoy**
with **Bonnie Langford**
in *Strange Matter*
The third of a four-part
adventure by
PIP AND JANE BAKER
The quarry is big and wet
and cold and full of BBC
staff.

Rani................KATE O'MARA
The Doctor.SYLVESTER MCCOY
Beyus........RONALD PICKERING
Faroon.......WANDA VENTHAM
Melanie.....BONNIE LANGFORD
Urak......RICHARD GAUNTLETT
Ikona......MARK GREENSTREET
Lanisha.................JOHN SEGAL
Special voices
PETER TUDDENHAM, JACKI WEBB
Incidental music KEFF MCCULLOCH
Visual effects designer
COLIN MAPSON
Script editor ANDREW CARTMEL
Designer GEOFF POWELL
Producer JOHN NATHAN-TURNER
Director ANDREW MORGAN
★ CEEFAX SUBTITLES

7.35–8.00 Doctor Who

starring **Sylvester McCoy**
with **Bonnie Langford**
in *Strange Matter*
The last of a four-part
adventure by
PIP AND JANE BAKER
The new Doctor is
established, three more
stories to go. Can Andrew
succeed? And what IS that
giant brain?

The Doctor.SYLVESTER MCCOY
Rani................KATE O'MARA
Beyus........RONALD PICKERING
Melanie.....BONNIE LANGFORD
Urak......RICHARD GAUNTLETT
Ikona......MARK GREENSTREET
Faroon.......WANDA VENTHAM
Special voices
PETER TUDDENHAM
JACKI WEBB
Incidental music KEFF MCCULLOCH
Lighting HENRY BARBER
Script editor ANDREW CARTMEL
Designer GEOFF POWELL
Producer JOHN NATHAN-TURNER
Director ANDREW MORGAN
★ CEEFAX SUBTITLES

CHAPTER 3
Time and the Rani II

The Invasion of the Scripts.

John invited me into his office with Graeme Curry, another of our upcoming writers, to watch Kate O'Mara, the Rani, being interviewed on a talk show in Birmingham. 'Come on darling,' said John to the screen. 'Get the plug in.'

The following Monday, I experienced for the first time in my life the physical shock of seeing my name in print. I was leafing through **Doctor Who Magazine** and suddenly found I was in it. It said something like, 'Since the new script editor, Andrew Cartmel, has just arrived, it seems likely that it was the producer who commissioned Pip and Jane Baker.' Very astute. I was glad that people could work out for themselves that I was not responsible for *Time and the Rani*.

Thursday 16 April 1987. Kate Easteal's birthday. I gave her a card for five-year-olds with a punch-out red devil mask. 'It's great!' said Kate. 'It's topical!' It was also the day of the producer's run at the Rehearsal Rooms in North Acton before we went into the studio for *Time and the Rani*. Shaking hands with Sylvester. Bonnie dancing in a mirror. 'This is the scene where I put the microthermister in,' said Sylv. 'Take it out, you mean.' For the purposes of rehearsal the microthermister was an empty vodka bottle.

The following Monday, we were in the studio for **Doctor Who** serial 7D, *Time and the Rani*. We were shooting the first block of material that hadn't been shot on location. I sat in the carpeted darkness of the control room looking at a big glowing clock that had an arrow for a second hand. There was absolute silence, lights placed over steps so people didn't trip. Being new to the process, I was thinking that the way things were shot was so fragmented, how could they begin to make sense of the story? The technical problems were so immense that the acting was the least of it. On one of the screens smoking blood ran down a trough. 'We'll do this rehearsal without gunge,' said Andrew. 'What I want to know, John, is what all those extra hips and legs are doing there.'

'Hello Pip,' I said to Pip Baker. 'It's Andrew,' said Jane Baker, who was standing beside him. Down on the studio floor, Andrew Morgan was eating an apple. The camera jerked into a close-up of his blue sweater. 'Cue the gunge.' We saw technicians' sneakers in the Tetrap eyrie. The mystery of the image as the camera drew back amongst black curtains and people and cameras and props. We saw Einstein at lunch. 'Kindly keep smoking to a minimum in the interest of health and comfort,' read the sign in the control room by the monitor screens. (It seems unbelievable now, but at the time people were indeed allowed to smoke in places like this. As an ardent non-smoker, I spent my years on **Doctor Who** gagging on cigarettes belonging to the old-school chain-smokers who still dominated the field.) Dave Chapman, the video effects guy with long hair and a beard, smoked hand-rolled cigarettes in liquorice Rizla papers. He was watching snooker on his black and white monitor.

Geoff Powell wandered through shot with a ladder. 'That's the shot,' said Andrew, 'if Dickhead can get out.' Geoff had chosen his own nickname, but it couldn't have been less appropriate. Even on our low budget he was a designer of genius. On the studio floor, Kate O'Mara said, 'I wasn't on my marks. I couldn't see the fuckers at all.'

'Where's Richard's head?' Excitement. Coloured lights. 'Recording is running up.' The cover for the TARDIS viewing screen squeaked something awful as it went up and down. Tetrap voices distorted. I left the quiet darkness of the control room to go down onto the studio floor. The hair on the top of my head was stirring under the heat of the lights. The studio had a lemon shampoo smell under the blaze of those hot lights. There were folded newspapers stuck in cameras as everyone waited to get started.

We were behind schedule. People were starting to blame other people. Tension was rising. Andrew was in the control room talking to Tony Redston on the intercom. 'We are slowing things down considerably,' said Andrew. 'We've got to give them a break,' said Tony. 'I appreciate that, old love,' Andrew responded patiently.

Actors in Tetrap suits were hanging upside down in front of a blue screen. They looked very hot in their hairy suits with their monstrous heads removed, red faces showing. The rostrum they were positioned on was getting in the way of the camera. I sat in the producer's booth with John as he's reminisced about the good old days of disciplinarian BBC floor managers who stood for no nonsense and would call out the first line of every scene, and so on. 'We had some wonderful lesbians,' said John wistfully, 'but they're all directing now.'

Andrew was in the control room saying, 'Well, move the fucking rostrum.'

I was arranging last-minute drafts of scripts from Malcolm Kohll and Ian Briggs, so that we'd have five out of six for the final production in typing before I went on holiday. Things were getting a bit hectic. A taxi was sent to pick up one script from Malcolm's house in Islington. Meanwhile, I'd just rung Fraser and Dunlop, my literary agents, where I'd set up an appointment for Ian (I felt he was a good writer who deserved an agent) and then asked Hayley, my agent's assistant, to grab episode two of *Dragonfire* from him and put it on a bike. 'They're coming from all over London!' said John. 'It's the invasion of the scripts.'

Nine days later, I was back from Spain, sitting in my office with my ears peeling from sunburn. There were green leaves spreading over Shepherd's Bush Green. I walked into the **Doctor Who** office that morning and there were two giant circular photographs of Sylvester McCoy, one in colour, the other black and white, bigger than the biggest wheels of the biggest vehicle you've ever seen. They were each the size of a kids' paddling pool, wrapped in plastic, propped up against the filing cabinets, with address labels on them. BBC Enterprises had ordered them for an exhibition but the contractor had fucked up, interpreting the dimensions as inches instead of centimetres. I loved it. It was like **Spinal Tap**. So anyway, Enterprises was unable to use them and simply gave them to us. I immediately grabbed the black and white one and stuck it on top of my filing cabinet (where it would remain for months). Sylvester's giant face looked down at my office, seeming to stare cross-eyed at the address label on his own nose.

Across the corridor, director Chris Clough was working on this season's three-parters (*Dragonfire* and *Delta and the Bannermen*). I was delighted to hear that he was considering Theresa Russell as the teenage English biker in Malcolm's *Delta and the Bannermen* script. I didn't tell him that she wasn't right for the script because I wanted to meet her. She had starred in Nic Roeg's **Bad Timing**, which was one of my all-time favourite films.

I went to the Rehearsal Rooms wearing a T-shirt I had bought in Spain (A Lichtenstein style comic panel of a crying girl's face and a word balloon reading 'Nuclear war? There goes my career'). I was here to watch the second producer's run – the scenes which would be recorded in the studio the next week. I was beginning to see it all come together, the bits from location and the previous studio stuff, and piecing it all together in my head. A priceless education. Chris Sandeman was loping fatly around, standing in for a Tetrap. Mark Greenstreet edged over to me and whispered, 'That's my favourite line.' His favourite line was, 'If you're not careful you'll find out from inside that cabinet.'

'Janet Fielding's got that one,' said John, looking at my T-shirt.

Back into the studio on Sunday for round two; the final three-day block of *Time and the Rani*. Reggae on Shepherd's Bush Green in the cold night, booming off the windows of Barclays Bank. It was a summer festival, though it didn't feel like summer. I went into the studio early to look at Geoff Powell's set. Gold paint and brown paint and black Day-Glo had been run together on the floor and the resulting blend ingeniously made the wood look like marble. Up that close, the set looked good, but it looked like a set. But through the cameras it looked real. Wandering around the sets, sitting in the control booth, I was becoming aware of the fabulous potential of this show. What a wonderful situation to find myself in.

Sunday morning Bank Holiday confusion on the studio floor. Andrew Morgan was down there. 'Let's start please, Tony. Go, go.' 'I don't think he's got his earpiece in,' said someone in the control room. 'Whose air hose is this?' asked someone else. There was the ringing of dropped pipes. 'The door at the back ought to be shut, Tony.' 'Dave, Roger, would you like to look at the blue and see if it's on the right axis? Is it too dense?' 'It's much too dense.'

Kate O'Mara lifted a machine panel. 'Jesus wept.' It was heavy. We could see a giant red brain glowing on a raised ramp. I seemed to recall that John had suggested this brain, way back in the first rewrite conferences we had had with Pip and Jane. I believe he'd said something like, 'What we need in this story is a giant brain. They're getting all these geniuses and sucking their intelligence into a giant brain.' And there it was.

Sylvester was shaking his arms to warm up. There was excitement and colour and movement on the screen. The red light came on outside the door. Running up to record. 'Relax and enjoy it,' said Andrew Morgan. 'A good note,' said Kate.

Andrew bit savagely into an apple as we waited for the special effects to be rigged for the third time. 'Jesus, this just isn't fair, mate.' Then, suddenly, it was a take. The scene sizzled. It was a revelation the way everyone woke up when the scene worked. 'We really must watch those booms, loves.'

Voices in the control room. 'Am I vibrating?' asked Sylvester. 'Sylvester's vibrating, yeah?' 'Just slowly.' 'If this was on the other way around, I could vibrate properly,' said Sylvester. Down in the studio, he lifted up his bum so Jo Newbery could slide his copy of the **Observer** out of sight under it. They closed the door of the cabinet and Sylvester vibrated wildly inside it, wearing a modified pair of earphones that were, according to the script, sucking out his brain impulses. Sylvester stopped vibrating. 'Bless me father, for I have sinned,' he said, suddenly equating the cabinet with a confessional booth. 'This may be the most ridiculous thing I have ever been asked to do.' Up in the control room, John murmured, 'You ain't seen nothing yet.'

John Nathan-Turner was a pillar of strength, when you consider the stress he was under. He had been flying up to Birmingham to see his father who had had a stroke while trying to escape from hospital after minor surgery ('He made a bid for freedom,' said Kate Easteal). His father had knocked down two nurses and a security guard before they could subdue him. Now he was paralysed. And John's mother was on the verge of the latest in a series of nervous breakdowns.

As I looked at Sylvester on the screen in the control room, I had the feeling that **Doctor Who** was entering a golden age. I was watching and learning, things coming together in my head. I was thinking about my idea for a TV series, 'R O Bott'.

We finished our studio work on Sunday on schedule and that made a tremendous difference to morale – at least to my morale. 'Is that the last shot with us?' 'It could be.' Donald Pickering was not at his happiest. But then he was being asked to roll down stairs in green make-up. Kate O'Mara was holding some prop, saying, 'What do I do with this? I daren't put it under my arm, dare I?' 'Give it to Urak,' said Andrew. 'Poor doll, he's got claws,' said Kate sympathetically. 'Will he be able to take it?'

We had lost 16 minutes of video effects footage – colour separation overlay for the viewing screen – which had been wiped by some idiot in the basement that morning. The fun just kept on coming. 'Boom well in,' said Andrew. Everything was slowing down. It was like quicksand. I was almost falling asleep in the quiet drowsy warmth of the control room. At that moment, I was glad I was not Andrew Morgan: the pressure would have killed me. No one had told him about the colour separation overlay yet.

Half asleep, I felt drowsily drawn to Kate Easteal, who was sitting in the chair in front of me. Kate was lovely, and sexy. I was feeling a certain erotic yearning for her there in the control room darkness. On the monitor Kate O'Mara was saying, 'Is it possible to get in a position where I don't have to kick you so hard? I'm terribly worried about hurting you, Donald.' 'It's all right, darling,' said Pickering. Dave Chapman and Anne Faggetter, the production associate, were in an adjacent control room discussing the lost CSO footage. The film **Waterloo** was playing on a light man's monitor. 'I saw this in 1970, Leicester Square.' 'Was it better then?' 'It was wider.'

The pattern of lights on the lighting control board flickered like a night sky, like a constellation, like a **Doctor Who** special effect. Geoff Powell had scripts on the brain. Literally. It was Tuesday, the third day of the last studio of *Time and the Rani*. It was also the birthday of my girlfriend Kate Druce. I sat in the corner of her bedroom while she knelt on the floor, unwrapping some of the presents I had given her. A green H. R. Giger poster. A Halo Jones T-shirt. Looking at the simple joy on Kate's face I felt happy in every corner of myself.

Back at the studio, the cavalcade of Kates continued, with Kate O'Mara standing in front of a gleaming red brain the size of a small elephant (I love this show!). Geoff, who had designed the brain, was getting angry because people kept leaving their scripts on it. I guess it was so big it was like a table or something.

My girlfriend Kate Druce came out to the TVC restaurant to meet me for a birthday lunch. We kissed in the ring road. 'I'm in a jazzy, smashing, rip-roaring mood,' said Kate. 'I'm in my flying and drinking and drinking and driving mood.' I showed her around the studio. The special effects men loved her. Colin Mapson made the veins on the giant brain thrash just for her. One of Colin's visual effects assistants, Mike Tucker, animated the animatronic Tetrap's head so it stuck its tongue out and Kate saucily tongue kissed it.

Pip and Jane Baker were there. My girlfriend Kate knew the story of the conflict over the script between me and Jane, and I thought Kate might beat her up in the control room. But Kate (Kate One) behaved herself. Meanwhile Kate Easteal (Kate Two) said, 'I'm going to have a word with the non-speaking Tetrap.' Then she went to drool over the non-speaking Lakertyan. I went to watch them set the charges to blow up the giant brain and listened to Kate O'Mara (Kate Three) cursing when she fluffed a line – something that seldom happened. Sylv was holding up his whirring electric hand-fan for her. 'That fucker gave me the wrong fucking cue,' said Kate Three.

The brain gantry – a platform in the air, red and smoky, huge brain seething – was taking on the aspect of a haunted house for the actors. Sylv freaked in mid-line. 'Someone's talking!' he shouted, 'I heard them!' Tension was high here on the tower of the giant red brain on this, our last night of shooting.

We got the shot. We blew up the brain. We finished the show. With the help of Mike Tucker and a giant metal BBC ladder, I almost wiped out a bank of lights in the process of filching one of Geoff's magnificent dragon heads. If we hadn't rescued it, it would just have ended up in the trash. We got it down safely. I went for a drink in the BBC Club. John Nathan-Turner rolled his eyes in amused tolerance when he saw the giant shape wrapped in a black bin liner. My souvenir. 'What's that, then?' he asked archly. Taxi back to Kate Druce's. The taxi driver thought the dragon's head was great. He reminisced about **Doctor Who** as we drove through the empty night streets. When he was a kid, it worried him a lot when the Cybermen turned to foam. He went to the cinema to see the first movie with Peter Cushing in it, and all over the cinema parents were having to explain the recasting of the Doctor to their kids who were saying, 'That's not him. That's not the Doctor.'

Kate opened the door and I stood there with this giant dragon's head, a grey black serpent skull carved out of foam packing, with tubes for eyes. It looked like something dreamt up by H. R. Giger or Ian Miller. (The dragon's head would preside proudly over the hallway in our basement flat in Baron's Court for years to come, precariously hanging by its bracket from a gas pipe.)

The following day I was at the office and my sister's friend Kelly Maxwell, over from Canada bearing birthday presents, came in. Kelly had a yellow jumpsuit and yellow eye make-up. I took her to lunch at Television Centre, then down to Studio Two to see the mammoth sets from *Time and the Rani*. But in Studio Two the floors were gleaming. The giant room was completely bare. Everything had already gone, like a dream on waking. The doors were open at the far end. Sunlight and green trees.

Wednesday 27 May 1987. There was an article about Sylvester in the latest issue of **Starlog**, an American science fiction magazine. What will his Doctor be like? 'He'll be a little smaller,' McCoy predicts.

My girlfriend Kate had taken her last sociology exam that day, and she dropped into my office, where I was talking to Ian Briggs, bearing a bottle of champagne. I got a bunch of blue and white striped paper cups from the BBC canteen. Kate took off a pair of worn-out socks and threw them in the bin in my office. I took them out of the bin and put them in the filing cabinet drawer with all the drafts of Pip and Jane Baker's script.

We diplomatically closed the office door so the sound of champagne corks couldn't be heard across the corridor where they were busy with pre-production matters. I poured blue and white striped paper cups full of champagne from the foaming bottle for Kate and myself and Ian Briggs. We proceeded to get drunk in celebration. I wrote a new label for the filing cabinet drawer: 'Pip and Jane and Dirty Socks'.

Two months later, John Nathan-Turner and I were sitting in the plush office of Jonathan Powell, watching the first episode of the new season of **Doctor Who**. I wasn't worried. I was beyond caring. I hadn't had any breakfast and was just concerned about my stomach rumbling while I was sitting on this smart white sofa. After the screening, Jonathan Powell said, 'Great hat. I like the hat.' He was referring to Sylvester's new headgear.

The next week, I took a day off from my holiday in Kent to come up to London for the press launch of the new **Doctor Who** season at BAFTA ('Naffta', John Nathan-Turner called it) in Piccadilly. I walked in and Kate Easteal and John stared at me in astonishment. I'd had a haircut and was wearing a suit and tie. Sylvester patted me on the shoulder and told me about his canal holiday. Andrew Morgan bought me an orange juice. Then we sat down in the screening room with the press. The lights went out and *Time and the Rani* started, the sluggish story limping across the screen. After the screening, there were pizza and drinks for the press. A guy in a leather jacket scooped up a few quick slices of pizza, then left. 'That's **Time Out** off,' said Kate. London's trendy weekly magazine wasn't ever going to be a fan of *Time and the Rani*. In fact, it was hard to imagine anyone who would be.

Bonnie Langford was talking to the press about Michael Grade. 'He

Me with a Tetrap head on location in Cloford Quarry
for *Time and the Rani*

Above, left: Myself, the swimming pool robot and Stephen Wyatt
on location for *Paradise Towers*

Above, right: Stephen Wyatt at a dinner party at his house

Above, left: Me pretending to use the drinks machine telephone
on the set of *Paradise Towers*

Above, right: Bonnie Langford, Stephen Wyatt and myself in front of a
TARDIS spattered with Red Kang graffiti. My t-shirt is **Life in Hell** — a
comic created by Matt Groening, still some years before he invented **The
Simpsons**. Don't say I wasn't there first.)

Stephen Wyatt and the lovely Catherine Cusack
in the studio for *Paradise Towers*

Me in the marvellous Bannerman spacecraft designed by John Asbridge,
from *Delta and the Bannermen*

Kate Easteal and Sara Griffiths on the party set
for *Delta and the Bannermen*

Sara Griffiths as Ray, with me in a particularly beautiful location for *Delta and the Bannermen*

Sara as Ray on the motorscooter with the Chimeron child (Jessica McGough) on location for *Delta and the Banermen*

Don Henderson as Gavrok being mean to Bonnie Langford
as Mel on location for *Delta and the Bannermen*

Sylvester and Sara Griffiths on location
for *Delta and the Bannermen*

Malcolm Kohll, Kate Easteal and myself on location for *Delta and the Bannermen*. We are in a holiday camp and Kate is riding a giant rabbit, one of the surreal playground attractions there

Me, looking rather goofy, at the Acton Rehearsal Rooms with Susie Brazier (a visiting friend) and Sophie Aldred, plus the creature from *Dragonfire*

Above, left: Myself and Leslie Meadows as the Dragon in *Dragonfire*. My T-shirt reads "Nuclear war? There goes my career!"

Above, right: In the studio for *Dragonfire*

Above, left: Sophie having her first promotional picture taken as Ace

Above, right: Tony Selby as Glitz on the set of *Dragonfire*

gets all the flak, poor soul.'

What a shame that we had to start a new season, and a new Doctor, with this story.

Monday 7 September 1987. The first episode of the new series of **Doctor Who** was broadcast. The following day, an agent rings me up to hassle me about the episode. 'I thought you were one of the good guys,' she said. 'How could you inflict that on us?' I was depressed enough as it was.

My girlfriend and I watched the episode in bed, gazing at on an old black and white TV perched on a chair. Pip and Jane's dialogue echoed in the autumn night. 'It's very wordy,' said Kate. 'They use pretentious words like "persona".' She put her head on my shoulder as the credits came up. 'Script editor,' she said.

7.35 Doctor Who
starring **Sylvester McCoy**
with **Bonnie Langford**
in *The Paradise Tower*
The first of a four-part
adventure by STEPHEN WYATT
Andrew meets a lot of
Kangs. Which Kangs are best
remains to be seen.
Yellow Kang...ASTRA SHERIDAN
Melanie.....BONNIE LANGFORD
The Doctor.SYLVESTER MCCOY
Young Caretaker
                    JOSEPH YOUNG
Bin Liner.....ANNABEL YURESHA
Fire Escape......JULIE BRENNON
Blue Kang Leader
            CATHERINE CUSASK
Deputy Chief Caretaker
                CLIVE MERRISON
Tilda.................BRENDA BRUCE
Tabby.........ELIZABETH SPRIGGS
Pex................HOWARD COOKE
Chief Caretaker
                RICHARD BRIERS
Theme music composed by
RON GRAINER
Theme arrangement and incidental
music KEFF MCCULLOCH
Costume designer JANET THARBY
Script editor ANDREW CARTMEL
Designer MARTIN COLLINS
Producer JOHN NATHAN-TURNER
Director NICHOLAS MALLETT
★ CEEFAX SUBTITLES

7.35 Doctor Who
starring **Sylvester McCoy**
with **Bonnie Langford**
in *The Paradise Tower*
The second of a four-part
adventure by STEPHEN WYATT
The caretakers are all too
young, the lighting's too
bright. We may never find
out which Kangs are best.
Chief Caretaker
                RICHARD BRIERS
The Doctor.SYLVESTER MCCOY
Deputy Chief Caretaker
                CLIVE MERRISON
Melanie.......BONNIE LANGFORD
Pex................HOWARD COOKE
Fire Escape......JULIE BRENNON
Bin Liner.....ANNABEL YURESHA
Blue Kang Leader
            CATHERINE CUSASK
Tabby.........ELIZABETH SPRIGGS
Tilda.................BRENDA BRUCE
Maddy...........JUDY CORNWELL
Incidental music KEFF MCCULLOCH
Make up designer SHAUNNA HARRISON
Script editor ANDREW CARTMEL
Designer MARTIN COLLINS
Producer JOHN NATHAN-TURNER
Director NICHOLAS MALLETT
★ CEEFAX SUBTITLES

7.35 Doctor Who
starring **Sylvester McCoy**
with **Bonnie Langford**
in *The Paradise Tower*
The third of a four-part
adventure by STEPHEN WYATT
Richard Briers is playing it
his own way. But we may
finally have discovered which
Kangs are best.
Tabby.........ELIZABETH SPRIGGS
Melanie.......BONNIE LANGFORD
Tilda.................BRENDA BRUCE
Deputy Chief Caretaker
                CLIVE MERRISON
The Doctor.SYLVESTER MCCOY
Bin Liner.....ANNABEL YURESHA
Fire Escape......JULIE BRENNON
Pex................HOWARD COOKE
Chief Caretaker
                RICHARD BRIERS
Maddy...........JUDY CORNWELL
Blue Kang Leader
            CATHERINE CUSASK
Video commentary
                SIMON COADY
Incidental music KEFF MCCULLOCH
Visual effects designer
SIMON TAYLER
Script editor ANDREW CARTMEL
Designer MARTIN COLLINS
Producer JOHN NATHAN-TURNER
Director NICHOLAS MALLETT
★ CEEFAX SUBTITLES

7.35 Doctor Who
starring **Sylvester McCoy**
with **Bonnie Langford**
in *The Paradise Tower*
The last of a four-part
adventure by STEPHEN WYATT
RED KANGS! RED
KANGS! RED KANGS
ARE BEST!
Chief Caretaker
                RICHARD BRIERS
Bin Liner.....ANNABEL YURESHA
The Doctor.SYLVESTER MCCOY
Fire Escape......JULIE BRENNON
Blue Kang Leader
            CATHERINE CUSASK
Melanie.......BONNIE LANGFORD
Pex................HOWARD COOKE
Deputy Chief Caretaker
                CLIVE MERRISON
Maddy...........JUDY CORNWELL
Incidental music KEFF MCCULLOCH
Lighting HARRY BARBER
Script editor ANDREW CARTMEL
Designer MARTIN COLLINS
Producer JOHN NATHAN-TURNER
Director NICHOLAS MALLETT
★ CEEFAX SUBTITLES

CHAPTER 4
Paradise Towers

Which corridor are we in now?

When one door closes, another one opens. As I closed the door of 312 Union House on Pip and Jane Baker after a particularly depressing meeting, I stepped through into my office where *Paradise Towers* author Stephen Wyatt was waiting.

Seeing Stephen cheered me up. I had been chuckling aloud, sitting in this cold office, scarf tucked into my sweater, when I first sat reading the script for his television play **Claws**. I promptly invited him in and took him out to the Bush Hotel Bar where we sat in a corner discussing his **Doctor Who** storyline. 'I'm busking madly!' he said.

Friday 30 January 1987. I rang Stephen to check on the spelling of his name; it was about to be typed on a commissioning brief. The following Monday, I dropped in on him in his office at the Script Unit. (The Script Unit was a wonderful organisation dedicated to finding and nurturing new writing talent. I hope I don't sound too cynical when I say naturally it's now gone.) I bestowed the news that he was being commissioned to do an episode of **Doctor Who** – with the deadline only a fortnight away.

'Oh shit!' he cried. 'Oh fuck!'

'Don't panic, Stephen.'

'I like to get my panicking out of the way at an early stage,' said Stephen, and began flicking through his diary.

A week later, he dropped in and delivered his first draft of the first episode. He left me to read it on my own. I sat turning the pages and laughing aloud, all alone there in the early morning BBC corridors.

On Tuesday 17 February (the day of the first *Strange Matter* production meeting), John Nathan-Turner gave me the thumbs-up for Stephen's script, which was the best news in a long time. But it would still be a rather rocky road. Two weeks later, John was on the phone to Stephen at the Script Unit. 'Hello, dear,' he said, and proceeded to rake Stephen over the coals, in a humane and good-humoured way. I felt somewhat betrayed by my new writer because I had told him in confidence that Sylvester McCoy was going to be the new Doctor and then reportedly he'd told half the Script Unit. Of course, I should have kept my mouth shut, so I was also in the shit, because this was big news, valuable publicity, and it was supposed to have been kept under wraps until the correct moment.

I went through Stephen's script, which was excellent, with John, talking about the technical limitations of the show and what was achievable in terms of special effects with our budget and our resources. He talked about the pacing of a chase scene involving a robot cleaner in the high-rise block and the need to keep the people moving slowly enough for the robot to give convincing pursuit. 'Having worked with robots before...' said John.

Monday 16 March 1987. As the tribulations of the first story continued, my little ray of sunshine was to read episodes three and four of Stephen's script. 'He smiles as only a zombie can,' read one of the scene directions. A few days later, John and Stephen and I sat down to have a script conference. John was concerned about the little old ladies in *Paradise Towers* who are cannibals. 'You realise that they're also lesbians,' said Stephen.

I continued working with Stephen on the script in my office. 'We could do the scene that way,' said Stephen. 'That would make it more – let me see if I'm using this correctly... *muscular.*' He was taking the piss out of my script editor's jargon. You could tell when my script conferences were going well by the demonic laughter echoing down the hallway of Union House.

Frances Graham, the production assistant on Stephen's story, didn't love me any more. That was putting it mildly. I had asked her to photocopy some scripts. She refused. Then, manifesting an admirable survival instinct, she darted to the producer's elbow just as I was about to lodge a complaint. She ended up photocopying the scripts, but she didn't love me any more.

That Friday, Stephen and John and I went out to the pub with Nick Mallett, who was going to direct *Paradise Towers*. Back at the **Doctor Who** office, Kate Easteal said, 'I'm actually going to read Stephen's episode two. I never felt any urge to read Pip and Jane's.'

The following Tuesday, Stephen delivered his episode three and four rewrites and I laughed aloud as I read them. With Malcolm Kohll delivering his episode one of *Delta and the Bannermen* and Ian Briggs about to be commissioned, the season was starting to fall into place. In fact, I'd started worrying about the next season. 'If there is one, and if we're working on it' – the television professional's eternal mantra.

I was worried about finding the writers, getting them into the right frame of mind. 'You're a very cunning taskmaster,' said Stephen, 'I'm sure you can draw these things out of people.' He volunteered to work with me again next season.

Friday 3 April 1987. Nick Mallett was conducting casting interviews for *Paradise Towers* across the corridor from my office. Prospective Pexes filing in. Kangs in the tea bar.

I bought a new T-shirt, this one featuring Calculus Cat, with the logo 'Death to television'. I walked into the **Doctor Who** office and Kate looked up at me from her desk and said, '"Death to television!" I love it. I want one.' John was in his office studying a receipt for Patrick Troughton's send off. 'Kate,' he called, 'That was a very reasonable price for that wake.'

In mid May, *Time and the Rani* still wasn't over. There were still post-production and special effects. I went out to North Acton to the Visual Effects Department to watch Andrew Morgan directing the model shots. I stood in a dark room full of technicians adjusting lights. They couldn't quite achieve what they wanted and shrugged in resignation. 'I'll just have to tell my old mum to turn the brightness up, that's all.'

There was a big red globe of a planet on a stand. The camera was moving back along a track to make the spaceship model appear to fly. The white spray that blazed out of its jets was air brush propellant.

I went wandering around the workshops, looking at stuff being made for future stories. The giant white robotic cleaners for Stephen's were very impressive, rolling smoothly on concealed wheels as if hovering on air. There was a tiny white crab model of the swimming pool monster, also from *Paradise Towers*.

John came into the office with his parents' dog, Pepsi. Because of the recent tragedies in his family, John was going to have to look after Pepsi. 'The cover of the *Radio Times*, dear,' said John and showed me an old yellowing cover from the 1970s featuring a young Pepsi and another pup.

Kate came into the office while I was talking to Stephen Wyatt and read us this brilliant letter from this kid, a 17-year-old **Doctor Who** fan in New Zealand. He described an earthquake that hit when he was at school. 'We were shit scared,' he said. The phone rang halfway through Kate's recital and I missed the rest of it. 'You missed the bit where they went out on the playing fields and the ground felt like jelly,' said Stephen.

I had just finished the 'Notes for New Writers', which I had started to write months earlier, when I first joined **Doctor Who**. We desperately needed this, to send out with all the mountain of unsuitable, unworkable (indeed, frequently near-psychotic) story material we had to return to the fans, before it buried us alive. I burst into laughter as I proofread it. Kate Easteal had typed it and at the bottom of the list of things hopeful writers must do she'd added 'PS Bugger off'.

John had put a yellow Post-it note on the 'Notes for New Writers'. It read 'Excellent'. I felt quite proud. Invigorated, I set about clearing the office of six months' accumulation of slush-pile scripts and correspondence. In many ways the American fans were the most memorable: 'I am interested in submitting a plot/story for the **Doctor Who** series and I would therefore like to know your specific operating parameters in detail.'

Kate Easteal poked her head in the door. 'Do you want anything from the tea bar?' she asked. 'Or are you waiting for the substantial finger food?'

The substantial finger food was at Nick Mallett's get-together above Albertine's wine bar. This was a practice peculiar to Nick as a director, where the cast and the production people got to know each other over copious free wine. What a great idea. I get to meet all the Kangs. 'Kang' was a conflation of 'Kid Gang' and they were futuristic female juvenile delinquents who inhabited the decayed urban wasteland of Stephen's high-rise story. Stephen wittily gave them names to reflect their environment. One blonde girl was Annabel Yuresha, better known as the Red Kang called Bin Liner: 'My boyfriend thinks it's a perfect name for me.' Fire Escape couldn't make it.

There was Astra Sheridan, who played the non-speaking Yellow Kang. She had a fascinating dark stain streaking out from the brown iris of her right eye. Her character got killed in episode one. There was Catherine Cusack, the Blue Kang Leader, wearing a purple dress. 'Cusack as in...?' 'I'm afraid so.' I liked her immediately.

Clive Merrison, the Deputy Chief Caretaker, was reminiscing about stealing knickers and flying them from the flagpole over Lime Grove in the golden days of **Doctor Who**. Stephen was talking to Richard Briers (the Chief Caretaker) at length. Everyone was drunk. All the heterosexual actors had got Annabel in a corner. I was complacently in love with my girlfriend, so I left them to it. Kate Easteal was pissed and red faced and laughing. I really liked Kate. She had apparently mooned an entire army convoy coming back from Tonbridge Wells the previous weekend.

The morning following this debauch I overslept. When I woke up, I just knew I was going to be late for the read-through in North Acton. I missed the tube by a matter of seconds and was left standing on the platform at White City, fighting off despair. I was going to be late. It was crucial that I get to the read-through but I was going to be late. Another train pulled in. And terminated. I was going to be late. I was grinding my teeth. Another train pulled in and I got on board and sitting at the other end of the carriage was Sylvester with his Sylvester and Tweety Pie briefcase, studying his script. 'I'm so relieved to see you,' I said, sitting down beside him. I could stop worrying. If I walked in late, I walked in with the star.

At the read-through there were unexpected pleasures. I had known Stephen's script was good, but there were moments of dramatic chemistry which I hadn't anticipated. The read-through was a wonderful success. Gales of laughter at the funny bits. The Rezzies (elderly female residents in the high-rise slum, played by Liz Spriggs and Brenda Bruce) imperiously tore out the superfluous script pages when I told them these had been dropped from the new draft. Nick was wearing a terrific suit and tie. Stephen had changed his earring especially for the occasion.

I looked at these pretty young girls who were playing the Kangs and I began to realise how easy it was in this business just to shag your brains out.

There was a real buzz to this read-through. Excitement.

The next day, we had the run-through, also at North Acton. We began to see what the story was like with some blocking of physical action for the actors.

Nick Mallett moved like a dancer, snapping his fingers softly to punctuate a scene. I believe he used to be a dancer, actually.

After the run-through, I met Mike Tucker for lunch in the canteen above the Rehearsal Rooms and he gave me a load of photos from the last studio (the *Time and the Rani* shoot). I sat with the Kangs (Catherine Cusack, Annabel, Julie Brennon) and Sylvester and looked through the photos.

Friday 22 May 1987. There was a rain smell of spring as I walked to the tube. Smell of flowers on the circular road at Television Centre. The guard on the gate said good morning. Soon I was passing traffic roundabouts, walls of green, endless beautiful green trees, big houses. We were in Chalfont St Giles. Stephen and I went in a chauffeur-driven car with Judy Cornwell (guest-starring as Maddy), going out to an Iraqi millionaire's mansion where we were shooting the swimming pool sequences for *Paradise Towers*.

Clive Merrison was already there, sitting in a parked car. He told Stephen that the Tricycle Theatre had burned down. Stephen was genuinely shocked. 'When?' 'Last night. This morning. Now.'

The house was amazing. Beautiful pink, red, yellow, orange, lavender trees across the shaggy green lawns. There was an incongruous mock-up of an elevator standing in the middle of the overgrown grass. Howard Cooke (Pex) and Bonnie Langford were stepping out of it.

There were black and yellow BBC frogmen standing in the swimming pool. I sat watching them on a monitor. When they rewound the tape, the water in the pool turned purple. The yellow and black robot crab hit the water buzzing, the lights in its eyes flashing on and off.

There was no heat or light or water on in the millionaire's mansion and the only loo available was an outdoor one with a broken lock. The cistern had to be filled with a hose every time it was flushed. Stephen, Sylvester and I were queuing outside when the cistern overflow pipe began to spew water onto the flagstones. Sylvester laughed his maniacal laugh and from inside Catherine Cusack called 'It's not me.'

Between shots, people were milling around. The robot crab lay dripping on a table. Bonnie was shivering in a white bathrobe. The black Blue Kang wandered past. I sat on a sofa with Stephen, surrounded by Kangs, thinking that we had started all this. Make-up women were busy with spray cans of colour, taking scissors to scrape the bangs of a Blue Kang wig and make it curl. I studied a Kang crossbow. On the monitor Sylvester was shaking hands again in playback.

Outside, the visual effects guys emptied water out of the crab. I asked if the hole in the crab's chest was for anything. 'Oh yes,' they told me. 'A great big fucking tentacle comes whazzing out.'

Kangs moved around in a mirrored bar. There was a hypnotic gleam to the white light bellying on the blue bulge of the swimming pool water. Stephen Wyatt noticed that the Deputy Chief Caretaker's suit was immaculate when it should have been shabby, tatty, stained. From the scanner, we got them to rip an epaulette. There was technical chatter in the scanner darkness as the Kangs came into shot. 'Dave, the extreme Red on the left. Her face is too shiny.'

I wandered through a wood full of bluebells at lunchtime with Stephen, talking BBC politics by the gravel tennis court. The Kang called Fire Escape was scratching her bottom in her red tights. Nick Mallett was discussing a shot, talking in ellipses. 'It's not… When she's… I'll edge back… It'll be okay.' He sat by the swimming pool watching a monitor. There was a microphone lead running into the swimming pool. Everyone moved as they struck the lights and I was caught up in a crowd of Kangs. 'Are you going to be in this shot too, Andrew?' asked Bonnie.

'We have to lose that lamp now, Nigel. What did I do with that Stanley knife?'

Friday 29 May 1987. The performances of the Rezzies were still deemed to be slightly over the top. 'It is a bit eating-the-scenery,' said John Nathan-Turner. It was the run-through for the first studio, and Richard Briers was there, as one of the living dead. Clive Merrison sat reading the **Evening Standard**. Annabel Yuresha was sitting backwards on a chair, her legs wrapped around it, doing things to my brain. Ian Fraser was pretending to be a robot. Catherine Cusack took off her sweater and showed me her James Dean T-shirt (I'm notorious for my T-shirts). Then Annabel got her legs on top of the chair. Bonnie was tied up in a chair of her own, her face covered with a black shawl, squeaking like a rubber mouse. Julie Brennon was slim and tanned and sexy, wearing a **101 Dalmatians** top.

Julie and Catherine and Annabel knelt to mourn their dead compatriot, three faces clustered together, two pale and one deeply tanned. It was a moving moment. Nick Mallett snapped his fingers to end the scene.

Wednesday 3 June 1987. At the Rehearsal Rooms, Bonnie and Sylvester stepped out of an as-yet-non-existent TARDIS, indicated by tape marks on the floor, to confront urban squalor in Paradise Towers. They kicked over some as-yet-non-existent rubbish and reacted to some ditto rats. Stephen and I turned to each other and simultaneously whispered 'Rats!' Neither of us had anticipated such authentic set dressing.

Clive did a wild double take in his scene with the robots. 'Top that,' said the Rezzies. There was a script in the sink of the Rezzies' makeshift kitchen. 'I've dropped my sausage,' said Liz Spriggs as they mimed the action. The run-through was fun, like a holiday. Stephen watched with fierce interest, his eyes gleaming. He was seeing his story begin to come to life. The word made flesh. Brenda Bruce was screaming into the sink. Kate Easteal stood by a window, quietly watching. 'Flaming Carrot Comics,' said Sylvester, reading my T-shirt before a scene. Between scenes, I talked to Catherine Cusack about T-shirts and the Derby. John Nathan-Turner snapped at me, the first of several such episodes as the season moved on and tension mounted up. It left me feeling sour and angry for the rest of the day.

Thursday 4 June 1987. 'Will you run to record please.' We were in the studio for the first day of studio shooting on **Doctor Who** serial 7E, *Paradise Towers*. Sylvester as the Doctor steps out of the TARDIS into the rubbish of the Fountain of Happiness Square and sees a tall metal pump and he takes off his hat and greets it.

'Oh Doctor,' says Bonnie as Mel. 'Well, you never know, Mel.' This was a pure Sylvester McCoy ad lib, and it's wonderful. The writer, Stephen, instead of asking for it to be taken out, was keen for it to be left in!

We watched the eerie gliding quiet of the cleaner robots. Voices in the control room. 'Strike the TARDIS. Watch the rubbish.' The next shot in the recording order called for *fully practical rats*. The shot description was 'tight on rats moving through rubbish'. Stephen was giggling. 'Don't go down to see the rats without me,' he said.

Sitting there in the control room watching Stephen's story come together, the first of my stories for the show, I was intensely happy. I was thinking of my work and my girlfriend, and I was wonderfully aware of the richness of both areas of my life, the personal and the professional.

Stephen and I went down to the studio floor. 'The rat lady is just coming across.' 'Ooo. Nice tit-for-tats,' said a BBC technician when he saw the cages the lady was carrying. Tit-for-tats being, of course, more rhyming slang.

The light men and the sound men erupted into a tribal argument about trying to position a boom where a light was standing. 'It *is* the Deputy Chief Caretaker,' said Stephen, alluding to a character in his script who stands as a symbol for moronic rule-besotted bigots everywhere.

One of the banes of our existence on **Doctor Who** was the occasional really troublesome fan. One such person, a 13-year-old whom we'll refer to by the pseudonym Nigel Feather (apologies to anyone who is actually called Nigel Feather) was a particular thorn in our side at that time. He specialised in being pestering and obnoxious, to the extent that we had a graffito on the notice board in my office that read 'Death to Nigel Feather (13)!'. To which Kate Easteal had added 'Back-biting scum'.

Well it turned out that, while we were busy shooting *Paradise Towers*, Nigel Feather had been trying to get into the studio. Kate told us that he had been caught with a forged letter. He had taken the letter we'd sent him saying he couldn't visit the studio, chopped it up, re-typed it and photocopied it. The little fucker.

'Is that a clear for the rats?' The rodent lady took our little furry friends away again. There was a purple neon *lift* sign and arrow against the green-lit set corridor. Sylvester and Bonnie and the Kangs seemed to be having so much fun that I wanted to be there with them. Non-speaking Kangs in the Television Centre Red Assembly (it sounds like something out of Poe, but it's a colour-coded studio tea bar) were being chatted up by BBC lads. There was a succulent honey-skinned extra holding a handbag; 'One of the other Kangs asked me to hold it for her,' she said. Stephen and I were talking about doing a Kang sequel. 'Teenage Hells Angels in Outer Space,' said Stephen, trying a title on for size. 'They meet a monster and instead of being scared they say, "Tell us what we want to know or we rip your tentacles off!"'

Bonnie yawned musically as Henry Barber (the lighting designer) stepped into shot to check the lights. Domestic tat was being added to dress the Rezzies' flat: Flying ducks, seashell ashtrays, purple fluted vases. 'More, more,' said Stephen. I was looking at Annabel's lovely bare Kang arm.

It was going to be a good show and Sylvester was going to be a great Doctor. That much was evident to me already.

Stephen was very concerned that the Caretakers should be suitably seedy looking and slovenly and shambolic. At this point, they still looked too spiffy and well organised. I'd already spoken to John about this once on Stephen's behalf (it was my job to bridge the gap between writer and producer). But still nothing seemed to have been done. The Caretakers looked too much like a crack cadre and not enough like a shower of scruffy losers. Stephen urged me to repeat the observation. So I moved forward in the control room darkness to remind John. He turned to me and snarled, 'Listen. Don't you check on me. I'm the producer.'

I retreated and sat down again, feeling humiliated and angry. That was the second time in two days that John had snapped at me. I was grinding my teeth with rage and doting on notions of revenge: that's the worst mistake he's ever made, and so forth.

'Are you sulking?' asked Stephen.

The following day I was still stung and fuming about John's behaviour. I talked to my landlady, a BBC news producer, about it. I told her my theory as to why it was happening. There's a story about Stanley Kubrick when he was working on Spartacus. Apparently he got along very well with his star, Kirk Douglas, until there was a screening of the work in progress for Howard Fast, who wrote the novel on which the film was based. Fast is supposed to have enthusiastically praised Kubrick's obvious genius and congratulated Douglas on finding such a talent. Thereafter Douglas took umbrage at the notion that someone else was getting the praise and conceived a bitter dislike of Kubrick. Anyway, that's how the story goes. And I put myself in a similar position to Kubrick. I assumed that someone had praised John on his script editor and John had reacted Kirk Douglas-fashion.

Looking back with the hindsight of years, though, I suspect there was a more straightforward explanation. The enormous pressure of making the show for John had been compounded by the even more enormous pressure of events in his family (his father's stroke, his mother's nervous breakdowns).

Back in the studio on Friday, I avoided John. Down on the studio floor, the door of the Rezzies' set was being drilled, in preparation for Pex's entrance and I could hear Bonnie and the Rezzies on the soundtrack reminiscing about dentists. 'Well, I was a dental nurse,' said Liz Spriggs.

There was a very effective shock – it shocked me three times – when Pex smashed down the door after the warm lull of Stephen's dialogue: 'Make the most of the peace and quiet.' *Smash.* 'It's called dramatic irony, guv,' said Stephen.

The eerie green lights of the corridor. The robot approaching. 'Less program on the feed to the robot.' More fully practical rats. A fully practical caged budgerigar. 'Andrew, what I want to know is if you're a fully practical script editor today,' said Stephen.

The robotic cleaner scooted backwards as the videotape was rewound. The non-speaking Kangs and the non-speaking Caretakers were playing charades in the Red Assembly. A Red Kang touched her arm. 'Two syllables. First syllable.' The non-speaking Rezzies remained aloof.

Catherine Cusack showed the other Blue Kangs how to do the hand signs. Blue Kangs handed their crossbows over to the Red Kangs at the end of a take: sharing limited resources. I shanghaied Catherine and took a Polaroid of her gnawing on the dismembered leg of a Yellow Kang. Another snapshot to treasure.

Kangs, rats, what more could I have asked?

A cluster of BBC technicians, strangely silent, intent, concentrating hard, waved us out of the way so they could see the monitor. Ah, of course. They were watching cricket.

Sylvester was worrying about the **Evening Standard**'s election headlines. 'They're really digging up the dirt,' he said. A kid visitor was inspecting a Kang crossbow. 'How the hell do you fire it?' he asked. You didn't. It wasn't fully practical. A Blue Kang was chatting to a black Caretaker.

The Red Assembly had taken on a late-night transport-café feel. The succulent Asian Red Kang had put on her spectacles to help with the charades clues. Catherine Cusack and I sat talking in the BBC Club. A giant purple Robbie Coltrane shouted over our heads. 'Hugh!' he bellowed.

Wednesday 10 June 1987. A writer friend of John's whom we'll call Patrick Rigg (apologies to any real Patrick Riggs) came in to talk about the possibility of working on the show. He didn't immediately come across as a natural for **Doctor Who**. But he and John and I retired to the Bush, the unofficial BBC pub for a drink; something I didn't normally relish but it was preliminary in the peace moves between John and me. After Rigg had gone, John and I talked and buried the hatchet. 'I was so angry I wrote it down. I had to do something,' said John. He meant that he wrote down whatever it was I said to him that set him off. I was reminded of the truth of the old cliché about there being two sides to every story. I hadn't realised I'd antagonised him so much. I certainly hadn't intended to. Anyway, the hatchet was buried.

This was all well worth doing but it meant that I wasted an afternoon sitting in a smoky pub listening to Patrick Rigg gloat about bonking a 19-year-old on the sitting room floor while her parents – his friends – were in the next room. He then gave us the latest facts about a cure for baldness. He told me about a story of his, involving two burglaries and a double cross and it was actually a very nice idea. Extremely clever. 'It earned me a lot of money.' He'd used the same idea again and again in lots of contexts. The script of his which I'd read was well enough written though screamingly right wing. 'I'm just a fascist,' Rigg said blithely, before going on to tell us more about his sexual exploits. Believe it or not, he was a member of Mensa.

Thursday 11 June 1987. I went in for a chat with Colin Rogers (deputy head of drama series and serials). We talked about **Doctor Who** and what I should do next. He was worried about violence: in particular the scene with the lesbian cannibals (the Rezzies) going down the garbage disposal. 'I have a ten-year-old of my own and I know how attached they get to characters.' I complimented Colin on the framed photo of Dylan Thomas he'd put up in his office. 'You're the first person to recognise who it is,' he said. Right, I thought, that was a good career move.

Richard Briers was reading a copy of **Family Circle**. We were out in North Acton again for a run-through of the second block. Catherine Cusack was wearing glasses and baggy purple trousers, running across the room in a Groucho slouch. At lunch, Stephen, Sylvester and I were sitting out on the balcony of the Rehearsal Rooms restaurant, looking out over a big green graveyard down below. I was eating ice cream: Stephen had his sunglasses on. Sylvester had his own publicity postcards at last, a great photograph of him outside the Iraqi millionaire's empty mansion in Chalfont St Giles (you could see the Iraqi millionaire's bluebells out of focus against the green background). I gave my girlfriend Kate one of the Sylvester postcards. 'Oh, isn't he great?' she said. 'He's a nut.'

Tuesday 16 June 1987. 'Nice and nasty please,' said Nick Mallett as the actors got ready to do a run-through in the Rehearsal Rooms. Clive Merrison was reading the **Guardian** while Astra Sheridan screamed at his feet. She was doing her death scene.

'From the top, where Bin Liner's blocking Catherine.' 'Suppose Camera 3 does the shots 2 was supposed to, until Bin Liner moves?' We were back in the studio. There was a Chaplin silhouette of Sylvester against a window at the end of the corridor. 'Lift the boom,' shouted someone. 'Which corridor are we in now?' asked Bonnie.

'Hold it Cleaners. Wait for your cue.' In the control room, Nick was jumping around in his chair, urging the cleaning robots on. He gave a note to Sylvester about running: 'Like the clappers.' In the studio, there was the smell of Kang perfume, the smell of smoke-gun smoke. I was tired and the motion on the studio floor was dreamlike. A girl in floral trousers was dragging camera cables like an Egyptian slave labouring on the pyramids.

'Has Jeff got it – a single of the Doc, Jeff?' 'Could I just confirm that I do have 37 and 39?' 'Yes, Jeff.' 'Okay.'

The Doctor lying on the floor, slim Kang legs standing beside him. A red light went on in the control room. 'We are recording.' Sylv fluffed a line ('Audio-architechnotonical') and he started eating the telephone in frustration, 'Ah, fuck it.'

'Nick, Bin Liner's a bit garbled on her, "I can see them through the eye-spy."' Nick's foot was pumping frantically as he sat in the director's chair. 'Build high for happiness, Alex,' said the lighting technician (quoting a catchphrase from the script, which warmed my heart). 'If Clive's on Camera 3 he'll find it,' said Shirley Coward, the vision mixer. 'There's your camera, Clive boy.'

There was an ashtray on Dave Chapman's special effects console, sitting on top of a five-and-a-half-inch floppy disc, and some liquorice Rizlas.

Down on the studio floor, the Caretakers were dressed in their fascist-militaristic uniforms and Clive (or was it Sylvester?) was singing 'Springtime for Hitler'. Sylvester produced a Penguin edition of G. B. Shaw from his pocket: **The Doctor's Dilemma**. A lovely smile from the Asian Red Kang.

'Fairy feet from Bonnie,' said John Nathan-Turner. 'Light on the trotters,' instructed Nick Mallett, passing on the suggestion. 'Careful on the rostra, Bonnie,' was the way Ian Fraser ultimately phrased it. 'Come with me Bin Liner, Fire Escape and… Air Duct!' said Sylvester, improvising brilliantly (there was no Air Duct in the script). I was watching Catherine Cusack's face, pale Irish beauty.

Thursday 18 June 1987. There was a chalkboard above the winch control panel with 'Elvis is King' written on it. We were rehearsing. Bin Liner was without her red Kang wig, so she was Annabel with her long lank blonde hair. In the control room, all the screens suddenly go blank. 'System fault.'

Shirley the vision mixer hooted with laughter as the robotic Cleaner rammed its phallic drill bit at the lift doors. Clive's black and white image from a screen was reflected in John metallic Garfield briefcase on the control room floor. Bonnie, in a big floppy T-shirt, was wandering along a blue-lit corridor between the large robots.

Tension and excitement after lunch. 'Strike clock. Cue robot.' We were shooting again. One of the extras, a Caretaker, hadn't come back from lunch. There was the possibility of panic in the air. 'We'll do 262. He isn't in that one.' 'Perhaps he's lying at the bottom of a lift,' said Stephen.

'The over the shoulder 249 is very wide isn't it?' 'I've tightened up.' 'Thank you.' As we sat there watching this story being shot, Anne Faggetter was behind us in the producer's booth watching the rough tapes of the previous story. Down on the studio floor, a chair began to fall apart under Sylvester, who leapt up and attacked it. Attacked it, smashed it to bits, knelt and mimed playing the harp with the remains of it, like Harpo Marx. Bonnie was being wonderful with the disabled children who were visiting the studio, sitting watching in their wheelchairs.

'We've got non-smoking robots.' 'Oh, I think we can have smoking ones.' Red and blue lights hung above were casting strange red and blue shadows around the outlines of everything on the studio floor. It made it look like something out of a 3D comic book. 'Okay. Nearly there. From the top. Opening positions,' said Nick. 'Can you go back to the first condition, please?' John's cigarettes were poisoning everyone in the control room as he chain-smoked.

Friday 19 June 1987. 'That was the crassest line in the script,' said Stephen, listening to some of his own dialogue – 'A monster that makes camp jokes.' Rich Briers wandered around in his Kroagnon outfit, looking like a sort of **Wizard of Oz** Nazi. 'The best-dressed-zombie competition,' said Stephen. Sylv did an acrobatic tumble out of camera shot. 'What a good fall. Nobody saw it,' he said. He fluffed a line and smacked his head against the wall.

We were showing around an American **Doctor Who** fan who was visiting the studio. He was called Zachary ('That's what they call me on the convention circuit'). Chatter from the studio floor: 'Somebody's whistling.' 'They are.' 'It's the robot arms.' 'We need a practical crossbow and a lightweight bolt.' 'Too much chat going on please!' shouted Ian. 'And in the room there!'

Henry Barber said, 'No. The tube goes up and Kroagnon comes out of it.' Julie Brennon was cackling her wicked laugh as the tube descended on Richard Briers. It was Friday, the last few hours in the studio for this story. There was a combination of extreme tension and end-of-term euphoria in the air. Ian Fraser shouted 'Fire Liner!' accidentally gene splicing Fire Escape and Bin Liner. I was sitting with Sylvester in the Red Assembly, flirting with the Kangs.

'Cue the lift doors and out you come, Cleaner.' Nick raced between the studio floor and the control room. 'Do the next one please: "Hungry, hungry."' 'That's two sets of carts and Rezzies' legs, red light, smoke, spooky robots.' I sat with Stephen in the dark control room, realising that this was the culmination of months of our work.

Red Kangs in a corridor jumped involuntarily as an explosion went off on the other side of the studio. Freeze frame of Catherine Cusack triumphantly throwing a hubcap from a wrecked robot.

'Sorry, so sorry to stop,' said Richard Briers. 'Isn't it better to have just one "hungry" each time?'

Afterwards, with the last shot complete, I bought a weary Nick Mallett a drink in the BBC Club. He wanted Perrier water. One of the Kangs and I were together in the crush of people at the bar. 'What about this girlfriend of yours then?' she said. 'We're like everyone else,' I said. 'We have periods when we get along really well, we have periods when we don't get along.' 'Well, when you're having a period when you're not getting along,' she said, 'why don't you ring me up. And do anything else you want with me.' A certain amount of Kang-snogging then ensued in the BBC Television Centre lift. A nice, deliberate kiss.

Back in the BBC Club, standing drinking vodka and tonics in the crowded bar. Kate Easteal was chatting with Catherine Cusack. She asked Catherine what she was doing next. '*Sophia and Fuckface,*' said Catherine, 'And I'm Fuckface. The young Fuckface.' (I believe Catherine was referring here, perhaps a tad disrespectfully, to *Sophia and Constance* from that acknowledged literary masterpiece **The Old Wives' Tale** by Arnold Bennett. The following week, I would see piles of boxes in Threshold House containing *Sophia and Constance* scripts and think of young Cusack and smile.) Catherine was drunk and young and attractively left wing, claiming she found the elderly prime minister of Russia rather sexy: 'Every time I see Gorbachev on the television, that mark on his head, I just about have a bloody orgasm,' she said. 'Tell us about it,' said Kate Easteal.

Down in the lobby of Television Centre, waiting for taxis. Catherine said I could call her Catta and I felt privileged. Her cab arrived and she hugged me and Kate goodbye, and then she was gone. Kate and I sat there, staring up at the brilliantly lit, intricate Television Centre ceiling. 'This is a bad ceiling to look at when you're drunk,' said Kate.

It was now the early hours of Saturday morning and *Paradise Towers* was in the can. I rode home in a taxi with a Kang crossbow in a plastic bag.

Thursday 20 August 1987. Stephen and I were reminiscing about the writing of *Paradise Towers*. Stephen said, 'There is an optimum time for writing. I think actually three scripts in a week is pushing it.' We were watching rough tapes of *Paradise Towers* episodes one to four and it was impossible to be objective, particularly about the geographical relationships of the set. You have these two corridors which are supposed to be miles apart in a huge skyscraper complex, but we *knew* they were next to each other in the studio. Stephen was wearing shorts and sandals. Graeme Curry and Ben Aaronovitch were watching with us, to try and get a feel for Sylvester, and it was great to have the reaction of an audience. Kate Easteal was looking for her keys in her **Thomas the Tank Engine** satchel. I then sneaked out of the building to avoid Pip and Jane.

Thursday 10 September 1987. We had a viewing with Colin Rogers, and we convinced John to scrap the less than inspired David Snell music for *Paradise Towers*. I felt strongly about this because to my mind the score was somewhat dreary synthesiser stuff that didn't work to help any scene. Indeed, I often felt it was working *against* them. So Keff McCulloch got to rescore it. Thank God. Colin liked Stephen's scripts. He speculated that there'd soon be girls playing Kangs in playgrounds all over the country. 'Shouting "Make her un-alive!"' said John.

Monday 28 September 1987. I heard that John Nathan-Turner had been freaking out over tapes. The technical fuck ups were quite unbelievable. *Paradise Towers* had been dubbed back again but it still had the wrong music, and people in presentation had borrowed Pip and Jane's latest episode – to be broadcast that evening – and damaged it. And there was still a hole in the soundtrack.

There was an **Open Air** discussion of **Doctor Who** the next day, and I'd selected a nice Kang clip for them to use: 'Boys? What are boys?' says Annabel Yuresha as Bin Liner.

Tuesday 29 September 1987. John and Sylvester and Bonnie were on television up in Manchester, on **Open Air**, in the firing line. Apparently the woman M. C. had the knife out for them and for **Doctor Who**. She sprung a **Daily Telegraph** article on them (or maybe it was the **Express**) which had singled Sylvester out as 'Wally of the Week'. She read a couple of paragraphs of abusive prose then looked across at Sylvester. Sylvester grinned happily and launched into a fantastically agile and good-naturedly diplomatic reply starting with the words, 'Well, I never read the newspapers, but…'.

Thursday 1 October 1987. Stephen was telling me about his television play **Claws**, a well-written black comedy about the intrigues and machinations and treachery among breeders of pure-bred cats. I had read **Claws** months earlier and it was one of the reasons I had hired Stephen. It had now been filmed and was going out that Sunday. Unlike the first **Doctor Who** story, it had also had a successful press showing. Apparently publications right across the political spectrum had given it a favourable response. 'If both **City Limits** and the **Daily Mail** think it's a boffo wheeze, we must be onto something good,' said Stephen.

A few days later, I was with John and he was talking about the good old days of Christmas parties at the BBC. 'They were spectacular… People would *screw…*' I discussed the reviews of **Claws** with Stephen. We were talking about the **Daily Mail**. 'It's a newspaper for *literate* subhuman fascists,' I said. 'My mother!' said Stephen.

I went to the identity card office to get my photo taken and my BBC identity card renewed. The plastic wafer came out of the camera and burnt my fingers.

A tremendous weight had been lifted off my mind. I wasn't worried any more. The sense of relief was physical and very intense. I hadn't realised it, but three things had been weighing on me. The first thing was simply the stress of production; when we had finished recording the season's stories, I began to feel saner. Then there was the worry of what happened when my contract expired; when the BBC renewed it, I felt better still. The final thing was Pip and Jane's story. For the previous four weeks this had been going out with my name on the credits. I wasn't consciously aware of how clenched and defensive that had made me until the night that the first episode of Stephen's

Tuesday 6 October 1987. We actually received a memo from Jonathan

Powell, congratulating us on *Paradise Towers*. This had never been known to happen before. 'First rate,' said Powell. He knew we were planning to bring back the Daleks the following season, and now he was talking about wanting 'the Daleks at Paradise Towers', which I translated to mean that he didn't want the Daleks on Lakertya (the gravel-pit planet in *Time and the Rani*), which I further translated to mean that he wanted the Stephen Wyatt-style scripts to continue.

Once the music score for *Paradise Towers* had been replaced by the new one composed by Keff McCulloch, John asked me if I wanted to hear episode two, which had just arrived. I politely declined. Then, in my office, I could hear the new music from down the corridor. It drew me into John's office, where I sat down beside a box full of new **Doctor Who** books. Sheer joy. The difference the right music could make to a story was hard to believe. Keff had taken the somewhat overlong Brer Rabbit rulebook scene (where the Doctor fools the Caretakers) and he'd put music at the beginning and the end, no music in the middle, and now it worked. He'd added lyrical music to the scene with the Kangs and the cans of soft drink, evoking exactly the sense of tenderness and communion, the coming together of the Doctor and the Kangs – the quality I'd always wanted the scene to convey. Keff's background was pop music and his stuff was in the happy upbeat pop idiom, but I was confident he'd develop. Already he was showing the instincts of a skilled film composer. Even if you didn't like a particular piece of his music, it was always there for a reason, and always the right reason. He understood the emotions we were trying to convey and he *helped*.

I rang Stephen to tell him the good news. My girlfriend Kate and I went to the theatre with Stephen to see Alan Drury's adaptation of Molière's **The Hypochondriac**. In the seats behind us in the circle, teenage girls were talking and laughing. 'It's the voice of the 1980s,' said Stephen. 'You hear it everywhere. Female, about 20, a little drunk.'

Thursday 8 October 1987. I was going on holiday and I rang up the Netherlands tourist bureau to check whether I'd be able to tape **Doctor Who** okay in Holland. I didn't want to miss an episode. I passed my videotape of *Paradise Towers* through airport security to be hand searched. I read a **Doctor Who** book on the plane. Kate looked over at a photo of some classic **Doctor Who** monsters. 'I remember those geezers.'

Rain sprayed off the wing in a blaze of light. We trundled along the dark, wet runway. Long lines of lights, the dark bulk of our wing cancelling them in sequence as we passed. The cabin lights dimmed. The sudden thunder of engines. We were airborne. Whispery thud of Walkmans up and down the aisles. Violent turbulence over the Channel. American students laughing: 'The steward guy fell down.' We crossed the coast of Holland and approached the airport. Coming in for landing. The moon floated past the wing then bounced up like a huge white rubber ball. An American student was saying, 'I'm confused. Holland's the country and Amsterdam's the city?'

I needn't have worried about the technical questions of taping *Paradise Towers* in the Netherlands. Everything worked fine. Indeed the Red Kangs had red subtitles, the Blue Kangs blue. We watched the show with our friends. It was the second episode of Stephen's story and I was proud of it. I felt that the history of the show was in the process of changing as it went out.

'Charming creatures,' said our friend Mylene as the Kangs taunted Pex.

A week later, when I got back to work in London, Graeme Curry rang to say how much better *Paradise Towers* was than the previous story. Ian Briggs wanted to tell me the same thing, and to pass his congratulations on to Stephen.

Thursday 15 October 1987. Suddenly there was talk of re-editing the knife scene in *Paradise Towers* in the light of another gun massacre ('A replay of Hungerford,' said John; *Not Again* bannered the **Daily Mail** headline) and a knife killing (Douglas Hurd, the Home Secretary, was about to change the law on the possession of knives). This scene wasn't in the script. Stephen and I specifically took pains to avoid a knife – the obvious thing to use in the scene – and instead specified sort of bizarre gladiatorial toasting forks. The knife was added over my protest. However, to cut the scene meant losing Stephen's zinger of a line, 'Have you seen the basil, Tilda?' ('Everybody's favourite line,' said John.) In a way, I felt insulated from the whole debate. I had a tape of the original. I was all right.

That night, as I slept, I was vaguely aware of storm sounds outside, the wind rolling some flower pots around in the concrete hollow outside our basement flat. I woke up the following day and heard that there were some trees down. I started walking to work because there were rumours of difficulties on the tube to Hammersmith. But when I got to Hammersmith there were no trains operating from there either. In fact, the station was sealed off with locked metal grids. As I walked the rest of the distance to work I began to realise that it hadn't been just a storm. It had been a hurricane and London was devastated.

Walking to work was lovely. The street was green with fallen leaves. People were wandering around bewildered and indecisive; they were programmed to commute to work and suddenly they found there was no way of getting there and they didn't know what to do. Routine had been disrupted and they'd received this little windfall of freedom and they didn't know what to do with it.

Outside the BBC, the road was covered with shattered roof tiles. I rang Chuck up as soon as I got into the office; one Cartmel brother making contact with the other across the wrecked city of London. 'There's been some looting in Tottenham,' he said. 'Brilliant. Great. I love it.' 'It's just like the Blitz.' 'That's exactly what I said.'

Then I rang Ben Aaronovitch. He said, 'My bedroom is in the attic of a four-storey house on a hill. I know what I'm talking about when it comes to storms, man.'

John Nathan-Turner's house in Brighton had been damaged, but then he listened to the news and he said, 'When you hear about people dying, fuck a window.'

We had a meeting with Colin Rogers, who was watching footage of the Kangs in *Paradise Towers*. 'We're waiting for Douglas Hurd's ruling on crossbows,' he quipped.

Friday 23 October 1987. We got the viewing figure for episode two of *Paradise Towers* and it was 5.2 million. That was higher than the first episode of the season when we were being hyped to the hilt and everybody had tuned in to see Sylvester's debut. Triumph. I headed down to Kent for the weekend, leaving John in his office proudly watching the first episode of *Delta and the Bannermen* ('Rock around the Clock' and buses crashing into satellites in outer space) with John Chapman, an up and coming young producer. On the train to Kent, I saw reminders of the hurricane everywhere. Broken trees by the river. Old tiled roofs in Folkestone with the tiles ruffled like feathers. Stretched plastic sheeting on various roofs in assorted colours. Missing tiles like missing teeth.

I got a letter from a fan called Neil Spencer, in which he begged me not to go on destroying **Doctor Who** with stories like *Paradise Towers*, pleading with me to cut the comedy and save his beloved show from the abyss, and so on. I found it a bit of a downer. However, he also implored me to watch two classic stories from the Tom Baker era, *The Talons of Weng-Chiang* and *The Seeds of Doom* ('both of which I have on video thanks to other **Doctor Who** fans in Atherton,' stated the letter). Well I actually did what this correspondent advised. I borrowed the tapes from the **Doctor Who** office and I watched them over the weekend while I was down in Kent. And it turned out to be valuable advice. I spent Friday night watching *The Talons of Weng-Chiang* and taking notes. It was a wonderful story written by the masterful Robert Holmes. My girlfriend Kate loved it, too.

On Monday, I went into work to discover that Michael Grade had heard about the knife scene in *Paradise Towers* ('I think someone told him about it on a golf course,' said Colin Rogers) and had ordered it cut from all repeats and foreign sales. The foreign sales cuts seemed an odd decision, since this piece of censorship was in response to a peculiarly English piece of hysteria. And, when I thought about it, the order about repeats was odd too, since this hysteria was also peculiar to this particular moment in history. Oh well.

I was on the phone to a friend who had invited Kate and me over for a meal. 'Sorry Mark, that night we're having dinner with the man who wrote *Paradise Towers*.' 'Ah,' said Mark. 'Ice hot.' A line from the show!

Friday 30 October 1987. The day before Halloween, John Nathan-Turner showed me a very succinct and intelligent letter from a woman who was disturbed by the scene with the kitchen knife in *Paradise Towers*. I agreed with her. This is the scene that Grade was having cut out from all future prints. John Nathan-Turner mentioned that he remembered me registering a complaint when they were shooting the scene. John was good enough to remember it now, although he had ignored me at the time. The joke was that it was John's advice I had been acting on, to avoid violence involving household implements.

After the King's Cross tube station conflagration, Ben Aaronovitch said, 'We couldn't write about guns after Hungerford. We couldn't write about bombs after Enniskillen [the IRA massacre]. And now we can't write about fires.' We actually got a complaint about the bus blowing up in *Delta and the Bannermen* because it was the day after Enniskillen.

Tuesday 24 November 1987. The **Sun** had the headline 'Crossbow Killer Rapes Mum'. I found it very odd that the madman and loathsome sex criminal going berserk with his crossbow hadn't managed to time his fit to coincide with the transmission of *Paradise Towers* which featured the heavy use of crossbows.

7.35 Doctor Who

starring **Sylvester McCoy**
with **Bonnie Langford**
in *The Flight of the Chimeron*
The first of a three-part
adventure by MALCOLM KOHLL
An all-location shoot is
always a good excuse for a
party. Goronwy is far too
keen on bees. Bees make
honey.

Gavrok..........DON HENDERSON
Delta..............BELINDA MAYNE
Chima....................TIM SCOTT
The Doctor.SYLVESTER MCCOY
Melanie......BONNIE LANGFORD
Toll Master..............KEN DODD
Weismuller..........STUBBY KAYE
Hawk...............MORGAN DEAN
Murray...........JOHNNY DENNIS
Bollit...............ANITA GRAHAM
Adlon...........LESLIE MEADOWS
Keillor..........BRIAN HIBBARD
Burton...........RICHARD DAVIES
Billy..................DAVID KINDER
Ray.................ROBIN ASPLAND
Lorells..........KEFF MCCULLOCH
JUSTIN MYRES, RALPH SALMINS
Vocalists
TRACEY WILSON, JODIE WILSON
Theme music composed by
RON GRAINER
Incidental music KEFF MCCULLOCH
Costume designer RICHARD CROFT
Script editor ANDREW CARTMEL
Designer JOHN ASHBRIDGE
Producer JOHN NATHAN-TURNER
Director CHRIS CLOUGH
★ CEEFAX SUBTITLES

7.35 Doctor Who

starring **Sylvester McCoy**
with **Bonnie Langford**
in *The Flight of the Chimeron*
Part 2 of a three-part
adventure by MALCOLM KOHLL
The new Doctor is really
finding his feet, and the new
companion, Ray, is going to
be a big hit!
Keillor..........BRIAN HIBBARD
The Doctor.SYLVESTER MCCOY
Ray.................ROBIN ASPLAND
Delta..............BELINDA MAYNE
Melanie......BONNIE LANGFORD
Gavrok..........DON HENDERSON
Billy..................DAVID KINDER
Vinny...........MARTYN GERAINT
Baby Chimeron....
JESSICA MCGOUGH
Goronwy...........HUGH LLOYD
Weismuller..........STUBBY KAYE
Hawk...............MORGAN DEAN
Burton...........RICHARD DAVIES
Murray...........JOHNNY DENNIS
Adlon...........LESLIE MEADOWS
Bollit...............ANITA GRAHAM
Young Chimeron
AMY OSBORN
Callon..............CLIVE CONDON
Arrex........RICHARD MITCHLEY
Vocalists
TRACEY WILSON, JODIE WILSON
Incidental music KEFF MCCULLOCH
Make up designer GILLIAN THOMAS
Script editor ANDREW CARTMEL
Designer JOHN ASHBRIDGE
Producer JOHN NATHAN-TURNER
Director CHRIS CLOUGH
Videos: 'Death to the Daleks ,
BBCV 4073,
The Day of the Daleks , BBCV/B2056
'The Brain of Morbius , BBCV/b 2012
are available from retailers
★ CEEFAX SUBTITLES

7.35 Doctor Who

starring **Sylvester McCoy**
with **Bonnie Langford**
in *The Flight of the Chimeron*
Last part of a three-part
adventure by MALCOLM KOHLL
With the Bannermen
defeated, the Doctor makes a
solemn promise never to
return to Wales ever again.
Gavrok..........DON HENDERSON
The Doctor.SYLVESTER MCCOY
Melanie......BONNIE LANGFORD
Burton...........RICHARD DAVIES
Callon..............CLIVE CONDON
Arrex........RICHARD MITCHLEY
Weismuller..........STUBBY KAYE
Hawk...............MORGAN DEAN
Ray.................ROBIN ASPLAND
Goronwy...........HUGH LLOYD
Billy..................DAVID KINDER
Delta..............BELINDA MAYNE
Young Chimeron
LAURA COLLINS
Chimeron Princess
CARLEY JOSPEH
Vocalists
TRACEY WILSON, JODIE WILSON
Incidental music KEFF MCCULLOCH
Visual effects designer ANDY MCVEAN
Script editor ANDREW CARTMEL
Designer JOHN ASHBRIDGE
Producer JOHN NATHAN-TURNER
Director CHRIS CLOUGH
★ CEEFAX SUBTITLES

CHAPTER 5
Delta and the Bannermen

Is it a little mutant?

Wednesday 25 March 1987. I was discussing Malcolm Kohll's script with John Nathan-Turner and we decided to expand the initial battle scene. It would now take place not in the studio, in a set of the bridge of Delta's spaceship, but instead on location, in a slate quarry.

'It wouldn't be *Doctor Who* without a slate quarry,' said Malcolm when I told him.

A couple of weeks later, Malcolm dropped in to see how things were proceeding. He'd delivered his second episode and wanted to know what John thought. He waited in my office while John called me in. 'What's happening with Malcolm?' he asked, and right away I knew something was wrong. 'Have you read his episode two yet?' I hadn't. John looked at me and said, 'I think it's the worst script I've ever read.' (Only much later would I wonder if this was some kind of karmic balancing act: being so incredibly negative about poor Malcolm's script because he had been so positive about Ian Briggs's script for *Dragonfire*, against all odds, only the day before). I went back down the corridor to my office where Malcolm was waiting, with a fixed smile. I invented a story. An hour later, just after Malcolm had driven all the way back to Islington, I phoned him and ask him to come in again. I had now had a chance to read the script and I knew what we had to do.

I told Malcolm the truth, that we needed a complete rewrite. I'd now read his script and John was more or less correct. His episode one was fine but two was sort of an episode of lukewarm sitcom, not **Doctor Who** at all. There was very little Doctor in it and almost no incident. But John was more worried than I was. I was confident that we could get Malcolm to rewrite it for us. I asked him if he was willing to try it and when he said yes, that was most of the battle won. I felt like a bastard, but I knew we'd be all right. I thrashed out a new storyline for the episode with Malcolm, then together we went into John's office to run through it for him. When Malcolm ground to a halt at various points, I jumped in to bail him out.

Later, I was walking up to Television Centre with John in the sunshine. He patted me on the shoulder. I'd done a good job in a script emergency. I had convinced him that it was going to be all right, and it was.

The rewrite on Malcolm's script hit on Friday and he worked madly through the weekend on his rewrite. On Sunday evening, I took a train up from Kent, where I'd been belatedly celebrating my birthday (6 April, it fell during the location shoot for *Time and the Rani*), and headed for London to work with Malcolm. I came out of the tube at Highbury and Islington and found all the glass smashed in the door of the phone box. But the phone was working.

I was standing waiting as Malcolm pulled up in his car outside a Chinese restaurant. My girlfriend Kate had been a trifle miffed that I'd had to cut my weekend short to work on Malcolm's script. 'Very nice, to have a script editor travel up especially to see him,' she had said. 'If he wants to do a **Doctor Who** he's just going to have to learn to get it right.' She'd never worked in television in her life, but she was already starting to sound like the hard-bitten wife of the script editor.

But I was happy to schlepp up to London and sacrifice my Sunday because I wanted to get this right. I loved doing this job. Who would have thought it? Here I was in gleaming dark London, standing under a streetlamp on a spring night, ready to work on a **Doctor Who** script. Avoiding the broken glass on the pavement, waiting by the Chinese restaurant as Malcolm's car arrived.

Ten minutes later, I was sitting in Malcolm's flat with a glass of water. Talking Heads played in the background. Malcolm was standing around nervously while I read his new episode two. I read and chuckle. About ten pages in, I told him to relax. I read the Chinese take-away menus on the wall of Malcolm's kitchen as I dialled Brighton, ringing John up at his home to tell him the script was going to be all right. And it was. Malcolm had been working day and night and he'd written an entire episode in 48 hours. The least I could do was sacrifice my Sunday evening and come back to London early to read the script and let him off the hook.

Malcolm's script was fine. He sagged with relief and smiled and dropped me off at King's Cross station. The surgical glow of Sunday night fluorescent lights. Punks and drunks. I caught the tube from King's Cross. I sat on the tube train, tired and spaced out. It was ten thirty at night. At Edgware Road, the tube doors opened and someone stepped into the carriage. My God, it looked like Ian Briggs — who was writing the other three parter to go with Malcolm's. Briggs too would have spent the weekend slaving on his **Doctor Who** script. Was it him? I got up. I walked past him. I said his name. He looked up. The long stare of disbelief. What I should have done was coolly demand, 'Where's the script Ian?' as if an avenging God had sent me. But that would probably have given him a heart attack. Instead I just explained that I wasn't stalking him and it was a weird coincidence, a piece of synchronicity.

Tuesday 14 April 1987. 'Is it a little mutant? So sweet,' said Kate Easteal, reading Malcolm's script.

Spring in West London. Cherry blossoms falling among the dog turds. Malcolm and I walked along Frithville Gardens, both weightlessly happy. We'd had a meeting that morning with John and Chris Clough, the director for

Malcolm's story, and it had become evident to Malcolm that his story really would get to the screen and we wouldn't tear it to pieces on the way. That's a screenwriter's dream come true.

Malcolm had a chance to ask Chris to please use the real sound of a Vincent rather than any other motorcycle and Chris took the number of the Vincent Club while John invited Malcolm to meet the guy who was doing the music (Keff McCulloch) and help choose the songs. This all left Malcolm shell shocked with happiness. Writers just don't get treated like this in television. He was so chuffed *he* bought *me* lunch.

It was interesting. I knew that Ian Briggs's script for *Dragonfire* was far and away the best of the season and whenever I read it I went crazy about how good it was. But it was Malcolm's, with its 1950s setting, that had awakened the interest of the cast and production crew. It was the one people were talking about.

Wednesday 6 May 1987. After the last block of shooting on *Time and the Rani*, exhaustion set in. I felt like those studio days had nearly finished me off, and we'd only just got started. I was back in my office and across the corridor they were discussing the casting for Malcolm's story. 'What about Kate Nelligan?' 'What does she look like these days?'

I talked to Mike Tucker in the darkness of the filming stage in the Visual Effects Department at North Acton. There were empty cans of airbrush propellant lying around – the 'rocket fuel' for the spaceship in *Time and the Rani*.

Mike was saying how much he liked the next story – and like everyone else he meant Malcolm's, the 1950s one. 'I want to build the Bannerman fighter,' he said.

Monday 18 May 1987. We were sitting in the Conference Room in Threshold House, John-Nathan Turner, Chris Clough, production manager Gary Downie and myself, listening to two young women in 1950s outfits sing along to a backing track of 1950s songs. The Wilson sisters, Tracey and Jodie, as **The Lorells**. I loved this job.

The Wilson sisters sang *Mr Sandman* and there was one line that went 'Mister Sandman, send me your magic beam' and I tried to talk John and Chris into using this for the scene in Malcolm's script where the bounty hunter sends a signal into space and gets zapped for his trouble.

Ten days later, we were gearing up for Malcolm's story. Chris Sandeman was sharing my office, sitting watching videotapes of **Life on Earth**, researching insects for the story (the humanoid aliens in it have an insect-style life cycle). 'The scorpion's sexual problems are much more complicated,' intoned the voice of David Attenborough. From John's office down the hall came the sound of singing. They were auditioning Billies while Chris looked at library footage of insect reproduction: 'The sperm emerges as a milky fluid.' Chris was in search of a shot of bees swarming against a clear sky. All in aid of *The Flight of the Chimeron*, as Malcolm's saga was called at that point.

'They were screaming with delight,' said John. The people who had done the computer graphics for the new **Doctor Who** titles were apparently pleased with their work. New titles, new music. If only I had been happy with the script, I felt, then the start of the new season could have been be something wonderful.

At the end of the day, Chris was still in my office, crouched in front of the video. Kate Easteal looked in. 'You missed the bit with the scorpions fornicating,' I told her. 'Well, rewind it.' 'We have. Twice.'

Friday 29 May 1987. I told Bonnie Langford that we'd got Ken Dodd to play the Tollmaster in Malcolm's story. 'And the best part is that we get to kill him.' 'Oh, Andrew!' said Bonnie.

Across the corridor from my office, Gary Downie was choosing leather-boys from **Spotlight** to cast as non-speaking Bannermen. Chris Clough showed me a Polaroid of the wonderful creature for the Dragon in *Dragonfire*, built by visual effects assistant Lindsay MacGowan.

Monday 15 June 1987. The actress who was supposed to play Ray in Malcolm's story, Lynn Gardner, was practising riding her motor scooter and she crashed. She was all right, but she needed to rest for a couple of weeks. So we needed a new actress with a Welsh accent who could ride a motor scooter.

The following day, on the notepad on my desk I wrote *How often does she ride a scooter?* 'Sounds like a good name for a band,' said Daren, our work experience guy. John was wondering if we could get away with using Lynn despite her injuries, but in the end the part of Ray went to Sara Griffiths and Lynn took a voice role in *Dragonfire*.

In the sound recording studio at Lime Grove, a lovely, soft, warm, clean-carpeted, spacious place, David Kinder was about to perform *Singing the Blues* in the role of Billy. He took a swig of port before going into the microphone booth. 'Brandy's good, too,' said Tracey Wilson. I mentioned that Louis Armstrong used to drink milk to coat his throat. 'But milk congests you,' said Tracey. The drummer got interested, took off his headphones and joined in the conversation about dairy products and congestion. I loved that studio. Carpet and pale wood. In the control room suite, there were more buttons than you've ever seen in your life. More than in the TARDIS. Keff McCulloch, who was composing the music for this story, strummed his white electric guitar and a warm full sound filled the studio. David Kinder sang in a trembly Buddy Holly voice. 'He's got a 50s voice.'

Saturday 20 June 1987. I travelled on the tube to North Acton in the morning. It was the first genuine day of summer, beautiful and hot.

Only a few hours earlier, we had been in the studio, wrapping up *Paradise Towers*. And even fewer hours before, we had been in the BBC Club celebrating. Now we were back at the Rehearsal Rooms for the first read-through of *Delta and the Bannermen*. I made it to the read-through with seconds to spare. 'John said you were three sheets to the wind last night,' said Malcolm. Actually, I wasn't. I had been drinking vodka and tonic and trying hard, but I couldn't get drunk.

Everybody at the table for the read-through introduced themselves. The 70-year-old Stubby Kaye said, 'Stubby Kaye, boy actor.' Don Henderson, wearing a CND badge and a straw hat, was smoking a rollie. The script worked well. After the scene in which the Doctor denounces Gavrok, Stubby Kaye said, 'Hot damn! He stood up to that big bugger, didn't he?'

I left Malcolm and Chris Clough in the lift talking about motorbikes.

Malcolm kept calling Stubby Kaye (a theatrical legend) 'Knobby'. There was a note from the Rehearsal Rooms re his script: 'Cut the following from the passenger list: Crovassi, Ethnon, Herret, Jaxos'.

Wednesday 24 June 1987. 'Action with the charges! Fire! Die!' Chris Clough was in a quarry outside London on a grey summer day, directing the battle scene from Malcolm's first episode. I'd met Malcolm on the iron bridge outside Royal Oak tube station that morning and we played the Stones and Buddy Holly on his car tape deck as we drove out to Sandwell Quarry, near Rickmansworth. Malcolm had his Wellington boots: *de rigeur* for quarries.

The grey sky cleared and we were out in the country with the sun shining and green all around and, like a fool, I hadn't started taking my hay fever stuff. The sunlight off the white surface of the quarry was blinding, my eyes were burning and itching and my nose was running like a tap. I was sort of wading through the awfulness of it like a deep-sea diver. Finally, I went down to beg for some antihistamines among the technicians and both guys in the scanner pulled out packets of the same kind of pill in a neatly choreographed movement. As the pills took hold, my eyes and nose dried up and I felt truculently calm, distanced from reality.

The make-up girls flinched as the gun charge spattered sparks past them. We could hear peacocks screaming in the garden of a house nearby. It was that kind of neighbourhood: peacocks in the garden. I said hello to 'Mitch' the cameraman (Alastair Mitchell). A helicopter climbed in the wide blue sky.

In his script, Malcolm described the Chimerons as 'puffy green

Michelin men' and unfortunately that's exactly what make-up gave us. They'd done an utterly shit job. 'Joke-shop masks,' said John Nathan-Turner. He wasn't pleased either.

Mike Tucker was spraying a fire extinguisher at the flaming cinder of a smoke charge. Peacocks, helicopters, yellow smoke. The Bannermen looked great against the sky. The stuntman fell off the cliff onto a pile of cardboard boxes and everybody ran to see that he was all right. John Asbridge, our talented, amiable designer, and a make-up girl were wearing matching green wellies. There were purple tissues on the ground, indicating where explosives were planted. 'Are we loaded?' 'Just loading... loaded.' Richard Croft, who was responsible for the costumes, was staring at the Bannermen extras standing on the cliffs above us. He observed, with considerable dismay, that they'd broken their banners.

The following day, I returned to the office. John had already gone on location in Wales. 'The cat's away. The cat's a-fucking-way! We're going to have a ball,' said Kate Easteal. There were *Paradise Towers* noises from the office next to mine where they were working on the rough edit. We'd now cut Ian's wildly over-length scripts for *Dragonfire* (if they were over-length, it was the bloody script editor's fault) and now they were timed at 25 minutes. I was feeling euphoric. I felt like a professional script editor.

'I've got to ring the scanner after lunch,' said Kate. 'It's after lunch. I've got to ring the scanner.'

I was walking past the Barclays Bank on Shepherd's Bush Green and I bumped into a familiar-looking girl in a black sweater with punky blonde hair. I realised that she and her then-boyfriend had been my flatmates in the East End after university. She told me it was the second anniversary of her coming off heroin. She was now working for a video company. 'I'm raking in the readies.' We said hello and goodbye.

It was Friday, and at the end of the working day I took Kate Easteal back to my girlfriend Kate's basement flat in Baron's Court to join us for dinner. Kate and Kate went out in the garden for a cigarette and the slugs attacked their Rizla papers.

The following Monday, I was driving out of London with Malcolm, singing along to Buddy Holly. We were on our way to Wales, to the location for *Delta and the Bannermen*. Blazing summer. Sweaty motorway. Swathes of cloud. The Severn Bridge. We checked into the Barry Hotel and joined the unit in time for lunch. Of course.

Tiny country roads. Green, wild, overgrown with ivy. Ancient ruined remains of a stone wall. Twisted trees, wild bird cries. We could hear the distant drumming of the Vincent motorcycle back down the road. 'It's the bell mouths that make that noise,' said Malcolm. Moss clung to a tree stump like a green monkey. A friendly Welsh cop had lunch with the unit, his helmet left resting on a fence post. A little green-faced child ran past – Amy Osborn.

We watched Delta's polka-dot skirt go up in a foam of chiffon as she climbed into the sidecar of the Vincent motorcycle. Sylvester had his new question mark umbrella (the question mark handle was his own idea). A Welsh dad and his son were watching the shooting: 'What did Bonnie Langford say to you?' The Vincent drove through a low ford and Bonnie screamed as the water flew everywhere. We moved to a field beyond a railway bridge for the next set-up. A field with sheep in it – we really were in the country. Sunshine and fresh air.

Embarrassingly, I'd been calling Sara Griffiths 'Lynn' because Lynn Gardner's name was still on the schedule. Sara was dressed in black and blue, with her lovely brown back bare. 'You see that man?' said the Welsh dad to his son, indicating a man standing beside Bonnie, 'He created **Super Ted**.' He was right, too. It was Mike Young, whom I believe knew Bonnie.

Non-speaking Bannermen were sitting on their helmets, just like real soldiers in a period of enforced idleness. Chris Clough called out, 'Stubby can you just be keeping your sausage more in the fire,' and the entire unit erupted in laughter. Sitting there in that field, I got sheep shit on my script. The special effects boys blew up a pup tent in two vast fireballs, huge double bang, echo punching off the cliff face. The riggers dumped bits of burning tent in the river. Ecologists. Not surprisingly, the sheep disappeared. 'What a shot that was,' said Stubby Kaye. 'World War Seven.'

Back at my hotel, I opened a drawer in my room and found the Holy Bible and dialling codes for Barry. Out at the airport hotel, where the cast was staying, up in the Jumbo Lounge, Sylvester was dancing like an Egyptian and Malcolm was reading about capital punishment for animals. That was almost what those poor sheep got that day.

The following day, we met Chris Sandeman at the desk of our hotel. He was picking up a box of moustaches. We joined the shoot bright and early, out at the Barry Island Butlin's holiday camp. Brian Hibbard was playing an intergalactic bounty hunter dressed as a teddy boy. 'That tie's going to need sorting out,' he said. Brian used to sing with **The Flying Pickets**. 'The Flying Dickheads,' he said.

I went and said hello to John Nathan-Turner. 'I've just bitten Chris Clough's fucking head off,' he told me. According to him, Chris, an eminently nice guy, had been going on about how cheap and crappy **Doctor Who** was. 'We're only £28,000 over budget,' said John.

John Asbridge had designed a beautiful smoky, grubby metallic **Alien-**

esque Bannermen fighter interior for us. Malcolm and I crawled around in it, awestruck and full of admiration. There were seagulls crying over the concrete island of the holiday camp. This was an eerie place even before **Doctor Who** arrived. Giant plastic bunnies held garbage pails beside the swimming pool.

A kitchen warehouse had become a makeshift studio for the Bannermen fighter and bus. The bus was a revelation, an image suddenly and powerfully made real when we saw the shots of it against the black drapes – creepy, darkened transcontinental touring bus interior, only the reading lights on above the passenger seats. It was like seeing the motorcycle the day before; you spent months with it as words and then suddenly it was *there* with all the impact of reality. 'It's another world in that bus,' said Chris Sandeman. I saw a 1959 **New Yorker** magazine lying in a box of period magazines. 'Jayne!' 'Is the hairspray there? Fab. Thanks.' Pulsing red lights against the black cloth. 'And a good big scream, please.'

The Bannermen fighter doubled as the other Bannermen fighter. 'Actually, it's also the *Nosferatu*,' said John Asbridge, referring to the ship in *Dragonfire*. We heard the incongruous sound of real holiday camp kids playing outside during the Chimeron death scene.

Next, we were shooting a scene in a dining hall. The extras were repeatedly being served the same meals and never getting to eat them as the waitresses took them away again for each retake. It was like something from one of the milder circles of Hell. Gary Downie took the time to brief a little girl sitting at one of the tables: 'You're a real holidaymaker and these are spacemen, so you're not too sure about them.' Sylvester had devised a bit of business which involved him *listening* to an apple at the start of every take. I saw a fur coat lying open with the words 'BBC Elstree' inside it. The dining hall was hot with summer heat and hot with the TV lights and packed with extras. 'Quartz colour daylight' said the light beside my shoulder. I could see the heat rising from it in waves. Sylvester poured more water and gave the apple back to the little boy for the umpteenth time. Eventually we got the shot. 'We need a wild track.' 'You can do a wild track of us de-rigging.'

Sylvester and David and Belinda Mayne (Delta) sat in the back of Malcolm's car singing along to Buddy Holly. Malcolm and I stepped out of the best Greek restaurant in Wales into an evening street and someone lit a spliff. The moon hung in the sky, clear and beautiful.

The next day, shooting continued. Don Henderson, as the bad guy, Gavrok, kicked Bonnie down in the dust. Bonnie on the kick: 'It hurt. It was good.' Don carried his packs of Gitanes around with him in his transparent BBC Series and Serials plastic bag. We were shooting in a tiny zone of space, hemmed in by local people on every side.

The tour bus ('Nostalgia Trips') was lifted by a crane above a rose bed and the door in its side slid shut with the steep angle. When the door shut, the logo on the bus looked like 'Neuralgia Trips'. Sylvester autographed the door of the crane. Squatting beside the TARDIS, in the sunshine, in the long fragrant grass, I watched a tracking shot. The old local doctor – moustache, pink shirt – who lived opposite the Butlin's holiday camp had heard we were going to blow up the bus. He asked us if we could blow up the camp, too.

Bonnie and Sylvester were being followed by a party of schoolkids, literally like the Pied Piper, heading to the motorcycle for a photo call. A woman appeared leading her ancient mother, giving her a running commentary. 'And Bonnie Langford's in the sidecar.' They approached with their autograph book. John Asbridge was adjusting giant fibreglass tigers on the putting green. The extras were summoned. 'Space tourists please.' Bonnie was tap dancing to keep warm. 'Get a sun gun.' Then Bonnie autographed the door to the crane too. 'Space tourists over here. All my space tourists. Thank you.' 'Cooking navipod, take one.' Cooking quarb crystal, they meant. Did no one read these scripts?

'There's that girl over there,' said a bystander, 'what's her name?' 'Bonnie Langford,' said another bystander. The public was like an accumulation of insects on something sticky, massing at our backs as we tried to shoot the scene. 'What time's Bulman due?' asked a local lady, alluding to the TV character Don Henderson was then famed for portraying. John Asbridge got blue paint all over his fingers from retouching the TARDIS.

We ended up doing ten takes of the scene with the quarb crystal in the jar. Sylvester went pootling by on the motor scooter, past the old lady in the wheelchair, with a flock of kids on BMX racer bikes following. Sylvester obligingly stopped to sign autographs, putting the publicity photos on kids' heads so he could write on them. Sara Griffiths was watching me make notes for my diary. 'Sara doesn't have an "h" in it,' she said. It seemed Sara could read my scrawl at a distance – and upside down. Sylvester was surrounded by kids and beached BMX bicycles.

Don Henderson was adjusting his eyebrows, using his reflection in the bus window. We moved the crowd back behind a ribbon so we could blow up the bus. 'Bazooka next.' A long BBC cable with a Healee plug snaked through the dust. A policeman said, 'That girl with lots of orange hair is Bonnie Langford.' 'Orange!' said Bonnie.

There was a wonderful hot wide blue sky behind the 'Shangri-La' sign we'd erected in the holiday camp. After completing a scene, Sylvester walked past us and said, 'You can have your words back,' putting the crumpled script page into Malcolm's teacup.

I stood talking to Don Henderson about UFOs and about his pal, fellow actor Lesley Grantham. The old local doctor came back and patted Don on the arm, 'I must just say good morning to the Prince of Darkness.' Don was our chief villain, in a fascistic black Bannermen uniform. His troops, the Bannermen extras, were busy dyeing their mouths with liquorice, spitting red liquorice gobs on the sunlit dirt. 'The Bannermen want to do their war cry again. They've got red mouths.' A giant fibreglass bear joined the lions on the putting lawn. 'You'll be unhappy to hear that my lovely T-shirt got black spray paint all over it. I was painting roses black last night,' said John Asbridge, our extremely gifted designer. Don smoked his Gitane as the Bannermen did a charge across the rose bed. 'I hope I'm not in this. Ah well. Too late.'

Stubby Kaye was failing to interest Pepsi, the producer's dog, in Hartz Dog Treats – Beef Flavour. There was genuine Bannermen *esprit de corps*. Apart from the liquorice business, Don was adding some details of his own: webbed fingers and raw meat to chew on. He was also immediately onto the Western image that Malcolm and I had wanted: sitting in a rocking chair with a rifle in his lap.

Sylvester paced the balcony practising his lines at lunchtime, wandering the putting green as the visual effects guys hammered the spaceship entrance together. We sat under the balcony with a horde of Fleet Street newspaper hacks as Sylvester approached on the Vincent motorbike for the big confrontation scene with Don. The shutters on their cameras clicked. 'Can't they get a Dalek on the bike?' 'Klingons?' 'Wrong show.'

After the scene, Don apologised to me and Malcolm because he'd had to use a handgun instead of a rifle, as called for in the script. This kind of courtesy to the writer and respect for the writing was refreshing. I arranged another group excursion to the Greek restaurant that night. 'I won't, but bless you,' said Bonnie Langford.

The next day, we shot in a deep alley at the holiday camp, blue and yellow cabins on either side, long grass in the middle uncut for years. Morning sunlight, shadows, sea haze, sea smells, gull cries and gull shadows. The night before, in the restaurant, I was talking to Sara about taramasalata, to David Kinder about Lawrence Durrell's *Alexandria Quartet*, to Morgan Deare about Ronald Reagan and to Sylvester about Mark Forstater, a producer of our mutual acquaintance (he did **Monty Python and the Holy Grail** and bought my first script). Mitch the cameraman was at the restaurant last night too.

Pepsi was barking. Brightly coloured 1950s extras were erupting from the cabins for the bad-guys-are-coming scene. The soundman was moving through the long grass with his sound cable rustling like a snake. Lost kids' toys lay abandoned in the grass. 'There's a script in shot. No. It's a kite.' 'You're going to be in shot, squire.' Sylvester dashed down the stairs prematurely, just before his cue. 'It's the retsina that does it,' said Mitch. Two newspaper hacks were talking to each other: 'Did you have a good night?' 'Apparently, yes.'

Brian Hibbard, looking greasy and evil in the role of Keillor, sang a beautiful brief fragment of a song. 'Sara, is your make-up in a continuity state?' 'Very quiet for sound please.' The newspaper hacks watched the shooting. They were impressed with the wonders of videotape: 'It's amazing. It's like a Polaroid. They develop it as they go along.'

We were shooting inside one of the camp's store rooms. There were racks and racks of chewing gum remover. In the eerie twilight length of the linen store there was a wonderfully strange glow to the stacked pink sheets. Blue-green glint of Sara's 1950s dance gown. Brian Hibbard was doing his Keillor lines in a South African accent ('Gunnict me with the Bannermen leader' for 'Connect me...'). Sylvester was writing his line about the ion beam on one of the laundry shelves. In the womb-like darkness of the linen store, people were moving quietly. There was a shrouded black and white monitor in the shadows, a smoke gun discreetly plugged into the wall with the word 'heating' lit up on it in red. 'It's melodrama,' said Chris Clough, 'but it's only slight melodrama.' 'That's one of the greatest directions I've ever had,' said Sylvester.

'Can you look more frightened Sara? Keep it tighter from the beginning I think, Mitch.' 'That boom was in again.' 'I think "again" is the wrong word,' responded the sound guy. Chris Clough was directing the actors. 'What you've got to do is scream and fall down vertically.' Brian was doing his Richard III bit.

That night, we were shooting the dance scene. Technicians' toes were tapping in time to *Why Do Fools Fall in Love?*. There was a spotlight and tinsel down at the far end of the hot hall. Green lights across the crane. The Wilson sisters bopping in their low-cut black dresses and black gloves. Chris Sandeman delivered Pepsi to John Nathan-Turner. 'She's just had a crap.' 'How lovely.' I thought that the band was playing the wrong song for this part of the scene, and I was right. But in that hot, crowded, rectangular, orange room it was impossible to move my brain to think what the right song should have been. All the colours and the physical activity of the dance were making the script come to life in an amazing way. Tension was growing. Chris had just called Mitch 'Chas'. Seven o'clock was approaching and the musicians were only hired until seven. The extras were beginning to enjoy the dance. In the end we got it, and it was a wrap.

Kate Easteal sat outside on a giant plastic rabbit with a broken ear and

Anne Faggetter took a picture of her and Malcolm and me in the coppery setting sunlight. We walked across the holiday camp to the dance hall, where we were having the unit party. Malcolm and I volunteered to serve behind the bar and, while we were pouring drinks and handing them out, something like a dozen people came up at intervals and said exactly the same thing to us: 'Nice to see you doing some work at last.'

'Greetings, sensation-seekers,' said Sylvester McCoy on stage. The unit party cabaret had begun. Sylvester's act involved putting the end of a giant piece of elastic in Don Henderson's mouth, unrolling it as he climbed over the audience, making his way away from the stage until the elastic was good and tight. Then he asked Don if he was ready and, of course, the instant Don opened his mouth to reply the elastic came shooting out and Sylv went catapulting across the room. Huge applause. 'That was Sylvester McCoy and the lovely Don Henderson.' There was also an enormous roar of laughter from the audience when someone came prancing on-stage in a wicked parody of John Nathan-Turner: effeminate gestures, curly hair, lurid Hawaiian shirt and a fake little poodle standing in for Pepsi. John took it with amiable good humour.

I left the party late and walked back towards the hotel. It was Saturday morning now instead of Friday night. The holiday camp swimming pool looked ghostly in the darkness, abandoned fun stuff bobbing in it. Cars' headlights flashed like lightning in the distance. I was walking along the dark road from Barry Island to the mainland. A quiet moment. Water lapped. Weeds waved. I stopped and stared out and imagined I could see Gatsby's green light across the water.

On the mainland, there were taxis shuttling back and forth, teenagers pissing against walls, girls laughing in the street. A drunk, wearing sunglasses in the night, holding a sharp vinegar-smelling cone of fish and chips, stumbled slightly as he walked up the hill. I rang the night bell of the hotel. Curtains billowed in the breeze on this hot night. A mere few hours later, it was five in the morning and I was knocking on Kate Easteal's door across the corridor. I was so tired I couldn't remember her name. It seemed that Kate was in there in a tryst with one of the handsome male members of the guest cast but we had to go back to London. Our ride was about to leave. Ann Faggetter drove us back to London, Kate asleep on the back seat under my jacket. Mist on the motorway. Red sun rising in it. Cardboard cut-out trees flashed by. Back in London, I had a coffee at Kate's then caught the tube to my girlfriend's.

Delta and the Bannerman was in the can.

Two months later, we had the rough edit of episode one, which was great. A week later, I was sitting with John Nathan-Turner and Chris Clough. 'Do we see enough of that?' 'Think so. We have a tracker dart theme as well.' We were watching a rough cut of episode two. We looked at the bit where Billy the mechanic is moving to kiss Delta. 'It looks like he's about to pounce on her mouth,' said John, 'Suck face, as the Americans say.'

Malcolm came in and saw a rough cut, and he loved it.

Tuesday 27 October 1987. We had another press launch, especially for *Delta and the Bannermen*. John had taken the unusual step of a second press launch that season because *Delta and the Bannermen* had such a star-studded cast (most of whom, it has to be said, were names unknown to me). But I was very pleased about this, because I saw it as a chance to recover some of the lost ground from the first launch, in which the press were invited to sample the new season of **Doctor Who** and were obliged to sit through 50 minutes of a story set in a gravel pit (thus confirming all their worst suspicions about the show).

Instead of BAFTA, the launch this time was at the Trocadero, a garish futuristic shopping mall near Piccadilly Circus, in 'Light Fantastic' – a hologram exhibition centre. I walked into the brightly lit mall and saw Kate Easteal serenely ascending on an escalator in this chrome and mirrored world. She waved. The screening took place simultaneously on two large screens facing each other on opposite walls. There was a bank of seats on either side of the room but, when Malcolm and I sat down in the front row of one, everybody followed us like sheep and sat behind us, leaving the other side of the room completely empty. The **News on Sunday** woman with the Sainsbury's shopping bag snorted and suppressed a laugh when we saw that first shot of the Chimeron face. She was absolutely right. But basically the story held them. They paid attention and there was a shimmer of amusement at the funny bits. When the screening ended, Don Henderson's wife loudly led the clapping. What a nice lady. Don was carrying the **Guardian** and wearing a CND peace sign badge and a sweatshirt that appeared to carry a cigarette pack caution label, but which on close inspection read 'Warning: H. M. Government can damage your health'.

The next week, Chris Penfold, a fellow script editor, popped in to tell me that his sons (11 and 12) both enjoyed **Doctor Who** the night before – the first episode of *Delta and the Bannermen*. They used to watch it when they were little and they'd both given up on it, until now.

7.35 Doctor Who

starring **Sylvester McCoy**
with **Bonnie Langford**
in *Absolute Zero*, a three-part
adventure by IAN BRIGGS
1: Andrew is not impressed
with the studio-bound
realisation of Ice World, but
both Ian Briggs and Sophie
Aldred make a good
impression.

Kracauer.........TONY OSOBA
McLuhan
            STEPHANIE FAYERMAN
Zed.................SEAN BLOWERS
Bazin...............STUART ORGAN
Pudovki...NIGEL MILES-THOMAS
Kane.................EDWARD PEEL
The Doctor.SYLVESTER MCCOY
Melanie.......BONNIE LANGFORD
Customer.........SHIRIN TAYLOR
Stellar.........MIRANDA BORMAN
Announcer.......LYNN GARDNER
Anderson...........IAN MCKENZIE
Glitz....................TONY SELBY
Ace.................SOPHIE ALDRED
Belazs.............PATRICIA QUINN
Creature........LESLIE MEADOWS
Theme music composed by
RON GRAINER
Incidental music DOMINIC GLYNN
Costume designer RICHARD CROFT
Script editor ANDREW CARTMEL
Designer JOHN ASBRIDGE
Producer JOHN NATHAN-TURNER
Director CHRIS CLOUGH

●FEATURE: *page 24*
★ CEEFAX SUBTITLES

7.35 Doctor Who

starring **Sylvester McCoy**
with **Bonnie Langford**
in *Absolute Zero*, a three-part
adventure by IAN BRIGGS
2: With this story in front of
the cameras, it's fast getting
time to get four more stories
into pre-production for next
year.

Melanie.......BONNIE LANGFORD
Ace.................SOPHIE ALDRED
Creature........LESLIE MEADOWS
The Doctor.SYLVESTER MCCOY
Glitz....................TONY SELBY
Kane.................EDWARD PEEL
Belazs.............PATRICIA QUINN
Pudovki...NIGEL MILES-THOMAS
Arnheim...CHRIS MACDONNELL
Kracauer.........TONY OSOBA
Announcer.......LYNN GARDNER
Archivist....DAPHNE OXENFORD
Incidental music DOMINIC GLYNN
Make-up designer GILLIAN THOMAS
Script editor ANDREW CARTMEL
Designer JOHN ASBRIDGE
Producer JOHN NATHAN-TURNER
Director CHRIS CLOUGH

★ CEEFAX SUBTITLES

7.35 Doctor Who

Last in the present series
starring **Sylvester McCoy**
with **Bonnie Langford**
in *Absolute Zero*,
a three-part adventure
by IAN BRIGGS
Kane's lolly melts, then Kane
melts. Then Mel leaves.
Can't think of a Mel/melt
pun. Sorry.

Creature........LESLIE MEADOWS
Glitz....................TONY SELBY
The Doctor.SYLVESTER MCCOY
Mel............BONNIE LANGFORD
Ace.................SOPHIE ALDRED
Kane.................EDWARD PEEL
Bazin...............STUART ORGAN
McLuhan
            STEPHANIE FAYERMAN
Stellar.........MIRANDA BORMAN
Anderson...........IAN MCKENZIE
Customer....SHIRIN TAYLOR
Announcer.......LYNN GARDNER
Incidental music DOMINIC GLYNN
Visual effects designer ANDY MCVEAN
Script editor ANDREW CARTMEL
Designer JOHN ASBRIDGE
Producer JOHN NATHAN-TURNER
Director CHRIS CLOUGH

★ CEEFAX SUBTITLES

CHAPTER 6
Dragonfire

Funny business, time.

I first met Ian Briggs when both of us were invited to the BBC Writers Workshop, an initiative by Tony Dinner, head of the Script Unit, designed to encourage new talent. Malcolm Kohlll was another member of the group, and so was Robin Mukherjee. When I joined **Doctor Who** one of my first actions was to ring Tony Dinner and get the phone numbers for these writers.

I duly summoned Ian to Shepherd's Bush and we started what would become hours of script discussions in my office. Our first stab at an Ian Briggs **Doctor Who** concerned the TARDIS and its infinite interior. One of the ploys of the amusing bad guy was to develop this vast interior for property development (in 1987, as now, the real estate market in London was superheated and the subject of much publicity).

John Nathan Turner's response to this land-scam story was unenthusiastic. 'I don't think the teenies will get it,' he said. 'The TARDIS is bigger on the inside than the outside. That's about as much as they will understand.'

He was right. It was not a great story. Back to the drawing board. I went back down the hall to my office to tell Ian to think again.

Thursday 5 February 1987. Ian's story was coming along a treat. The previous week, I had thought it was dead but he came in and sat down and talked to me across my desk and everything he said, every idea he proposed was *right*. I loved it. I got Ian's latest draft of his outline and it seemed perfect to me.

Friday 27 February 1987. I was working with Ian Briggs on his outline for a **Doctor Who** story called *The Pyramid's Treasure*. We'd been developing this painstakingly for over a month by now, and we were down to the fine tuning before I handed it over to John. There was a character in it called the Fatboy, a loathsome villain. In one scene, Ian now had him wearing a Hawaiian shirt. Now, John had a well-known penchant for wearing such shirts. Indeed, lurid Hawaiian shirts were John's trademark. (Fifteen years later, Sylvester and Sophie attended John's memorial service wearing Hawaiian shirts as a tribute.) So, with immense paranoia, I removed the Hawaiian shirt line, explaining to Ian why I was doing it. 'Perhaps we should also drop the reference to the gay television producer in the last paragraph,' said Ian. I like Ian.

Wednesday 4 March 1987. I showed Ian's storyline to John. We sat in his office and went through it. John didn't like it at all – even with all the Hawaiian shirts removed. I suppressed the urge to panic and started salvaging what I could. I'd have to get Ian to take another crack at it. Thinking about John's reaction after the meeting, I found myself suppressing not panic but anger. Three quarters of what John had said was accurate, practical objection. But a quarter was prejudice against Ian. The more I thought about the struggles we'd had with Pip and Jane's script, the angrier I got. I was determined to commission some writers of my own, like Ian, to balance things. Headache and nausea haunted my day. I was trapped in hallways with the painful stink of new paint and in story conferences with the Dachau stink of cigarettes. I'd been having classic anxiety dreams. In them, I'd been commissioned to write a script for **EastEnders** which was due in on Friday evening and it was Friday morning and I hadn't started it yet.

While the turbulence continued over *Time and the Rani*, I was working with Ian Briggs, trying to restore his confidence – and mine – and come up with a new storyline that John would accept. I took him to lunch at Television Centre. As we sat down, the guy at the next table began to snap his fingers and point at me. It was the director Chris Goddard. I'd met him some months earlier before I'd landed the job on **Doctor Who** and was still trying to find a way into television.

By the end of March, it looked like Ian was finally going to get the go-ahead for his episode one.

Thursday 2 April 1987. John was on the phone to an agent, checking an actor's availability. 'If the script goes firm, I'd like to go firm on Tone.' This was Tony Selby, the guy who had played Glitz in the previous season. (Glitz was a character created by the late great Robert Holmes, so at least this would mean some royalties for his widow.) The script in question was Ian's, and the inclusion of a character from an earlier story to make John happy seemed like a small price to pay.

Glitz had a sidekick called Dibber. 'I got the hots for Dibber, actually,' said Kate Easteal. Kate was coming down to location the following week on the coach, bringing the Tetraps' heads with her. Sylvester McCoy was pacing around the rehearsal room in his panama hat and a pair of baggy blue tracksuit trousers. I was reading **City Limits** magazine, which had an article about sex toys featuring a Dalek dildo. John Nathan-Turner asked for a photocopy of the article. I wondered if a Dalek dildo lawsuit was in the offing.

Thursday 9 April 1987. Ian Briggs's new **Doctor Who** story was called *Dragonfire* and it was splendid, full of vivid, funny dialogue that rang true. I had episode one on my desk. I got Ian this far despite John's initial prejudice against him. Today, the crunch came and John was to pass judgement on the script: either we'd go ahead with Ian or I'd be forced to ditch him. I felt like my whole future was in the balance. I wanted to do scripts that I believed were good. I wanted to choose the writers. In the end, I wanted to shape the character of the show. Create a sense of wonder. Make the Doctor an enigma again. Fuck the explanatory lumber of my 20 years of predecessors. And Ian was a writer I wanted and knew to be good. And John's judgement so far was dead against him. Ian had fucked up the preliminary chat-with-the-producer and then I had encouraged him to come up with a wacko initial storyline that John hated.

John had got back from the *Time and the Rani* location the previous night. He got into the office late today. The **Doctor Who** office was full of sunlight; I hoped that was an omen. Kate Easteal was dressed all in black; I hoped that wasn't. I sat talking with Graeme Curry, trying not to feel the tension while John shut himself away with Ian's episode one. At least I was having a good time with Graeme. In fact, a great time. His story was taking shape nicely. Then John summoned me into his office…

I came out walking on air. I took Graeme down to the coffee bar. Sunlight streamed through the windows. I couldn't believe it. John had accepted Ian's script. It was all actually working! It was like feeling a car begin to start three months after you push the accelerator. I was grinning like a fool. I rang Ian to tell him the good news. John had actually said that it was good. 'He's got the format,' he said. I don't know if I'd ever been so happy. I was grinning all the way back to Hammersmith. Cold spring evening. Waiting for a train. The sheer *relief* I felt when John said he liked the script.

Tuesday 14 April 1987. Ian delivered his second episode in the usual brown London Business School envelope. This one had 'Episode Two – read it and weep. PS. Has this been commissioned yet?' written on it. Ian's script was brilliant, with his 'Crewmen / Women' (equal opportunity among futuristic space thugs; it was so nice and so right and I wouldn't have thought of it). And then there was his fabulous character Ace, making exclamations like 'doughnut!' and 'Mega!' Ace was great. I suspected that she might end up being the new companion when Bonnie left, things coming 360 degrees around after all we'd been through. John was interviewing Kangs for *Paradise Towers* and he came in and said about one girl, 'She's Ace. She's not a Kang. I think I've found Ace.'

John Nathan-Turner was talking about another actress. 'Sort of like Sarah Sutton with balls.'

Wednesday 15 April 1987. This was the day of the wake for Patrick Troughton at Television Centre. Afterwards, a small nucleus of mourners came back to the **Doctor Who** office. It was a sunny day. John had the windows wide open and the office door kept slamming in the breeze with great violence.

There were giant bottles of red and white supermarket wine to hand. John was introducing me around. I tried to tell Janet Fielding how much I admired her performance in the screen test but I'd miscalculated the time and place and it just sounded like the usual bullshit. I sat on a filing cabinet drinking white wine with Kate Easteal, as Nicholas Courtney (the Brigadier) and his girlfriend rang for a taxi. Nick's girlfriend was blonde, an American with an admirable command of idiomatic English. 'We haven't been there for yonks,' she said at one point.

Wednesday 20 May 1987. Mike Tucker introduced me to a guy called Lindsay MacGowan, who had done creature design on **Legend** and **Aliens**. There was a possibility he'd be doing the creature for *Dragonfire*, which would be fantastic. Lindsay was only in England because his work permit for the States had lapsed, and he was only at the BBC for another month or so. I took a look at his portfolio and it was staggeringly good. I hoped that the BBC bureaucracy wouldn't screw this possibility up. I loved special effects, the whole business of it. It was becoming clear that science fiction and fantasy films were something I should pursue. I loved the stuff.

A fortnight later, Chris Clough showed me a Polaroid of the creature for Ian's story – the Dragon – and it was wonderful, since Lindsay did get to build it after all. A striking image of his design, bleached white by the Polaroid flash. Fantastic menacing white scales and bone. An insect head.

I met Colin Rogers in the lift. He said he liked all the **Doctor Who** scripts by the new writers. I arranged to meet him for a proper talk the next week.

Thursday 9 July 1987. I got back from shooting *Delta and the Bannermen* in Wales and went straight on to *Dragonfire*. Full speed ahead. Talking to Ian Briggs in my office, I kept calling him 'Stephen' and 'Malcolm'. Yet again I felt like a father of many children. I opened a letter on my desk, another note from Bill Joule (a pseudonym; apologies to any real Bill Joules). Ian applauded. He is familiar with the Bill Joule situation. Bill Joule was this guy who had written a **Doctor Who** script called (let's say) *Digital Man*, which had been rejected once, but he kept insisting that this script would 'save **Doctor Who**'. He would send recorded delivery letters demanding that we reconsider. 'I have one question,' he said in his letter '– have you read *Digital Man?*' Having written to John Nathan-Turner, then to me, he tried writing to Michael Grade, who basically ran the BBC. I ended up with all these letters on my desk. Kate Easteal looked at my face as I open this latest one. She said, "This is the effect *Digital Man* has on our script editor. Digital-Fucking-Man.'

Early next week the famous script arrived. After weeks of shrill clamouring by its author, it was being given a second (and very final) chance. The results were unequivocal. It was unbelievably bad. We added the writer, Bill Joule to the notice board in my office, which was now known as the 'death board'. There was a drawing of Bill Joule, a stick figure being hanged. Out of his mouth came a word balloon: 'I have one question. Have you read *Digital Man?*'

Now Ian Briggs added another word balloon: 'Yes – it sucks.'

Thursday 16 July 1987. At ten o'clock on a Thursday morning in North Acton we had the read-through for *Dragonfire*. I was sitting beside the production assistant Rosemary Parsons, with my Welsh suntan beginning to flake off. (In the Television Centre canteen fellow script editor Valerie Ryan said, 'Have you got a suntan or is it a trick of the light?') Sylvester cracked jokes in mid speech as he read his part in the script.

An actress called Sophie Aldred was there to play Ace, this wonderful anarchic teenager Ian had written, who sort of grew out of a Cockney checkout girl from a storyline that I'd invented in January that was scrapped and changed. Sophie turned up in shorts and Doc Martens and she looked good in them. I asked Richard Croft, the costume designer, if she could wear the DMs when she was Ace as well. There were scripts on the table, a model of the set, lipstick on a BBC paper cup.

Back at my office, I was chatting with Ian when Ben Aaronovitch dropped in. I give him a copy of the letter I wrote praising his abilities to the sky (every word true) in an attempt to get him on the BBC Writers' Course (I failed miserably). Ben was literally blushing as he read it. The letter contained phrases like 'fiercely inventive' in describing his abilities. Ben put the letter down when he'd finished. 'This is a great ego massage.' The phone rang and it was the Rehearsal Rooms saying they needed a more futuristic fruit drink name for the scene in the refreshment bar in *Dragonfire*. I asked Ben to come up with something. 'This is where the fiercely inventive bit comes in,' said Ian. Stephen Wyatt also dropped in, and for the next quarter of an hour we had three of the best young writers in Britain trying to come up with a name for some futuristic fruit drink. Betty the BBC post lady opened the door to deliver the mail. 'I thought it was another writer,' said Ben.

(The name we finally settled on for the drink was Astral Cascade.)

Just after Ian left, we got another phone call from the Rehearsal Rooms asking us to add some technical-sounding gibberish to extend the scene between the Doctor and Arnheim (I loved Ian's names). So I lifted a passage about semiotics from a very pretentious text book about **Doctor Who** I happened to have on my shelves, and paraphrased that. I sent it off to the team at the Rehearsal Rooms and then took off with my girlfriend for a well-earned holiday in the south of France. While I was away, Ian attended the run-through of the script and laughed aloud when he heard this semiotic dialogue. 'Who wrote it?' he asked. 'We thought you did,' they told him.

A week and a half later, we began shooting *Dragonfire*. There was a blue light shining in the studio. 'Oh, it's all lit up!' cried Ian. Then, 'Sorry, I'm getting very child-at-Christmas here.' 'The Chimeron baby was cool,' observed Lindsay MacGowan, in reference to one of the effects from the last shoot. Lindsay came into the studio yesterday to see what they'd done to the monster he'd designed. What they'd done was added a neck, broken all the spines off and got the colours wrong. He was there until 3.00 am trying to put things right and he was back again now. The other special effects guys didn't understand his concern. 'Are you *still* working on it?' Poor Lindsay. He was talented and he cared about what he was doing and he'd tried to make **Doctor Who** look good; and someone stole his airbrush last night.

Everyone was still at lunch and in the studio at Television Centre there was a cluster of cameras like a huddle of robots all standing staring intently at a colour code chart. There was a huge white plastic box with dry ice smoke spilling out. This was all part of Ice World, the environment dreamt up by Ian for his very groovy script. 'Props please. Chris Sandeman, we need a carrier bag.' We did a retake of the materialisation scene and Bonnie and Sylvester and Mike Tucker all came out of the TARDIS (a theoretically infinite space but in practice very tiny and cramped and crowded) and it was carried off again.

The monstrous 'dragon' picked up Miranda Borman (playing Stellar, the little girl). 'Right. Okay. Cut. Well done.' A little boy in a wheelchair talked to Leslie Meadows, who was wearing the monster suit. 'I saw you pick her up, I did,' said the little boy. He and all his brothers were dying of a rare form of M. S. Kate Easteal sat on the studio floor with one of the poor little guys sitting huddled protectively between her legs. I borrowed Sylvester and got him to pose with the children and shot off all my remaining Polaroid films and gave them to the kids.

I was sitting with Ian above the studio floor in the control room when this dark, somnolent, subdued place suddenly erupted into life – England had scored against Pakistan at cricket. 'Back to the curry house, boys!' said one of the technicians triumphantly. Some might say I should have been dwelling on the political incorrectness of the remark. But I was actually thinking, 'If only they'd take this much interest in the programmes they're making.'

'Can John Asbridge look at the shot?' asked a control room voice. 'We have a Forbidden Zone shoot-off.' The two-hander scene between Ace and Kane (Edward Peel) was genuine magic. 'I was getting quite caught up in that,' said John Asbridge. That was thanks to Ian's superb writing, in happy conjunction with some talented actors. The dry ice streamed eerily in. I could *feel* the series improving, like a ship turning onto the correct course.

Down on the studio floor, Patricia Quinn, playing Belazs, was saying,

'The black from the guns rubs off. It's hazardous, darling.' There was a butterfly floating above the freezer centre set. A Shepherd's Bush butterfly that had wandered in from the sunlight outside. 'Look,' said Ian, 'a Red Admiral.' Mike Tucker had to turn on the TARDIS light while holding the door shut. 'There's no end to my talents,' he said. The TARDIS really was a shabby wreck. Considering that it was a television icon known all over the world for over 20 years, it was a bloody disgrace. It wobbled as they shut the door. The lines in the script 'This is our space craft,' and the disbelieving response – 'I'm not stupid' – sounded terribly apt.

We were into the second day in the studio for *Dragonfire*. 'It's bloody freezing down here,' said Kate Easteal. 'It's Ice World,' said Mike. They had just botched the wonderful scene Ian wrote in which Kane kills the sculptor and *the sculptor doesn't resist*. The way Chris Clough shot it, there's no indication that the sculptor submits willingly; Kane grabs him from behind. If they'd shown us during rehearsals how they were intending to shoot it, there would have been a chance to correct it. Instead, a great scene became a routine scene.

The little kid alone in the set flooded with dry ice looked monumentally eerie. All the minor characters and two-handers and dialogue and conflict in the script were outstanding. Ian's script was going to be the best of the lot that season. Cool smoke flooded out of the dry ice vats, floating eerily among the cameras as it drifted through the studio. 'Temperature gauges full up. Melted statue in, please.' We stopped shooting because the tiny curls on Glitz's sideboards (sideburns) were too tight. John Nathan-Turner was very concerned about this. 'I think they're darker than last year but they're exactly the same in terms of spacing and curl,' said Tony Selby, who played Glitz. 'They're definitely darker than last year,' he added after ten minutes. The whole production had ground to a halt. Gillian Thomas from make-up was up in the control room with another set of fake sideboards. 'They're lighter.' 'These are the ones,' said John. They were talking about re-shooting all of Tony Selby's scenes. You could bet they wouldn't re-shoot the fucking Kane/sculptor scene.

The tension was growing. Ian and I rewrote a line and John dismissed it with a snarl. 'Pure panto,' he said.

But the shooting of *Dragonfire* was also the occasion for one of my best memories of this show. Walking into the warm crowded noisy cafeteria in the Red Assembly to find it full of frozen mercenaries, space customers and Ice World guards. The visual effects guys showing us the silver deodorant cans (they were silver because, after all, this is the future) which in the story Ace cheerfully packs with her home-made explosive Nitro-9. 'We went through 16

Pamela Salem, Sylvester and Karen Gledhill on location in Hammersmith for *Remembrance of the Daleks*

Back row: Graeme Curry, JN-T, Stephen Wyatt, *front row*: director Andrew Morgan and writer Ben Aaronovitch in a screening room

Photographs courtesy of Andrew Cartmel and Steve Cook

Above, left: Kate Easteal and Ben Aaronovitch in the **Doctor Who** office with one of those giant photos of Sylvester McCoy looming in the background

Above, right: Sylvester with one of the Doctor's sworn enemies

Photographs courtesy of Kate Druce

Above, left: The Dalek spaceship in the schoolyard at the Hammersmith location

Above, right: Myself and Kevin Clarke in the same location

Above, left: Kevin Clarke posing with a Dalek during a visit to the *Remembrance of the Daleks* location

Above right: Ian Briggs holding a maquette (miniature scale model) of the creature from *Dragonfire*

Simon Williams, Karen Gledhill, Pamela Salem, Sylvester McCoy and Sophie Aldred on location for *Remembrance of the Daleks*

Photographs courtesy of Andrew Cartmel

Above, left: Me with the amazing Jessica Martin as Mags, the werewolf, on location for *The Greatest Show in the Galaxy*. (As you will have gathered I was a T-shirt nut in those days, this one is an image of a classic 1950s Wally Wood science fiction cover for EC Comics)

Me, Jessica Martin and Stephen Wyatt in the makeshift studio
for *The Greatest Show in the Galaxy*

Sophie, me and Sylv on location for
The Greatest Show in the Galaxy

Stephen and I on the set of *The Greatest Show in the Galaxy*

On location for *The Greatest Show in the Galaxy*, which was being shot in a makeshift structure in the car park at Elstree studios as a result of an asbestos discovery at our normal studios

Ian Reddington and Sophie Aldred taking a break during
The Greatest Show in the Galaxy

Sophie, Stephen Wyatt, Sylvester and TP McKenna on location
for *The Greatest Show in the Galaxy*

Photographs courtesy of Mike Tucker and Andrew Cartmel

Above, left: Me on location for *Silver Nemesis* with writer Kevin Clarke standing just behind me

Above, right: Stephen Wyatt and Graeme Curry on location during the *Silver Nemesis* shoot

Photograph courtesy of Andrew Cartmel

Kevin Clarke being menaced by Cybermen on location for *Silver Nemesis*

pints of Sainsbury's cream to get these.' 'You heroes,' said Ian.

Gary Downie was giving the zombie extras speech instructions: 'Just snarls and growls. Jim Hawkins acting.' A nice, somewhat larger-than-life woman called Sue Moore (John Nathan-Turner nicknamed her Foghorn Lil) was there with her model team to provide the extraterrestrials for the refreshment bar sequence, most notably a nasty little fanged goblin called Eric. Terrific work. They also had a fabulous half-flayed skull for the scene where Kane's head melts. I couldn't believe we'd get away with that.

If anyone is keeping track, we seemed to be referencing **Star Wars** in the refreshment bar scene and **Raiders of the Lost Ark** in Kane's melting. And we were exploring the tropes of **Alien** and **Aliens** when the Dragon appeared. It felt great that the show was actually addressing proper science fiction and fantasy again.

Before we went into the studio, I spent a long working day watching all the videos of the previous season's **Doctor Who**. Up to then I'd been devoting myself to earlier, more classic episodes. 'More classic' is being tactful. Just before I joined the show, **Doctor Who** had been entering a bit of a slump. The script editor, the able Eric Saward, had eventually fallen out with John Nathan-Turner and the stories showed a certain lack of inspired commitment. Or perhaps it was just exhaustion. In any case, watching those final episodes I felt like I was having sludge slowly pumped into my brain, like I was being gradually given an anaesthetic. There were no stories in those scripts. Even Robert Holmes (a great writer whom Eric Saward stalwartly supported) wasn't at his best) and the story by Philip Martin, who wrote the brilliant **Gangsters**, was a major disappointment.

Crucially, there was no feeling for science fiction or fantasy in the show at the point where I took over. Basically the scripts were failed thrillers full of confusing incident and boring characters with science fiction *detail* arbitrarily heaped on, but nothing genuinely science fictional about them. No core or centre to these stories.

I believed that, with *Paradise Towers*, *Delta and the Bannermen* and then *Dragonfire*, we were beginning to tell proper stories again, and ones that were actually also science fiction.

Glasses and tables went flying, cupcake shrapnel at our feet after the scene where the zombies clear the refreshment bar. Eric the puppet yawning between takes. Halfway through a take, Sylv said, 'Sorry, I fucked it up.' 'I don't remember that line,' said Ian. 'Can we clear this table please,' said one of the floor managers, 'Eric has made rather a mess.' Sophie looked great in her waitress apron, black skirt, red half-stockings, black Doc Martens, Batman earrings, Tintin wristwatch.

'What scene is this?' 'The metaphorical pianist.' 'Ah yes. The metaphorical pianist.' In the control room, an argument was going on about the angle of acceptance on Edward Peel. This was technical stuff about camera placement and the viewer's perception. 'It's his shoulders. His shoulders have crossed the line.'

A bit more teeth at the bottom if you can,' came the instruction to the actor from the control room. 'Grow them,' said Ian. Three special effects people pointed fiery hot paint strippers at the wax effigy of Edward's (Kane's) face. It began to melt and reveal the skull and muscles underneath. Detergent bottles full of washing up liquid and yellow paint were squeezed and horrible yellow stuff came running out of the melting face.

'How were the fleeing customers?' 'They were fine.' John Asbridge was up on a stepladder desperately wrestling down the 'Closed' sign above the docking bay. Tony Selby said, 'Have you got the dicky birds there Andrew?' Rhyming slang again. I handed him the script he wanted, containing the words.

The Arnheim scene, in which the Doctor discusses philosophy with a thuggish guard, was a genuine small masterpiece. I made a point of buying the guy who plays Arnheim a Bacardi and Coke in the BBC Club afterwards. But the scene ran on into overtime and Ann Faggetter told me it cost £700 for the ten-minute overrun. I made the mistake of mentioning this to Ian and, oddly, he insisted on blaming himself. He was terribly upset. He felt that if he'd written simpler dialogue everything would have gone more smoothly. But it wasn't his fault. Ian could hardly talk. It was just the emotional stress of his story coming to life, being shot. I bought him a brandy. Ian was sitting on the floor of the crowded BBC Club, bereft. Kate Easteal gave him a hand up. 'Any cheap trick for a bit of physical contact,' she said, smiling.

The following week, Sylvester was agitating for the leave-taking scene I wrote as his audition piece to be grafted onto Ian's script as the ending. I'd been resisting it. I felt it just wouldn't be right there. Besides, Ian might not have welcomed a chunk of someone else's writing being crow-barred into his story.

The work on the final draft of *Dragonfire* continued as we approached the last studio dates. Kate Easteal was typing out the latest draft. 'This is quite good. Did you write it?' 'No. Ian.'

Friday 7 August 1987. On the phone to Ian bitching about how Chris Clough missed all the nuances in his scripts. 'There was no problem with Malcolm's scripts because they didn't have any nuances.' This was a trifle unfair on Chris and Malcolm, but not entirely. Ian characterised Malcolm's scripts as 'gung-ho' and perhaps that was a fair description. But gung-ho wasn't necessarily a bad thing for a screenplay to be. Straightforward energy and drive and a clear, unambiguous story can translate well into television drama. But it's true that the filming of *Dragonfire* was full of missed opportunities, all of which were present and correct in the script.

The following Monday, I was out in North Acton with Ian for the producer's run of the remaining parts of *Dragonfire*. Coffee smell in the BBC lift. John Nathan-Turner was musing good naturedly; 'What can I say to the press about Sophie? A right little raver and a terrific fuck. We're delighted to have her on board, if only she can stay sober.' Needless to say, John was indulging in some rough and tumble humorous fantasy here. Sophie was outgoing but not *that* outgoing. And, under her extrovert exterior, Sophie was actually a rather dedicated and level-headed actress. She had a terrific quality of vulnerability blended with tomboy toughness. Plus she was very good looking.

Although Sara Griffiths was in the running for a while, it looked as though Sophie was going to be the new companion.

They were still screwing around with Ian's ending for *Dragonfire*. I learned a little lesson here. Because Sylvester was always unwholesomely keen on the leave-taking scene I wrote for his audition, Chris Clough asked me for a copy of it at the rehearsals. I let him have it after some discussion. I thought it was a good scene but wasn't entirely convinced it would work here. I gave them the scene just to prove that it was inappropriate and that Sylvester's memory was playing tricks on him; it wasn't as great as he thought. But of course, the next thing I knew they were photocopying the scene and it was being gene-spliced into the script. 'The lunatics have taken over the asylum,' said John Nathan-Turner.

Wednesday 12 August 1987. The zombie had a hyphenated name (Nigel Miles-Thomas, as it happens). Bonnie Langford was singing *Running Up That Hill*, doing rather a good impression of Kate Bush. We were back in the studio for the last of *Dragonfire*. Ian and I did the final rewrite of the final scene on a napkin in the Red Crush bar. Chris Clough was sitting at the table with us, talking about it. John Nathan-Turner came over and said politely, 'Excuse me, Chris. I think we may have cameras.' 'Oh Christ,' said Chris. They hurried off to the control room.

Sophie said she knew the journalist who had just interviewed Sylvester. 'I met her at the Equity A. M. I was being really raucous and right on.'

On the studio floor, they were climbing the ice face. Sylvester was trying to attract Gary's attention. He raised his hand. 'Please, sir. Can we take the wires off?' Sylvester is a natural acrobat and was happier climbing without the safety wires. Bonnie wandered in. 'Do I have to scream? No?' She wandered off again.

Sophie stood at the foot of the ice face for the photographers, 'snow' falling on her – Sylvester was crouched by the railing above, sprinkling confetti. 'Visual effects by McCoy.' Ian was happily chatting to the camera crew about maskers and framers. Mike Tucker said, 'See you guys tomorrow.' 'You're not stopping?' 'I've got to build the *Nosferatu*.'

Sylvester was hanging by a wire on the ice face. The powers that be had deemed that it was unsafe to work without wires. 'We want to know where the umbrella is,' said the control room. 'Sticking in my right testicle,' answered Sylvester.

Ian had invited two guests to the studio, two teenage girls from the drama class he taught who were reportedly his models for the character of Ace. 'Would you like to meet Bonnie Langford?' we asked them. 'No, we'd like to meet Philip Schofield' (a teen heart-throb of the day). The girls studied the studio. 'It's like a sweet factory,' said one of them. 'A sweet factory?' 'All the colours.'

stood up on the gantry making notes in my pocket diary in my microscopic handwriting. Henry Barber, the lighting director, walked past. 'Just you wait. In ten years you won't be able to read that.' Sophie told me about this 'great Batman book' she had bought. She meant Frank Miller's **The Dark Knight Returns**. The zombie was doing some prolonged crouching for the next shot and Gary Downie was saying, 'No matter how big and strong somebody is, their legs will start packing up in this position.'

We finally got to the farewell scene. I sat in the control room with scraps of paper all over me. It was a different gallery (control room), but the words I was hearing over the speakers were the same I had heard in the darkness months ago when I first set foot in a television control room, the night we shot the screen test. When I first joined this madhouse. All those months earlier. Everything coming full circle. Janet Fielding was even here again, sitting in the producer's booth.

'Funny business, time.'

Thursday 13 August 1987. Leslie was surrealistically dressed in his dragon's head and a Noel Coward dressing gown. In the gallery, one lighting technician was explaining the story to another lighting technician. 'It's not really a dragon. It's a bio-mechanoid.' Cathy the property buyer had got some knickers for Ian because Ian was complaining about the lack of strewn underpants in Ace's living quarters. Sylvester was practising his sliding on the plastic snow. John Nathan-Turner was talking to Kate Easteal about the end-of-shoot party that night: 'Just invite some lovelies. No old bitches.' There was Styrofoam snow on the control room floor, tracked in from the studio below.

'Meanwhile there's that poor dragon still waiting,' said vision mixer Shirley Coward, as an endless argument ensued about Glitz firing a gun and the Doctor grabbing his arm. 'This is getting silly, this is.' The terrible frustrating pain of trying to convey to the people on the studio floor just exactly what you wanted, and just what you could see in the control room. 'Can we have lights in the alien chamber please.' While Ian was down on the floor socialising, I was perched on a high chair in the dark gallery, keeping a finger on the pulse of the script. Watching the screens. The gaffer's blue trousers were eerily turning into trouser-shaped sections of the ice cave on the CSO. 'How's that, Dave?' 'If John Asbridge is going to continue the flattage upwards it's okay, yeah.' 'Do we have a single on the Doc?' 'Three's offering us a single.' 'He's on the blue, though.' On the Chromakey (the CSO), two pieces of flattage which have black (not blue) outlines painted on dumbfounded us and stopped the entire production until John Asbridge, a hero, hastened in with a spray can of yellow paint.

Tension was high. It was madness working so close to the line. It was already 9.30 pm. It was just silly doing things under that much pressure. 'We've got to tweak a lamp.' 'We've got an overlay problem.' Fraught discussion with Ian in a hot corridor. We were trying to change some dialogue to compensate for a fucked-up special effect (the star chart). Ian wanted to take his time and discuss it, but there was no fucking time. I was freaking now.

The control room wanted to know if the actor playing the dragon was out of his costume yet. 'Is Leslie out of his head?' 'He's been out of his head for years,' said Sylv. Richard Wilson, the technical coordinator, had a slight problem: 'My machine stayed servo unlocked.' A cameraman was talking to the director. 'Could you run through the shots, Chris, for we bears of little brain?' The lighting guy was talking about Sophie. 'She's black hair, darkly lit, so expect some solid blacks in.' Sophie was holding her ears after Bonnie's epic scream. Chris Clough said, 'Can we just give them a general note to put a little more zip in it?'

'Zip?' said Sylvester.

The dragon was presented at different angles on every monitor, an eerie presence in the darkened control room. The creature was magnificent, despite steam only coming out of one of its nostrils. 'Looks quite nice all that.' 'Excellent.'

Despite everything, we got it all done and finished on time. Bonnie passed out tiny personalised boxes of chocolate to everybody at the party and she in turn was presented with a bouquet of flowers. Ian finally got around to giving me the bribe he promised if *Dragonfire* got made. A box of multicoloured paper clips plainly labelled 'script editor's bribe'. The party was subdued. Everyone was exhausted. Once we'd gone home, someone broke in and stole the leftover booze.

Tuesday 22 September 1987. '"Last one back's a gooey mess." I wish I was Ian Briggs sometimes,' said Ben Aaronovitch. We were watching a rough edit of *Dragonfire* and it was looking wonderful. However, this initial euphoric impression was to fade as I saw more of the footage, in a more finished form and just over a week later…

Wednesday 30 September 1987. I was watching Ian's episode one with him and aching – aching at the cheapness and nastiness with which it had been shot. I told him, 'It's a B-movie, but it's a good B-movie.'

Thursday 15 October 1987. John Nathan-Turner said, 'This excellent idea – which Andrew had.' It was at times like this that John was a great guy to work with. He was happy to give credit where it was due, and not everyone is like that. The idea in question was to use a voiceover on the P. A. in Iceworld to suggest a substantial time lapse between the climax of the story and that final farewell scene we had had so much trouble over. I said, let Ace make a bing-bong announcement. John said, let Glitz do it, and he was right.

On Monday, there was a letter from Ian Briggs waiting at the office. It included a sheet of character notes on Ace for the next season's writers. 'I feel as if I'm giving away my only child,' said Ian. 'Look after her please.' Along with the notes on Ace, Ian had also included a photocopy of the famous napkin scene for me. Meanwhile Kate Easteal had been watching a tape of the first episode. 'I thoroughly enjoyed it,' she said.

On Friday a couple of weeks later, we got the fine cut and dubbed cassette of *Dragonfire* and Dominic Glynn's music (I hadn't known what to expect; but Dominic was a brilliant composer then and has only improved since) was scary and very atmospheric. Plus the script was good and the show was altogether good.

Monday 16 November 1987. I watched *Dragonfire* with Ben and he provided a running commentary, 'Oh, those ice corridors work quite well, don't they? Wicked. That's a good bit of writing. I like that.'

A couple of days later, John and I sat with Colin Rogers for the official viewing of episode two of *Dragonfire*. He said the monster was good (Lindsay's work) and he talked about Edward Peel ('Old Eddie Peel') being a trifle over the top with lines like, 'After 3,000 years the Dragonfire shall be mine.' He chuckled mildly at the philosophical discussion that Ian wrote, which I thought was crucifyingly funny. And that's about all he said. This was my favourite episode of the season. I really hadn't expected Colin to leap out of his seat when he saw it, but he was only mildly pleased. I was beginning to realise that **Doctor Who** was an exercise in masochism. Even when you were good, no one noticed. I asked Colin what they'd said about the last episode at Programme Review and he said, very gently and kindly, 'They don't watch it, Andrew.'

Tuesday 24 November 1987. There was a superb article on **Doctor Who** in general and *Dragonfire* in particular ('The writing is sharp') in the **Daily Telegraph**.

Don Henderson wrote to congratulate us on the ratings for *Delta and the Bannermen*, enclosing a detailed list of the shows we'd beaten. 'He's obviously studying the top 100 like a banshee,' said John Nathan-Turner. Sitting on the sofa in Colin Rogers' office, John looked like a haggard, chubby Teddy bear. The recent shit-storm of abuse and vicious criticism had actually probably brought people back to watching **Doctor Who** for the first time in years. Bill Cotton told Colin, 'I saw **Doctor Who** this week and it was rather good.'

We watched the third episode of *Dragonfire* and Ian's script was wonderful. Despite my reservations about the way it was directed, it was still the strongest story of the season. Colin Rogers seemed to appreciate how good the writing was. He hated the model work, though. Personally what I hated was that cute little kid.

Thursday 3 December 1987. Ian Briggs sat in my office watching a preview of *Dragonfire* episode three. When it was over, we looked at each other and began to bitch about the way it turned out. The list of scenes which had been butchered was just absurd. Ian said he could sit down and re-edit the episode that night and do a better job. 'It might sound big headed...' said Ian. It didn't. I believed him.

A few days later, my view softened somewhat. I watched episode three for the umpteenth time, as it went out in the evening, and was surprised at how good it was. The departure scene was moving and eerie. Now I could see why Sylvester had been so insistent about incorporating his audition scene in there. It's a wonderful scene for him; maybe his best of the season.

Early in the New Year, as a kind of coda, Ian Briggs was on the phone about his *Dragonfire* novelisation. 'I may have to lose the Iceworld Pussyfresh deodorant for a start,' he said.

7.35pm Doctor Who

starring **Sylvester McCoy**
in *Nemesis of the Doctor*
Part one of a four-part
adventure by
BEN AARONOVITCH

Andrew meets Ben, the
Daleks appear and racism is
fought.

Rachel..............PAMELA SALEM
The Girl..........JASMINE BREAKS
The Doctor.SYLVESTER MCCOY
Ace..................SOPHIE ALDRED
Mike.........DURSLEY MCLINDEN
Harry...............HARRY FOWLER
Gilmore........SIMON WILLIAMS
Allison..........KAREN GLEDHILL
Embery
   PETER HAMILTON DYER
Ratcliffe.........GEORGE SEWELL
Headmaster...MICHAEL SHEARD
Dalek operator HUGH SPIGHT
Voices
ROY SKELTON, JOHN LEESON
Stunt arranger TIP TIPPING
Theme music composed by
RON GRAINER
Theme arrangement/incidental music
KEFF MCCULLOCH
Costume designer KEN TREW
Script editor ANDREW CARTMEL
Designer MARTIN COLLINS
Producer JOHN NATHAN-TURNER
Director ANDREW MORGAN
● FEATURE: *page 101*
★ CEEFAX SUBTITLES

7.35pm Doctor Who

starring **Sylvester McCoy**
in *Nemesis of the Doctor*
Second part of a
four-part adventure
by BEN AARONOVITCH

Just how many bacon
sandwiches is 'four bacon
sandwiches'? Is that four
rounds or one sandwich cut
into four? Harry knows...

Rachel..............PAMELA SALEM
The Doctor.SYLVESTER MCCOY
Ace..................SOPHIE ALDRED
Headmaster...MICHAEL SHEARD
Kaufman.........DEREK KELLER
Girl................JASMINE BREAKS
Mike.........DURSLEY MCLINDEN
Gilmore.........SIMON WILLIAMS
Rachel..............PAMELA SALEM
Allison..........KAREN GLEDHILL
John..............JOSEPH MARCELL
Ratcliffe..........GEORGE SEWELL
Vicar..............PETER HALLIDAY
Dalek operators
   JOHN SCOTT MARTIN
  HUGH SPIGHT, TONY STARR
     CY TOWN
Voices
  ROY SKELTON, ROYCE MILLS,
  BRIAN MILLER, JOHN LEESON
Stunt arranger TIP TIPPING
Incidental music KEFF MCCULLOCH
Make-up designer
CHRISTINE GREENWOOD
Script editor ANDREW CARTMEL
Designer MARTIN COLLINS
Producer JOHN NATHAN-TURNER
Director ANDREW MORGAN
★ CEEFAX SUBTITLES

CHAPTER 7
Remembrance of the Daleks I

Strong women and no latex.

Friday 22 May 1987. We were in the middle of shooting *Paradise Towers* and had just shot the swimming pool locations at the Iraqi millionaire's deserted mansion in Chalfont St Giles, and I was heading home for the weekend, on the train to Kent, watching rabbits running up a green slope.

I'd just started reading an unsolicited **Doctor Who** script called *Knight Fall* by a maniac called Ben Aaronovitch. Caroline Oulton passed it on to me. I wanted to buy Caroline lunch, with champagne. Ben Aaronovitch's script was so good that I set it aside. I wanted to savour it. Picking up and reading a script like this was like hitting a seam of gold. And I was only on page eight. The possibility of a glowing season of **Doctor Who**, a triumphal tour, appeared before my eyes.

It was a bank holiday weekend, so it was Tuesday before I could see Caroline at the BBC. I was sitting flipping through a copy of Luis Buñuel's autobiography in her large new producer's office (I borrowed the book and I've still got it, Caroline). Caroline had moved up from being a mere script editor. I was waiting for her to finish talking on the telephone. Caroline had a macabre laugh and she used the word 'festive' as a peculiar term of approval.

Caroline discovered Ben Aaronovitch and according to her he was 'a young fat guy whose mum answers the phone'. She met him when he sent in a script called **The Dole Queue Detective**, which was similar enough to **South of the Border** that she felt she owed him an explanation. 'He's completely loopy. I think he even calls me Miss Oulton.' He had such a bizarre imagination that Caroline suggested he write a **Doctor Who**. And the rest is history…

Or at least, it was going to be if I could get through to directory enquiries and obtain his number.

Wednesday 27 May 1987. 'This is Ben Aaronovitch's dad,' said a voice on the **Doctor Who** answer-phone. It had been impossible to find a number for Ben so I took a chance on ringing a Dr Sam Aaronovitch who lived in the same part of London. (Actually, I took a chance on getting Kate Easteal to ring.) And bingo.

Thursday 28 May 1987. It turned out that it wouldn't have mattered which Aaronovitch we'd chosen in the phonebook; they're all related to Ben. Ben took a can of Diet Pepsi out of his blue plastic sports bag. He was talking about **Doctor Who** novelisations. 'I noticed that several of them were by C. P. members.'

'What's C. P.?' I asked.

'The Communist Party.'

Ben Aaronovitch was an interesting character. He pronounced

(Raymond) Chandler 'Shandler'. He'd spent the last few years doing more or less what I had been doing. On the dole, writing scripts and pursuing further education at home (the list of A-levels he'd failed was quite staggering, which was odd because he was the most intelligent person I'd ever met; an indictment of the conventional school system). All the while, he'd been desperately trying to break into television writing. He had an educated and instinctive understanding of science fiction which was way beyond that of any other writer I knew. Except maybe me.

I thought that he might just write something great.

Wednesday 3 June 1987. Ben Aaronovitch was biting his nails. 'I know what it is,' he said. 'They've tapped into Hell.' He was talking about his proposed **Doctor Who** story *Transit*, which involved the perilous construction of a futuristic transport system involving teleportation. Whenever I made a suggestion he could respond to it, equal it, or top it. I admired this guy. He could well have been the ultimate **Doctor Who** writer. And he was certainly on my wavelength. There was a tremendous excitement to working on a story with him.

Monday 8 June 1987. I was a trifle hung over because my girlfriend and I had been experimenting with cocktails ('This is the fun bit, smashing the ice up,' Kate had said, walking into the kitchen carrying a hammer). We drank port flips, with crushed ice. That morning there was a thin miserable summer rain falling and the grey city smelled like warm piss. I hadn't shaved and I felt seedy. My fingernails needed cutting.

'Sweet,' said Caroline. She'd looked into my office and caught me writing my diary. We discussed Ben. 'He really has tenacity,' said Caroline. I very much wanted to see Ben succeed. He was a natural television writer. He could write fluently and he was inventive and still at a point where his imagination and energy hadn't been blunted. He knew what he wanted and was working very hard for it and all he needed was a break. 'He's me two years ago,' I told Caroline. 'Sweet,' she said.

I got on the phone to Ruth Baumgarten, another script editor I knew. I was trying to scheme Ben onto the Writers' Course this summer. Ruth told me that the main concern was getting a balance of race and gender on the course. I almost ate the fucking telephone. If they couldn't get someone like Ben on it, what was the point of their course?

Wednesday 10 June 1987. I saw two writers called Ben – Steed and Aaronovitch. I couldn't find any common ground with Ben Steed (great name, though). But Ben Aaronovitch continued to delight and surprise. I liked him a lot. He was full of energy. I found myself worrying about the way he dressed. This was a reversal: my agent would complain about the clothes *I* wore (mostly lurid T-shirts) while I pretended not to be concerned about things like that. I wanted to see Ben do well. He was me a couple of years before.

A couple of days later, I was talking to Ben about his gate-to-Hell story for **Doctor Who** before he flew to the USA for his holiday. He had been up most of the night working on it. Fell asleep at the word processor. He looked through my filing cabinets for a vintage **Doctor Who** script and was having trouble remembering where Q comes in the alphabet. We walked out into the Shepherd's Bush sunlight to catch the tube to North Acton. I was wearing pale trousers and a white T-shirt (Calculus Cat – Death to Television) and a suit jacket. 'You're looking smart,' said Ben, 'I don't like it. I prefer your heavy rocker outfit.' The last few times I'd seen him I'd been wearing black trousers and sinister black T-shirts (featuring V from **V for Vendetta**). 'My friends were asking what you looked like,' said Ben. 'And I said, "He looks like one of us."'

At North Acton, we had lunch with Lindsay MacGowan in the Rehearsal Rooms. 'Once you had slime on it, you couldn't tell it was a leotard,' said Lindsay. Ben had been asking him about the costumes that Lindsay had worked on for **Aliens**.

The cast of *Paradise Towers* came in and I introduced Ben to various Kangs. I told Catherine Cusack, as she stood chatting to us, that if she held her glass upright the juice would stop running out of it. 'Oh, cutting,' said Ben. Sylvester came in. He was depressed about the election results, and quite rightly so. It was a landslide for the Conservatives. Margaret Thatcher had a 100-seat majority. I sat up the night before with my landlady and her friends, watching the results. 'We'll open the champagne when Labour takes its first marginal,' she had said. But the champagne remained unopened. I read the headlines on other people's newspapers as I travelled to work in the morning and the gloating of the gutter press was appalling.

Lindsay took us down to the workshop to show us the model of the superb monster he'd been sculpting for Ian's story, *Dragonfire*. Ben was asking intelligent questions.

Afterwards, Ben and I stood in the sunlight on a bridge overlooking the tube tracks at North Acton. 'I never expected anyone to sponsor me,' said Ben. I was thinking that, even if I couldn't succeed in pushing through his **Doctor Who** story, I'd do my damnedest to get him something else. We travelled back towards Shepherd's Bush and Ben continued on into the West End to change some money for his holiday. 'I'll take advantage of the exchange rates. I might as well get some benefit from the Conservative victory.'

Monday 3 August 1987. There was a headline in the **Sun** today: 'Charles' Cruel Argy Sex Pest'. It was almost a précis of the gutter-press lexicon; such a concentration of clichés that the syntax had almost evaporated.

(Argy means Argentinean, a race still subject to vilification for invading the Falklands and being defeated by our army.)

Ben brought his friend Anna to my office to meet me. She had blue scarves knotted in her black hair. I liked Anna; she was almost like Ben's agent. She sat across from me at the table in the coffee room and apologised about Ben in front of him. 'I can eat my own words, thank you,' said Ben. I explained about the difficulties of trying to get Ben on **Doctor Who** without personally having sole commissioning power and with the ground constantly shifting beneath my feet.

I saw my name come up on the **Doctor Who** titles for the first time that day, and I must confess it gave me a queasy little thrill. Ben was reminiscing about the Brixton riots: 'A bunch of style freaks burned down Burton's. Everyone heaved a sigh of relief when Spud-U-Like was unscathed.'

Tuesday 8 September 1987. I got home, depressed because John Nathan-Turner was thinking of bringing the Daleks back in the next season. In itself that was good news, but it meant that Ben Aaronovitch was going to have to abandon a storyline and start from scratch *again*.

Friday 30 October 1987. Lindsay MacGowan rang to say he'd got the job with the visual effects department. Excellent news. Even better news: John agreed to commission Ben Aaronovitch. I immediately rang Ben to tell him. When he heard, he was convinced it was some kind of sick joke I was playing on him. I called Kate Easteal into the office to speak to him. She assumed a Russian accent: 'Aaronovitch. You are commissioned.'

I invited Ben into the office and we discussed special effects in **Doctor Who**. '*Weng-Chiang* had a wanky rat in it, though,' said Ben.

John had been haggling with Terry Nation. Successfully. I rang Ben to give him the good news. He wasn't in, so I just left him a message: 'Tell him we've got the Daleks.' I'd waited all my life to legitimately leave a message like that. Ben rang back at the flat tonight. 'Tell him it's Davros here.'

The next day, we sat in the office discussing Dalek storylines and watching **The Rock and Roll Years**, doing research on the 1960s. We were planning to bring the whole 25 years of **Doctor Who** full circle in some interesting way. And to restore that initial mystery that had been eroded over the years as viewers learned that the Doctor was something called a Time Lord, that there are a load of other Time Lords, that he's not even in charge, that he can be put on trial… until he's just a midget version of the fantastic character he was when it started with scary old William Hartnell. (Maybe kids prefer to be scared by their heroes.) Now I'd been able to sneak in my ideas about restoring the mystery and putting a shiver down everyone's spine. By now, John thought that those ideas were his, or had at least quietly accepted that they were good ideas.

Saturday 14 November 1987. Ben rang me up at the flat. He was still saying, 'Davros here.' I explained to my girlfriend Kate that Davros was the creator of the Daleks. She said, 'Ben is Davros, in a sense, then, isn't he?' I told her Terry Nation was really the creator of the Daleks if we wanted to get pedantic about it.

On Monday, Ben was sitting in my office watching a duff old monster on a **Doctor Who** story from our video vaults (the much-pilfered and disorganised single shelf in John's office). 'My story is going to have two characteristics – strong women and no latex,' said Ben.

On Wednesday 25 November 1987, I rang up the BBC Gramophone Library to request some 1960s pop music compilations for Ben's Dalek story. I carefully explained who I was and what I was doing; after a long silence, the woman (whose name was Pamela) on the other end flatly refused to issue any records, saying it 'sounds a bit fishy' *and hung up*. At that moment, I felt locked into this sprawling antiquated bureaucracy where there was supposed to be a department to serve your every need but actually they only existed to torment you and make your job harder. I was literally incapacitated with rage. At this point, Ben came into my office and John followed shortly afterwards. Despite my best efforts, Ben and the producer hadn't been getting along very well. Now, as I sat there at my desk, exhausted after feeling so enraged, I wasn't even worrying about how they got along. But the aftermath of the Gramophone Library incident and my weariness seemed to have cleared a sudden space in which everybody could get along. Ben suggested crackling blue voltage from the fingertips of the sinister little girl in his script and John thought it was a great idea. Suddenly the ice was broken.

Maybe it was worth that damned phone call after all.

Monday 30 November 1987. 'You don't know how many positive things I've heard from women about Ace,' said Ben. He lent me a book called **Neuromancer** by William Gibson and that morning I started reading it on the train up from Kent and I kept setting it down and looking out of the window – the book was so good I wanted to savour it. Gibson's novel was a remarkable post-**Blade Runner** vision of science fiction. It was also a superb cynical thriller. And it introduced Cyberspace – a sort of illusional alternative world consisting of the global computer network; an intoxicating vision for anyone who'd ever enjoyed writing software. As I read the book, a whole world of possibilities swept open for me. I had never realised a science fiction novel could be as good as this. It had the quality of the writing of Tom McGuane at times. I wanted to write something like it.

I walked with Ben along Shepherd's Bush Green after a good discussion of his Dalek story. 'Move over *Weng-Chiang*,' he said. 'And mine will be politically correct, too.' Working with Ben was exhilarating. We finished the outline for episode two in an hour. It was a good speedy story conference, both of us bursting with ideas ('That's just what I was about to say').

I asked John Nathan-Turner what colour the things inside the Daleks were. 'A yucky green.'

Friday 18 December 1987. It was a week before Christmas. As I came into the building that morning, the guy in reception said, 'I think Ben's in already.' Ben had become something of a fixture. He was indeed in already and he gave me his revised and completed Dalek storyline and then went off for a coffee. He'd put a hell of a lot of work into it. I sat reading it at my desk in the quiet, holiday-abandoned BBC building, savouring it.

Ben and I were talking about the draft of the first episode he'd brought in. 'It is a McGuffin,' said Ben. 'It's a well-integrated McGuffin,' I told him. Ben looked blitzed, almost falling asleep in the chair. He'd been up all night finishing this. Some of the dialogue went on too long, but basically it was superb. The first Dalek fire fight was full of splendid detailed incident. I left a draft of Ben's episode one and his outline of the story at the **Doctor Who** office, to be forwarded to Terry Nation in LA. Then I was off to catch the train to Kent for Christmas.

Monday 28 December 1987. After the holiday weekend and still in Kent, I was back on the phone to Ben. 'I went to a well wicked rave-up on Boxing day,' he said, then went on to describe a scene in episode two of his Dalek story. 'You'll quite like it. It's nice and visual… Association types dribble out like rats and converge on him.' (The Association was Ben's version of a British fascist, Oswald Mosley-type organisation.)

The New Year arrived and our work on the scripts continued. 'I'm thinking of fiendish ways of working in the racial purity,' said Ben, who was always on the lookout for a bit of social criticism in his scripts.

Wednesday 13 January 1988. 'It's a textbook example of Communist Party science fiction,' said Ben. He was in my office, returning the cassette of *Frontier in Space*, written by C.P. member Malcolm Hulke. I was reading the latest version of his Dalek episode two while Ben was in the *Doctor Who* office, talking to Kate Easteal and 'having a euphemism' (smoking a cigarette). He'd borrowed my big green **Encyclopaedia of Science Fiction Movies** and his cawing laugh echoed down the corridor.

This was the day of the get-together in the **Doctor Who** office. This was the end result of a lunch I had organised with some of the writers and Sophie Aldred and Lindsay MacGowan, which had made John Nathan-Turner furious because I had neglected to include him. But he had then decided it was a good idea and instituted a formal get-together with all the directors and writers and Sophie and Sylvester as well.

It was a tremendously good idea for all these people to meet, in John's red office, full of cigarette smoke, with boxes of red wine and stale **Doctor Who** special offer crisps and Kate Easteal's Proclaimers tape on the tape deck. Ben was talking about racism as a gargoyle on the back of his black friends which had to be beaten off with a stick. Stephen Wyatt thought we should employ more short writers – Kevin Clarke, Graeme Curry and Ben are all over six feet tall. Graeme had just arrived from singing the *Messiah* ('Another Messiah,' he sighed) at Abbey Road Studios for Deutsche Grammophon. Sophie Aldred and I were comparing Tintin key rings.

Two days later, and Ben was getting as enthusiastic as a kid as he described the spectacular ending of his Dalek story to John Nathan-Turner and June Collins, our production associate. Listening to Ben's ambitious description, John was being witty about **Doctor Who**'s minuscule budget: 'It would be nice to have some money left to do Stephen's.' As always, a good script conference with Ben.

Wednesday 20 January 1988. I had decided I wanted Ben to follow me as script editor on **Doctor Who**. I didn't really wield any power to make this appointment and I didn't know how to arrange it, but still I was plotting towards it. Ben had a clear vision of the possibilities of the show. He could have been the perfect man for the job.

A week later and the production cycle was starting again. **Doctor Who** was coming to life. Activity in the various offices around me. Alan Wareing was using the phone in the room next door. 'The story, the story, you'll love it. It's about a psychic circus.' Ben was due in to deliver his episode four and hard copies of one to three, but he still hadn't arrived. 'Where's shyster?' asked Kate Easteal, 'Where's shit-face?'

Ben turned up eventually, having spent most of the night writing. He said he was having creative problems until he realised it was just low blood sugar. 'I just went and ate some glucose. Twenty minutes later I was writing fucking episode four.' He went into the **Doctor Who** office to 'have a euphemism' and chat with Kate and I sat reading his episode four, laughing with joy. 'Unlimited rice pudding,' said the Doctor, interrupting Davros's tirade about his plans to take over the universe.

As many fire teams as the budget can stand slam into place,' said a scene direction. I was looking forward to these scripts coming to life, meeting the actors who'd play Rachel, Mike, Gilmore. I wanted to hear these lines spoken.

Ben came and sat in my office, chuckling at his own dialogue. 'I don't remember half these lines because I was asleep when I wrote them.' We did a final fix on the scripts and Ben tottered off home. Kate photocopied the scripts and we taxied them to Andrew Morgan, who was the director for that story.

The following day, which was a Saturday, I rang Andrew to see that he'd got the scripts okay. 'It's a pity they've gone to printing already,' said Andrew. 'But never mind. We can always add the pages with my changes later.' I laughed aloud. The season had started in earnest.

'The game is afoot,' I told Andrew.

John had gone on holiday. I spoke to him at his hotel in Florida (he and Gary had moved on from Honolulu). He was deeply worried about the lack of response from Terry Nation. Terry Nation had given us permission to use the Daleks but he had yet to approve Ben's scripts, or at least Ben's storylines.

The following Monday, Andrew Morgan officially joined the production. His team were across the hallway, in the office directly opposite mine. Andrew was in there saying hello to them. Happy busy voices. They were working on a Dalek story, but Terry Nation had yet to officially grant us permission to make it. He'd deputised everything to his agent Roger Hancock and Hancock had been going to read Ben's scripts over the weekend and give his permission today. I phoned him that morning and his first words were, 'I read the first two [scripts] on Friday and my reaction was, frankly, "Forget it".'

I was polite and charming for the rest of the phone call, but completely freaked out. That night I hardly slept.

But in a couple of days we got the go-ahead from Roger Hancock, who had struck a better deal for his client in the process.

Andrew Morgan came into my office and went through Ben's script. '"Bits of Dalek ricochet around the cellar..."' he read. 'You'll be lucky.'

Thursday 11 February 1988. The production team were watching a load of old Dalek tapes. The sound of Davros going spare echoed along the corridor. I rang Ben and gave him an update on various script changes being proposed by Andrew. Ben said, 'Don't get uptight. Everyone's stating their bargaining positions. I'm Jewish. We can't lose.'

The production team did a read-through of Ben's scripts that afternoon in John's office, to time them. 'We'll all take it in turn to do Daleks.' 'Grab a Dalek as you go.' Everybody had bright green scripts in their laps as afternoon coloured the sky over Shepherd's Bush.

The following day, Kate Easteal said to Ben Aaronovitch, 'Don't wear plaid boxer shorts under white tracksuit bottoms,' and she was quite right, too. Later she would say, 'I've never heard a script conference with people *laughing* before.'

Ben and Andrew and John and I were in John's pillar-box-red office discussing Ben's episodes one and two and I suppose it did go very well, with people laughing pleasantly and me sipping pineapple juice and crunching my health food bars while the other three chain smoked cigarettes. Someone queried a point and Ben paused to think about it. 'I'm trying to recover the logic that got me there,' he said.

Things did hit a snag when John suddenly objected to the Doctor creaming a Dalek with a rocket launcher. Who could object to such a thing?

Tuesday 16 February 1988. 'He was pissed. He must have been pissed,' whispered Andrew. John had fallen over the night before and smashed his ribs on his metal Garfield briefcase. Andrew rang up Ben and I joined him on an extension and we had an impromptu script conference. 'Two people on the same telephone and they're both called Andrew,' said Ben. We were talking about the scene John wanted rewritten because all of a sudden he thought it uncharacteristic of the Doctor to blast a Dalek with a rocket launcher. Ben described the rewrite. 'If you do it that way, Ben,' I told him, 'You can keep the Doctor's line about humans being expert at killing and put it at the end of the scene.' There was a pause on the line and then Ben said to Andrew, 'You see, Andrew, great minds think alike.'

Thursday 18 February 1988. Ben and I sat in the big empty office at the end of the corridor, 301 Union House, using it as our rewrite office. Working on episodes one and two. 'I want to see this filmed,' said Ben, 'I want the honour and the glory. I want to be interviewed by poisonous fanzines.'

The following day, I had another script conference with Ben, John and Andrew. Despite my admiration for Andrew and John as practical programme-makers, it was obvious that Ben and I were on a different wavelength. They understood how a story works, certainly, but they didn't have any feel for science fiction. They didn't grasp the scale or the potential of what Ben was doing in his script. And, like a lot of other directors I've encountered, Andrew was a highly effective craftsman but at the same time, it seemed to me, had a disturbing immunity to nuance.

John again brought up the issue of the Doctor destroying Daleks, saying it was bloodthirsty and immoral and out of character. And I flipped and we actually came close to shouting. 'I'm already letting you bend the character of the Doctor as much as I can!' said John. Luckily, the guy with my new computer turned up at this point and I had to go into my office to show him where to set it up, which gave me time to cool off. When we resumed after lunch, John had decided to be funny and charming, which he genuinely was, and told us amusing stories about making **Doctor Who**.

Monday 22 February 1988. It was Ben's birthday. I walked back from Television Centre with him after lunch. 'You I trust,' said Ben. 'And my friend Anna I trust. Everybody else pays cash.'

John Nathan-Turner gave Ben a kiddie's birthday card with a badge that said, 'Ban homework' but which John had amended to read 'Ban rewrites'. At the end of the day, we left John and Tony Holland (the **EastEnders** script editor) in the **Doctor Who** office, drunk as lords, working their way through a giant bottle of wine.

My girlfriend had a terrifying nightmare that night in which I was leading her through an abandoned house, coaxing her on to look for the body of a dead nun. She woke up and said, 'Why were you making me look for it, Andrew?' I held her in the dark.

7.35pm Doctor Who

starring **Sylvester McCoy**
in *Nemesis of the Doctor*
Third of a four-part adventure
by BEN AARONOVITCH
Ace beats several shades of
cream out of an Imperial
Dalek and the BBC manages
to land a spaceship in a
playground!

Rachel.............PAMELA SALEM
Ace.................SOPHIE ALDRED
The Doctor.SYLVESTER MCCOY
Mike........DURSLEY MCLINDEN
Gilmore........SIMON WILLIAMS
Rachel.............PAMELA SALEM
Allison..........KAREN GLEDHILL
Ratcliffe..........GEORGE SEWELL
Harry.............HARRY FOWLER
Girl................JASMINE BREAKS
Emperor Dalek
　　　　　　　ROY TROMELLY
Dalek operators
　　　　　JOHN SCOTT MARTIN
　　　　　TONY STARR, CY TOWN
　　　　　　　　HUGH SPIGHT
Voices
　　　BRIAN MILLER, ROYCE MILLS
　　　ROY SKELTON, JOHN LEESON
Stunt arranger TIP TIPPING
Incidental music KEFF MCCULLOCH
Visual effects designer
STUART BRISDON
Script editor ANDREW CARTMEL
Designer MARTIN COLLINS
Producer JOHN NATHAN-TURNER
Director ANDREW MORGAN
★ CEEFAX SUBTITLES

7.35pm Doctor Who

starring **Sylvester McCoy**
in *Nemesis of the Doctor*
The final part of a four-part
adventure by
BEN AARONOVITCH
Davros returns with a plan
involving unlimited rice
pudding, burn marks and a
coffin.
Rachel.............PAMELA SALEM
The Doctor.SYLVESTER MCCOY
Gilmore........SIMON WILLIAMS
Allison..........KAREN GLEDHILL
Ace.................SOPHIE ALDRED
Mike........DURSLEY MCLINDEN
Ratcliffe..........GEORGE SEWELL
Girl................JASMINE BREAKS
Black Dalek operator
　　　　　　　HUGH SPIGHT
Dalek operators
　　　　　JOHN SCOTT MARTIN
　　　　　CY TOWN, TONY STARR
Voices
　　　ROYCE MILLS, ROY SKELTON
　　　　　　　BRIAN MILLER
Stunt arranger TIP TIPPING
Incidental music KEFF MCCULLOCH
Lighting HARRY BARBER
Script editor ANDREW CARTMEL
Designer MARTIN COLLINS
Producer JOHN NATHAN-TURNER
Director ANDREW MORGAN
(Next week 'The Crooked Smile)
★ CEEFAX SUBTITLES

CHAPTER 8
Remembrance of the Daleks II

Unlimited rice pudding.

Wednesday 24 February 1988. There was a fantastic front of grim storm light moving in, swallowing the daylight. Like a black and white photo in the window of the office across the corridor. In a few seconds it had gone from day to night. 'I hope it isn't the end of the world, Ben.' 'If it is, it'll really bugger up the production schedule,' said Ben Aaronovitch, and in the office across the corridor Rosemary Parsons laughed. Ben's found an old girlfriend in **Spotlight**. 'A right div brain. Good in bed though.' He kept looking through the actresses. 'How about her for Allison? She's in the four to a page section. She'll be cheap.'

Our production manager, known only to Ben as 'that white-haired guy', was persisting tenaciously in trying to get us to agree that the scene which it was critical to set in a period junkyard (to tie in with the very first episode of **Doctor Who**) didn't actually have to be set in a period junkyard at all.

Sophie Aldred was on the phone in the **Doctor Who** office and Kate Easteal passed her to me. She wanted to tell me how much she liked the first two episodes of Ben's script. She was surprised at how well written Ace and the Doctor were. She wanted to know what happened after the cliff-hanger of episode two. 'To me, I mean Ace.'

'We kill you off, Sophie,' I told her. It wasn't true.

Kate was on the phone later, dictating John Nathan-Turner's corrections for the **Doctor Who Magazine** proofs. 'In the sentence that reads, "Andrew Cartmel appears to be", insert "Producer John Nathan-Turner and Andrew Cartmel appear to be".'

Wednesday 9 March 1988. I returned to the office after being away ill for five days, and Andrew Morgan called me in for a chat. He looked worried. He showed me the pages for the junkyard location, all of which had to be shot in three days. Then he showed me the pages for the school – also a three-day shoot, but there were more than twice as many pages. Welcome back to **Doctor Who**.

The next day, Ben came in to do yet more revisions on his script and he was weary. 'It's like the NHS,' said Ben. 'There's nothing left to cut.' John Nathan-Turner exploded at Andrew as we sat in his office. 'It's going to be an unhappy show,' he said, 'I just know it's going to be an unhappy show. We offer people good parts and now we're slashing them to buggery. We're going to have unhappy actors.'

'Yes, that worries me too,' said Andrew.

'We've moved stuff out of the studio into the OB [Outside Broadcast] for you and now you're saying you've got too much OB,' snapped John. 'I'm fed up with this!' John had a point. The rewrites on this script had been endless and Ben was right when he said, 'We've cut all the flab, cut all the unnecessary flesh and waste matter. Now we're cutting healthy living tissue.' Ben liked his National Health Service analogies. 'John, you're being unfair,' said Andrew, 'I just want what we all want. To do the best job possible.'

Personally what I suspected was that Andrew had been somewhat wound up by his production manager and chief prophet of doom ('that white-haired guy'). I was beginning to think that, after all the cuts they'd demanded, the episodes might under-run.

Sophie popped into the **Doctor Who** office to borrow some video tapes of the show. She had a cold or a bug of some kind, maybe glandular fever. 'Don't know what it is.'

'The Green Death, Sophie,' said John.

Thanks to John, we convinced Andrew and his production manager of the simple sanity of taking a day off the three-day junkyard shoot (35 pages) and adding it to what was the three-day school shoot (70 pages). The school shoot had twice as many pages, but it now also had twice as many days. 'Oh no, can't take a day off the scrap yard,' were the white-haired guy's last words on the subject, but that seemed to be what eventually was done.

Monday 14 March 1988. Working late, I showed Andrew a tape of *Destiny of the Daleks*, directed by Ken Grieve. ('I bet this overran in the studio,' said Andrew.) By now, I'd seen just about every Dalek story ever made and this was the only one – or at least the only one in colour – which succeeded in making the Daleks *look* sinister.

Andrew sat patiently while I wound the tape to the various scenes I'd noted on a list. I hadn't analysed it before, but watching with Andrew it became clear that the reason the Daleks look good in this is that they are seen from low angles or vignetted – just a bit of a Dalek at the edge of the screen, up very close.

'I'll ask for lots of ceilings,' said Andrew, 'and have them in the foreground a lot.' He was obviously taking on board what I was saying and coming up with an intelligent strategy. I couldn't tell whether he was serious or just placating an obvious imbecile, but I hoped the former.

Sylvester McCoy came into the office, praising Ben's script and especially the scenes with the 'No Coloureds' sign and, more importantly, the tea stall scene where the Doctor talks with its black owner John (who would eventually be played, splendidly, by Joseph Marcell). Maybe we'd get to do it after all.

Andrew had some more rewrites he wanted done, what else is new?

But interestingly he'd added a line to Ben's script himself which was a very good, weird Doctor-ish line. 'Maybe Andrew is turning into a science fiction person,' said Ben.

A couple of days later, I saw a woman walk past my office in a blue headscarf. It was Sophie. She, Kate Easteal, Elaine (assisting in the office), Ben and I were going out to lunch together. On the way to the Hat Shop (that's what it was called, but it was a restaurant) I went into the pub to invite John along. He wouldn't join us, but it was just a courtesy gesture really, because last time a bunch of us went out like this without inviting him he'd got annoyed. 'Creep,' whispered Sophie, smiling.

On Friday morning, in the reception area at Union House, Andrew Morgan's team was clustered, standing around waiting for their coach so they could go on a recce. The visual effects assistant was carrying Ace's silver, aluminium-cored baseball bat. I rushed upstairs to ring Ben and tell him.

The following Monday, I'd just cracked a very difficult piece of revision for Ben's script. 'I'm a genius,' I told him on the phone. 'I know you're a genius,' said Ben, 'Get writing you bastard.'

Kate was typing more rewrites for Ben's scripts. 'I must read these scripts. The bits I've read are quite jolly.'

Monday 28 March 1988. We had the read-through at the North Acton Hilton – as the Rehearsal Rooms were nicknamed. The girl who played the spooky little child walked in with her mother. 'Little girl and handler,' whispered Ben. When the little girl started to read the wrong line, Andrew said, 'That's not you. That's another Dalek.' Sylvester was cracking jokes as he hesitated over a line: 'With integral… with integral… I've got double integrals.' It was a calculus joke, at that.

In her first story as a full companion, Sophie was proving to be a deft, effortlessly effective actress. Andrew was reading one of Ben's descriptions from the script: 'Model shot of the Dalek Mothership hanging…' he hesitated. 'Meaty,' said Sophie, providing the next word. 'Hanging meaty and sinister above the Earth,' concluded Andrew. What a terrific description.

When we got to the scene with the battle computer (the little girl) collapsing and Ace picking her up, Ben said, 'I think that's one of my most innovative ideas, you know.' Sylvester came to the 'I am more than just a Time Lord' line and delivered it with great power, aiming it like a gun. Sylvester and Sophie were excitedly humming the **Doctor Who** theme as they finished reading the script. They were a terrific team. Sophie with her AirWair Doc Marten bag and Sylvester with his Sylvester and Tweety Pie briefcase.

Ben and I walked to the tube together. We crossed the bridge where we stood in the summer, back when I was still trying to get Ben commissioned and this story was still just a dream. 'I'm really nostalgic about this bridge,' said Ben. We stood on the platform waiting for the train. 'I'll tell you what I wasn't very happy with,' said Ben. 'I wasn't very happy with the amount of coffee we got.'

Three days later, we had a run-through of the location stuff in Ben's script, which would begin shooting the next week. Sophie in a black T-shirt and black gym trousers swinging a baseball bat at a Dalek. 'All in a day's work,' she said, and struck a pose with the bat. All the Daleks were actually little silver-haired old geezers. 'Scene four,' called Ian Fraser, the new production manager (the 'white-haired guy' had moved on to another project). 'I'm lost, dear,' joked Andrew Morgan, 'What's that?'

Sophie and Sylvester were great together. They were obviously going to be a hit. There was a prop labelled 'Hand of Omega' which someone had altered to read 'Hands off Omega'. The Dalek procession with the coffin looked eerie, even with the little old men in their acrylic jumpers.

On Monday 4 April 1988, we started shooting. They'd opened the pub especially for **Doctor Who**. I was watching the Daleks roll out of a very nice period warehouse yard on sheets of plywood. They wobbled. They bumped into the gates, their heads came off, the visual effects assistants had to grab their 'arms' and drag them out of shot at the end of the plywood. And did I mention they wobbled?

Ah, the other fifth wheel,' said Ben as I arrived. It's true, the writer and script editor weren't exactly regarded as a vital part of the working team by this stage of the production. Cool empty London street, a small Waterloo street, south of nowhere in the warehouse area on a quiet bank holiday Monday morning. Sophie joined us, her hair scraped back and plaited, her face radiant and beautiful, pale with make-up. The Daleks wobbled some more as they come off the plywood. 'Go for it, Daleks,' shouted Sophie. Ben lit a cigarette.

I suddenly realised to my horror that I'd rather be here in this cold South London street under a grey sky watching the Daleks fuck up for the umpteenth take than cosy at home in the bosom of my family, warm and asleep.

I'd got up at the dead-man crack of dawn that morning to get there and of course British Rail screwed up and cancelled the train I was on. I sat around for an hour on stalled trains and cold platforms, writing story notes on my laptop computer.

They finally got the shot right. I turned and asked Ben, 'Was that good for you?' 'I'm smoking a cigarette, aren't I?' The Special Weapons Dalek had an unholy epoxy paint and plastic special effects smell. The floating, howitzer-bearing weapons platform in Ben's script had become, for budgetary reasons, the Special Weapons Dalek, a mean-looking, rust-stained, big-gunned, sort of First World War-style of Dalek – a splendid piece of visual effects design by Stuart Brisdon. I also loved his rust-crusted coffin for the Hand of Omega. However, things weren't all perfect. There was the matter of those wobbly wheel mechanisms on the standard Daleks and the heads that kept popping off.

I was standing there thinking that it didn't matter how good the scripts were, all those months of work by Ben and me, if the Daleks wobbled.

There was the smell of cut wood in the timber yard. One of the extras playing the Association men was black. I couldn't believe it. The whole point about the Association was that it was intended to be a fascist, racist, National Front, Oswald Mosley Blackshirt type organisation. Did no one read the fucking scripts? Did no one care? Oddly, Ben didn't seem too bothered. He said that these types of racist organisations do sometimes have black members. I found this hard to believe but, as usual, it turned out he was right.

John Nathan-Turner was watching Sophie on the monitor. 'Find the camera, you dizzy cow.' 'That noble profile,' said Ben looking at Sophie's face. Her Batman earring appeared on the monitor screen in close-up. 'Remember this is all creepy-creepy,' said Andrew Morgan, 'Little children behind the sofa for this one.'

There was grit sifting down onto me, squatting down in this warehouse yard to watch the monitor they'd set up in an abandoned outdoor toilet. Activity all around me. 'Dalek plonkers in shot.' 'Where's the reflectors, Danny?' 'We'll lose the wobble in the editing.' I certainly hoped so.

Escargots for lunch in a clean, warm, white bus decorated with video nasty posters (**Driller Killer**, etc). Sophie was signing autographs for a gang of little kids on BMX bikes. I joined her. 'Is that your boyfriend?' asked a little kid. 'No, he helps to write the scripts,' said Sophie. I thought that was a pretty good, succinct job description. A black woman was teaching her little sons how to pronounce 'Daleks'.

The chemistry between Sylvester and Sophie was great. Even from the first seconds, it was obvious they were going to be magic as a team. The viewing public wouldn't know what hit them. It would be the greatest thing since Diana Rigg and Patrick Macnee in **The Avengers**. The next season of **Doctor Who** wouldn't be a hit, I thought; it would seep into the public consciousness like a slow-acting drug. The season after would be huge.

Sophie showed me the **Watchmen** badge she'd added to her jacket. Sylvester the anarchist tried to get me to join them in the garden where they were hiding, just before a take.

The camera was mounted on the back of a blue Citroen 2CV. The car's brake lights flared as it was pushed into position. We were in a tunnel directly beneath Waterloo East station. Stuart Brisdon detonated a Dalek at the far end of the road. (I should perhaps mention here that when I asked Mike Tucker and Lindsay MacGowan about Stuart, they said, 'He's good at bangs.') There was a vast explosion. The tunnel became a mouth of fire. Massive sound. A wave of black smoke. Fragments of Dalek flying through the air. An alarm began to ring above us, on the railway platform. Sirens in the distance. Within a minute and a half, the emergency services had begun to arrive. The police, four fire engines. Local people were pouring out of the council estate across the road. John Nathan-Turner and Ian Fraser were walking around looking like guilty schoolboys.

Later I was reading the script, waiting for a tube going home. The girl on the bench beside me leant over. 'Someone said they were bringing the Daleks back. I'm BBC as well. When's it going to be transmitted?' Smell of naphthalene on my hair.

The second day of shooting fell on my birthday, 6 April. I arrived on location and walked around to the catering wagon to see if they'd got any breakfast left. I walked back with a sausage bun. As I passed a van, the back doors sprang open. Sylvester and Sophie were inside. 'Good morning, Andrew,' said Sophie. 'Pull him in here with us,' said Sylvester mischievously. They dragged me into the back of the van and I hid under a seat, clutching my sausage butty as the engine started and we roared forward into a take.

This location was the back yard of the Living Steam Museum on Green Dragon Lane in Kew. The museum was the site of a BBC visual effects Christmas disco that Kate Druce and I went to. The back yard was full of junk. Steam engines. Flakes of rust floating in rainwater pools in the metal grooves of big abandoned machinery. Sylvester and Sophie leapt out of the back of the van. They got the take. I emerged from hiding. The sun came out over the Steam Museum. I grabbed an upright pole as I pulled myself into the van. The pole was attached to the dummy aerial on the top of the van. The aerial was now considerably lower than it had been. I may have been immortalised in a continuity fuck-up.

'It's my birthday today,' I told Sylvester. 'I wanted to do something special, like come to work stoned. But I didn't think it would make any difference.' 'You have done something special,' said Sylvester, 'You left half your sausage bun in the back of the van.'

Sylvester delivered his line – 'What's the situation?' – and opened the side door of the van. He opened it energetically. In fact, so energetically that he pulled it completely off the van. 'We won't have any more door acting,' said Andrew.

'I'm going to get my chunky gun out,' said the actor playing Group

Captain Gilmore, Simon Williams. He was taking the piss out of one of Ben's scene directions. 'Do you want me to arrive, or shall I be there?' he asked Andrew. 'Arriving, please,' said Andrew.

A stuntman flew backwards through the air on a wire as a Dalek shot him. The stuntman hit a wall of corrugated tin and slid down. Spontaneous applause. On the corrugated junkyard walls were tatters of posters: 'No More Apartheid Murders', with photos of the victims and the dates. One of the kids was killed on my birthday, 6 April 1979.

Ben said, 'I do like that truck, man. It's such a mean-looking truck.' The truck disgorged soldiers. Ben had named the Special Weapons Dalek 'Christina' because he said it reminded him of an ex-girlfriend. Simon Williams and Sylvester showed us coin tricks at lunch. Sophie talked about the poll tax. Ben was wearing a bright cotton shirt with African motifs on it. 'I hate this shirt,' he said, 'It was bought for me by the Special Weapons Dalek.'

I still have a folded page of yellow script from that shoot with a map printed on one side with the legend: 'Totters Lane Junkyard Location… Wed 6th & Thu 7th April'. There's a big fat arrow pointing to the Kew Bridge Steam Museum. On the other side I've written a note to myself: 'Early Warning synopses and blurbs for Autumn Launch brochure'.

Monday 25 April 1988. We were doing the second block of location shooting, at the school on Macbeth Street. Sophie cheekily pinched Ben's bottom. She stood happily swinging her baseball bat on top of the wooden stairs. When they performed the Ace-Mike argument it made my eyes sting with tears. Sylv produced a calling card out of thin air. Ben was chuckling uncontrollably at his own lines.

Sophie opened all the remaining windows in the chemistry lab to get the cigarette smoke out. Sylvester was leaning out one of the windows. He said 'enjoy the view' as a nubile black woman swayed past in tight jeans. Andrew came in and sighed over his shoulder. I overheard some discussion of a future location shoot and I heard the word quarry and my heart sank.

Another few yellow scraps of script record my impression of the studio shoot (on the other side of the script are some scenes in the Dalek Mothership Bridge, with some additional Dalek dialogue written in by hand: 'Davros will save us. Where is Davros?')

Thursday. Here's a picture of me, a snapshot in time as I set off to the BBC for the *Remembrance of the Daleks* studio filming. It was morning at my girlfriend's flat and I was flossing my teeth, listening to Bo Diddley, gloriously happy about the Dalek story though a little worried that I was becoming infatuated with the lovely Sophie. I stepped out into the street and it was a glorious day. Cherry blossoms were falling on my face. It was the last daylight I'd see for a while. We were now shut up in the studio in Television Centre.

The screen in the Dalek shuttle had the BBC test card of the little girl on it (just like you'd get when the BBC was off the air for the night). A surreal moment. Sophie was running around in striped trousers and a tank top, wielding her baseball bat, with a look of horror on her face. 'Human female is now leaving the building. Exterminate.'

Between takes, the unreconstructed male cameramen were scanning Sophie's breasts, her crotch, her Tintin wristwatch as she sat on the stairs. She was looking spectacularly and wonderfully anachronistic in the 1963 suburban parlour in her 1980s workout gear.

Andrew was talking to Scott Talbot, our sound man. 'Scott are you going to do some ding dongs? Are you going to do that for us? Doorbells?' Andrew had staged the staircase conversation between the Doctor and Ace brilliantly, with soldiers bursting between them at intervals to give a sense of urgency and authenticity. They were making a considerable noise, though. 'Can I just say fairy feet again? Especially to the soldiers.'

'Is that wire meant? Sorry? That wire by Sophie's feet. Is it meant?' Sylv lost his concentration, distracted by some movement by one of the soldier extras. 'The Hand of Omega is the mythical name for... someone's playing with his helmet down there.' General laughter.

'We're going to split the feeds on this, so Camera 4 you'll be on the ISO. Can we have the dead Dalek in the back of 4's shot?' I sat in the gallery, watching a white Dalek going up a set of stairs in a cellar set. Dave Chapman was watching billiards on his TV monitor, waiting for the shoot to reach the point where his visual effects expertise was needed. Voices from the studio floor echoed in the darkness. 'No, we have to do it again because of a boom shadow, darling.'

On the monitor, there was an eerie frozen image of the little girl in mid blast in a suburban doorway. While we waited for the next shot, the little girl talked to the stuntman about living dangerously: 'How many miles an hour does it go?' she asked. Not that many.

Ben was sitting with me, uncharacteristically subdued and pale. He'd thrown up with the stress. We were watching the little girl stalk Ace. It's a striking scene. It ends. In the control room silence afterwards I said, 'Well it scared me.' Ben said, 'It's creepy, man. I don't want children anymore.' We were both in awe of Jasmine Breaks, who played the sinister little girl (later revealed to be the Dalek battle computer). Ben asked Andrew, 'Where did you find her? An agency called Creepy Kids?' 'She is good, isn't she?' agrees Andrew Morgan.

But it wasn't just Jasmine Breaks who was brilliant. This whole story was superior. There was the BBC 1963 call sign up on the shuttle screen, with angular Dalek 'Arabic' script across it. I decided that **Doctor Who** is wonderful in cosy suburban surroundings. The contrast of the frightening and familiar, the alien and domestic, is great.

John Nathan-Turner gave a long spiel about why Sophie's Tintin watch would have to go. Apparently it looked like a prop in one of his earlier **Doctor Who** stories. There seemed to be a bit of conflict between John and Sophie at the time. Shame about that watch. She'd be upset to part with it. Meanwhile, on the control room screen, Sophie looked positively Pre-Raphaelite and radiant with her hair loose in the artificial morning sunlight of the parlour set.

Sophie's big scene commenced. It was interrupted almost instantly by drilling from somewhere in the dark mass of Television Centre. We all stopped and stared up in silence. The savage sound of the drilling spread through the big metal beams of the cathedral-like building, like a big insect buzzing. We ground to a halt.

The next day we were back in the studio.

Pamela Salem and Karen Gledhill (Rachel and Allison) walked by in curlers, carrying a TV. In the warehouse with George Sewell, I had the ticklish feeling we were doing something really wonderful. Sylv and Sophie inspected the glittering plasma globe that our prop department had bought to serve as the time controller. 'It's like the inside of my head,' said Sylvester. No, Sylvester, what it was really like was a naff prop that someone with no understanding of science fiction thought was futuristic and which would already be dated and old fashioned before this episode was even broadcast.

Technicians moving cables, slapping them on the floor to avoid the Daleks running over them. Camera rehearsal: Sylv was clutching a baseball bat and leaping out of a dry-ice-filled coffin. Jasmine Breaks was sitting behind a camera, wearing a seatbelt (to keep the little kid from toppling off), talking to fanzine reporters. Lynn Grant, the assistant floor manager, was having her back massaged by an off-duty Dalek. Fucking London Transport made me miss the smashing of the transmat.

'That was a little slow.' 'There was a boom shadow in the mid-shot.' In the gallery you could look from a control screen depicting the battle computer and the black Dalek to Dave's TV featuring Mrs Thatcher and the transition seemed terrifyingly natural.

Andrew was so tense he took a bar of chocolate out of his bag and began to glumly crunch it. A sign of extreme strain in our normally unflappable director.

'Time controller on please. Thank you.' I loved the idea of the Doctor zapping the time controller, of his unearthly powers. During the warehouse interior scenes, I sat in the gallery muttering, 'Lovely, lovely, lovely.' 'I want one of those for my coffee table,' said Shirley the vision mixer, referring to the time controller (a chintzy globe with electrical sparking effects inside it). Actually, I still thought that in a few months she'd be able to have one and this prop would seem about as exotic and futuristic as the digital clocks you see in 1960s futuristic movies, huge lumbering behemoth tape drive mainframe computers or a lava lamp. People in **Doctor Who** just didn't understand science fiction or real science technology.

Ben had gone down and fetched tea for everyone in the gallery. 'Thank you mum, thank you dad,' said John.

Memo from Turner: there was a memo from John lying around complaining about Sophie's badges on her costume. Ace's bomber jacket featured an assortment of badges, both as souvenirs of her travels and a kind of advertisement of her personality. The problem was that Sophie had been adding some badges of her own without going through channels (ie the costume department) and there had been continuity problems as a result. And John had flipped. When I walked into the producer's booth, I found John and Alan Wareing talking about Sophie. 'And now she's complaining because I won't let her have a late-night taxi.' Alan waves a disgusted, dismissive hand. For some reason, perhaps because this was the first proper story they'd done together, John and Sophie were totally in conflict. John talked to me about Sophie, and he was being very diplomatic and good about it all. But he said, 'It's the worst relationship I've had with any of the companions.' God knows why they'd got each other's backs up, but they had. Maybe it was just because they were such different people. A sort of ideological difference. I wished they weren't at loggerheads. They weren't for long. Sophie and John would bury the hatchet over several drinks in a country pub during the shoot for *The Greatest Show in the Galaxy* and they remained on good terms thereafter.

Sylvester was brilliant at being scary with the coffin, talking to it. Watching him, I decided I should write a script for **Doctor Who** and call it *Unearthly Powers*.

Ben and Kevin Clarke were interviewed for a US fanzine. 'My interview was a model of evasion,' said Ben. 'They were both very good,' said Kate Easteal.

'We're losing time,' said Andrew. 'I'm getting concerned.' Ian Fraser said, 'You're not the only one.' Martin Collins, the designer, was because they were threatening to shoot his set (the Bridge on the Dalek Mothership) without the special neon lights he'd painstakingly designed and built – because they couldn't find the plugs. He was threatening to go down to the studio and stand in the middle of the set so they couldn't shoot it until someone did find the plugs and they could switch the neons on. Time was running out but Martin was entirely in the right. He had worked hard on the lighting design and he knew it'd be great and he refused to just abandon it. Where were those bloody plugs? Finally, they were found, the neon lights went on, and the shooting continued.

I was sitting here in the warm womb-darkness of the control room watching the action unfold on the Dalek Mothership. This whole scene – the Dalek bridge, the map, angular Arabic scrolling on the screen, the Emperor Dalek – all assumed the lineaments of a dream I once had. *Déjà vu* amidst the gallery chatter.

'What's on desk effects Dave? Anything useful?' 'Am I breaking up?' 'You were but you're better now.' 'Will you tell Terry he forgot to say "Prepare the Assault Shuttle?"' 'Andrew Morgan – lighting here. Does the transmat come on during this scene?' Terry Molloy as Davros asked, 'Do I take my cue for closing the shutter from the screen going out of focus?'

John suggested another way of doing a shot on the Dalek bridge which just wasn't working ('It's just inanimate objects talking'). John was absolutely right – and I was beginning to understand why. Learning the grammar of television storytelling was like learning a new language.

It was 9.30 at night. 'Why is Ian talking in a Dalek voice?' asked Ben. 'Shut up Ben, please,' said Andrew.

Sylvester was repeating the final scene. Pam Salem was saying, 'You weren't ready that time.' She added firmly, 'Tell them in the control room to wait.' 'Supportive actors week,' said Sophie with approval, sitting beside me in the gallery.

Then it was over. Once again, despite the odds, we'd managed to do it all. Champagne in the BBC Club bar. Sylvester drinking champagne and Guinness.

Months later, more than a little battle scarred, I sat with John Nathan-Turner for the viewing of *Remembrance of the Daleks*. The viewing was a ritual in which the producer and the script editor sat down with the head of drama series and serials at the BBC so he could check on their output. The former head of drama was Jonathan Powell who had now moved on to a more lucrative and powerful position. The man we were dealing with now was Mark Shivas, an experienced and respected producer who had made his name with **The Six Wives of Henry VIII**, which had been a big international hit for the BBC.

Doctor Who clearly was not Mark Shivas' top priority, but he sat and watched the episodes with us patiently enough. I was rather excited because one of the best and finest moments in *Remembrance of the Daleks* was coming up. It was the scene where Ace is at the boarding house and discovers a sign on the window which says 'No Coloureds'. I was very proud of this scene, which I thought gave an authentic insight into the racist attitudes of the period and powerfully showed Ace's repugnance for them. The look of horror and disgust on her face is clear.

I felt it was a superior and unusually adult dramatic scene for our show and I was keen for Shivas to see it and give us his reaction to it.

So John and I were sitting on the sofa in Shivas' office, watching the tape with him, and the No Coloureds sign scene was coming up. It was just about to begin, when Shivas' phone began to ring on his desk.

'Excuse me,' he said, 'keep watching.' Shivas went to his desk and took the call. The No Coloureds scene unfurled on the screen. Shivas was on the phone, preoccupied with the conversation. His back to us. The scene ended. The story moved on to the next scene. Shivas' phone call ended. He rejoined us. He'd missed the whole thing.

I was aghast and furious, so I did something unprecedented for a script editor in a viewing. I insisted that the head of drama *rewind the tape and watch the bloody scene*. John looked at me with a combination of astonishment and amusement. But Mark Shivas indulged me. He rewound the tape. He watched the scene. He looked at me.

All he said was, 'You should have had her tear up the sign.'

Maybe he was right.

Just before *Remembrance of the Daleks* was transmitted, John took Ben out to the Bush, the local pub for BBC drama series and serials. He proceeded to buy Ben drink after drink, getting him drunk as a skunk, and telling him story after story about true transmission disasters that had befallen shows in the past.

Ben reeled home, deeply intoxicated and profoundly paranoid, to join a riotous party of his friends, get drunker still, and watch the first episode of his first television script go out without a hitch.

7.35–8.00pm
Doctor Who

starring **Sylvester McCoy.**
*Doctor Who and the
Psychic Circus*
by STEPHEN WYATT
Andrew is surprised to find
the quarry isn't as
disappointing as he'd
expected. Clowns, junk mail
and a hearse add to the
drama.
Ringmaster.............RICCO ROSS
The Doctor.SYLVESTER MCCOY
Ace.................SOPHIE ALDRED
Nord.............DANIEL PEACOCK
Chief clown..IAN REDDINGTON
Bellboy.....CHRISTOPHER GUARD
Flowerchild...........DEE SADLER
Stallslady...........PEGGY MOUNT
Captain..............T. P. MCKENNA
Mags...............JESSICA MARTIN
Whizzkid.......GIAN SAMMARCO
Bus conductor
            DEAN HOLLINGSWORTH
Morgana.....DEBORAH MANSHIP
Theme music composed
by RON GRAINER
Incidental music MARK AYRES
Costume designer ROSALIND EBBUTT
Script editor ANDREW CARTMEL
Designer DAVID LASKEY
Producer JOHN NATHAN-TURNER
Director ALAN WAREING
■ CEEFAX SUBTITLES

7.35pm
Doctor Who

starring **Sylvester McCoy.**
*Doctor Who and the
Psychic Circus*
Second of a four-part
adventure by STEPHEN WYATT
Asbestos! Argh! Run! Hide!
Captain..............T. P. MCKENNA
Mags...............JESSICA MARTIN
Ringmaster.............RICCO ROSS
Bellboy.....CHRISTOPHER GUARD
The Doctor.SYLVESTER MCCOY
Ace.................SOPHIE ALDRED
Chief clown..IAN REDDINGTON
Morgana.....DEBORAH MANSHIP
Bus conductor
            DEAN HOLLINGSWORTH
Mum.........JANET HARGREAVES
Dad.................DAVID ASHFORD
Little Girl.....KATHRYN LUDLOW
Nord.............DANIEL PEACOCK
Deadbeat................CHRIS JURY
Whizzkid.......GIAN SAMMARCO
Incidental music MARK AYRES
Make-up designer DENISE BARON
Script editor ANDREW CARTMEL
Designer DAVID LASKEY
Producer JOHN NATHAN-TURNER
Director ALAN WAREING
■ CEEFAX SUBTITLES

7.40pm
Doctor Who

starring **Sylvester McCoy.**
in *Doctor Who and the
Psychic Circus*
Part three of a four-part
adventure
by STEPHEN WYATT
John likes the Whizz Kid,
Ace doesn't like clowns, the
Whizz Kid likes the Psychic
Circus and the Doctor likes
Peggy Mount's sweetcorn
slop.
Visual effects designer
STEVE BOWMAN
(For cast see page 68)
■ CEEFAX SUBTITLES

New from BBC Video
Doctor Who in
The Terror of the Zygons
The Talons of Wang Chiang
price £9.99

7.35pm
Doctor Who

starring **Sylvester McCoy.**
*Doctor Who and the
Psychic Circus*
Last of a four-part adventure
by STEPHEN WYATT
The Gods of
Rrrrrrragnarrrrrrrok
rrrrrreveal theirrrrr
dastarrrrrdly plans! Andrew
settles himself in for another
year on *Doctor Who.*
Mags...............JESSICA MARTIN
The Doctor.SYLVESTER MCCOY
Captain..............T. P. MCKENNA
Ringmaster.............RICCO ROSS
Dad.................DAVID ASHFORD
Mum.........JANET HARGREAVES
Little Girl.....KATHRYN LUDLOW
Bus conductor
            DEAN HOLLINGSWORTH
Ace.................SOPHIE ALDRED
Deadbeat................CHRIS JURY
Chief clown..IAN REDDINGTON
Morgana.....DEBORAH MANSHIP
Stallslady...........PEGGY MOUNT
Incidental music MARK AYRES
Lighting DON BABBAGE
Script editor ANDREW CARTMEL
Designer DAVID LASKEY
Producer JOHN NATHAN-TURNER
Director ALAN WAREING
■ CEEFAX SUBTITLES

CHAPTER 9
The Greatest Show in the Galaxy

I love his mad laugh.

The Greatest Show in the Galaxy represented a watershed in my thinking on **Doctor Who**. With the previous story in production, *Remembrance of the Daleks*, I had felt we were providing first rate scripts and providing them for the best incarnation of the Doctor in years, if not decades. On top of all this, and we had just signed up a new companion worthy of this new Doctor. All the elements were in place.

From this point on, I was less caught up in the process of shooting of each episode. The novelty of that had worn off. I had realised that as a script editor there was a limit to how much effect I could have on a show once shooting began. There wasn't much more I could do without becoming a director or a producer and either of those possibilities was some years away.

So from now on my policy was create the best script possible and see how it fared in the production process. As I said, all the elements were in place. Now we had to see if the shows lived up to these elements.

As a result, starting with *The Greatest Show in the Galaxy* I was increasingly critical of failures in the design and special effects, traditionally the Achilles heel of **Doctor Who** – and areas where as a script editor I had little influence. I always felt we had provided the best raw materials and it was unspeakably frustrating to see how often the resulting shows didn't live up to their promise.

One story that succeeded was *The Greatest Show in the Galaxy*, a title I never liked and one that is ironically unworthy of the show it denotes. One reason for its success was that it showed some brilliance in the areas of design; the quality of the make-up and the costumes added immeasurably to its impact.

The creation of *The Greatest Show in the Galaxy* began on 6 May 1987. I was sitting in conference with John Nathan-Turner and Stephen Wyatt just after we had wrapped the shooting of *Time and the Rani*. Stephen's script for *Paradise Towers* had turned out well and we were going to commission him to do another story for the next season. That was the good news. But my blood ran cold when I heard about the story that John was proposing. While I had been blissfully on holiday in Spain with my girlfriend, sitting in the sunshine on thyme-scented hills, John was talking to Stephen about a story set in a fairground.

I couldn't imagine a worse location. It was so trite and kitsch and boring. As I said, my blood ran cold. But halfway through the meeting, which proved to be a rather dead-end discussion, John suddenly said, of his own volition, 'I'm going off the idea as we talk about it.'

So we ended up with a circus instead of a fairground. A circus was also trite and kitsch and boring, but to my thinking universes better than a fairground, especially since we had the **Circus of Dr Lao** (Charles G. Finney's marvellously waspish 1935 fantasy novel) as a reference point.

A week later, I was still thinking about the new story. I decided I needed to get hold a copy **The Circus of Dr Lao**. It's a vinegary classic of sardonic dark fantasy and I thought it could have a bearing on the fairground story which John and Stephen seemed intent on cooking up. Circuses and fairgrounds as a locale turned me off. But if we had to do a story like that, we should do it well.

There are certain honourable antecedents in the genre: Ray Bradbury's **Something Wicked This Way Comes** which followed Finney's wonderful book. I wanted Stephen to read **Dr Lao**. I didn't have a copy of the book in London, and the Fantasy Centre in Holloway didn't have a second-hand copy in stock, so I phoned an old flame of mine, Linda Simpson. I felt a strange pang of nostalgia. I knew she'd have a copy because the book was sort of part of our whole love story. Some people had songs. We had this book.

We biked Linda's copy of the book over from Plaistow and I passed it on to Stephen.

A few days later, Stephen and I went for lunch in the Television Centre restaurant and talked about the book. I wasn't proposing that Stephen borrow from it for his story. I wanted him to soak up its mood and see the possibility for a fairground setting in a dark fantasy story. Stephen wasn't especially knocked out by the book. He changed the subject and said he thought that we should collaborate on creating some fabulous hit series and sell it to the Americans and get very rich. He daintily picked up his lamb chop and gnawed the meat off it in a few quick, savage movements.

The next day, at the office, I was talking to Stephen, feeling happy about this circus story. I rang him up that morning to tell him that I'd had an idea that just about solved all the problems for us. Stephen chuckled. 'The support system for writers is very good on this show,' he said.

Three months later and *The Greatest Show in the Galaxy* was still in the discussion stage. Stephen and I and my girlfriend Kate Druce and her mum went to see Circus Oz in Waterloo, ostensibly as further research for Stephen's script. Circus Oz were amazing. Black lights and didgeridoo music, women in business suits crawling like spiders, a Raymond Chandler hardboiled detective story vignette performed upside down, hanging from the ceiling, a guest appearance by Death and his slaves ('Come on Wayne, come on Rupert. I tire of this. Back to the Pentagon.')

Back at the office in Shepherd's Bush, I'd arranged a lunch with Sophie

Aldred with Stephen and Graeme Curry, so they'd have a chance to meet the new companion. Kate Easteal came along, too, and we were sitting in the Hat Shop restaurant. Sophie was talking to Stephen about the Polka Theatre Company and to Graeme about South London football clubs. It was a good idea getting these people together. Sophie had already received her first fan letter, 'Very neatly typed on graph paper. A real anal retentive.'

On Friday, I headed home to Kent for a long weekend. Stephen rang me up about the script, *The Greatest Show in the Galaxy* (John's title; we let him have it; it made him happy). In fact, he rang me up twice. I'm glad and amazed at his progress. 'Take care, dear,' he said, and rang off.

A few days later, John was reading the first draft of Stephen's episode one. 'Griophos again. He's building up to a Griophos story.' (Griophos was a planet in *Paradise Towers*; apparently Stephen just liked the name.)

Monday 2 November 1987 was a bad day for the **Doctor Who** script editor. The detailed storyline we'd worked out for Stephen's script fell apart before our eyes. I walked up to Television Centre and had supper with Stephen, feeling useless because he'd still got three episodes to write and I couldn't think of a single helpful idea I could offer. Walking through the Uxbridge Road traffic, Stephen wasn't nearly as depressed as I was. We saw a truck on Shepherd's Bush Green and on the side it read 'B East & Son'. That cheered us up.

Wednesday 4 November 1987 was a good day for the **Doctor Who** script editor. Stephen's storyline was coming back into being, in a workable new form, almost entirely thanks to Stephen. I just polished a few points.

Roy Scammell, a stunt man and fight arranger on several **Doctor Who** stories, and his young sidekick came in to show John a new trick. Basically, Roy dressed up like a giant version of a Japanese toy robot with big flared boots concealing his roller skates, and he skated up and down the Union House hallway. He got his young friend to pull him along on a wire and the wire *snapped*.

John and Kate Easteal and Stephen and I were watching. Kate and Stephen were clench-jawed with repressed laughter. I was desperately not looking anyone in the eye. Roy scooted down the hallway and around the corner to build up speed, his roller skates whirring on the floor. Chris Penfold walked through the door behind us and said, 'Is it safe?' I loved that job.

After the stuntmen and Stephen had left, I was sitting in my office and the phone rang. The guy on the reception desk downstairs said, 'There's a sausage in reception for you.'

'A what? A sausage?' The voice on the phone was garbled.

A sofa sausage,' said the garbled voice.

'A Sophie Aldred?' I was clutching at straws.

'Yes.'

'Send her up.'

By December, Stephen had delivered all four episodes and John had read them. In episode three, an obnoxious little brat (the Whizzkid) who'd collected all the Psychic Circus' posters, etc, got splatted. 'I adored the barker,' said John happily as he read this.

In the New Year, we began gearing up to go into production on *The Greatest Show in the Galaxy*. Stephen's script was full of good satirical detail, like the mysterious miniature robot that breaches the TARDIS's defences and materialises in the control room. We expect it to be some kind of malign invader or booby trap. But instead it's an advertising robot which comes bearing a junk-mail type message, inviting the Doctor and his companion to the Psychic Circus. This was all rather prescient of Stephen, with the junk-mail robot as a sort of premonition of the spam which would be clogging everybody's computers a couple of decades later.

For the shoot, the robot was built in two versions, a full-size model by Tony McKillop and some miniatures made by the estimable Mike Tucker, whom I was delighted to have back on the show.

The Greatest Show in the Galaxy was one of two four-episode stories that season, which meant it was shot half on location and half in the studio. The rumours I'd heard during the shooting of *Remembrance of the Daleks* proved true and the location work on *The Greatest Show in the Galaxy* took place in a quarry. Specifically Warmwell Quarry in Dorset. Quarries were the bane of **Doctor Who** but this one was much more visually arresting than most and Alan Wareing's skilful direction put it to good use. The shots of the sand dunes when the Doctor and Ace first arrive are breathtaking and convincingly alien. And the green water of the man-made lake provides an arresting backdrop. It's a shame that the TARDIS prop looks as abjectly battered and shabby as it does when it appears on the dunes.

I went on location with Stephen Wyatt on a cool grey day and found Sophie running around the quarry to keep warm while the rest of us were huddling around heaters. I was impressed. It had never occurred to me that this was an alternative way to warm oneself up. But Sophie was always sporty and athletic, a feisty Fenland belle who went in for running, cycling, canoeing.

The Greatest Show in the Galaxy is a good story with a lot of strong elements. Surprisingly, it begins with an early example of rap music, although at that time we probably would have called it electro or hip-hop. In this first scene, Ricco Ross' Ringmaster chants a rhythmic introduction to the story, to a backbeat. Ricco was an American actor with an impressive track record. He had appeared in **Hill Street Blues** and was also one of the Colonial Marines in James Cameron's **Aliens**.

I think that at the time Stephen was concerned about Ricco's less-than-musical delivery. But over the years it's added a certain contemporary grittiness to what might otherwise be an utterly fantastical story.

For me, *The Greatest Show in the Galaxy* was in the tradition of the dark fantasies of writers like Ray Bradbury, Charles G. Finney and Robert Bloch. And like all good dark carnival stories, it used sinister clowns to good effect. The early sequences in *The Greatest Show in the Galaxy,* featuring the Chief Clown in undertaker's garb and driving a hearse, are remarkable. They're reminiscent of classic British television fantasy such as **The Avengers** or **The Prisoner** (particularly the opening sequence of the **The Prisoner** where he is gassed and kidnapped by men in undertakers' garb). This all immediately put *The Greatest Show in the Galaxy* on a whole new level.

There is also a hint of **Quatermass** in the ancient stones that the Doctor spots in the main ring of the circus. These stones reveal the connection of the circus with a bloody arena where men died for the delectation of the Gods of Ragnarok. The Gods are present in the story from the beginning, in the bodies of a normal-looking family who insatiably demand entertainment. The 1940s suburban dowdiness of the family was a masterstroke of costume design echoing Terry Gilliam's **Brazil**. (Stephen and I were both big fans of **Brazil** and he once gave me a copy of the screenplay.) Luckily when the family turn into the dark gods in the final episode, their new costumes also turn out to be pretty effective.

I wanted *The Greatest Show in the Galaxy* to follow the strategies I'd been formulating, to try and make the story foolproof in design terms. I'd seen how unpredictable aliens and monsters were on **Doctor Who**, so I wanted the characters, as far as possible, to be human beings.

We still needed some science fiction antagonists, naturally, so Stephen and I drafted a couple of robots into the story. There's the metal bus conductor, ably played by Dean Hollingsworth, for whom Stephen wrote with considerable wit, giving him double-edged lines of dialogue that were drawn from the spiel of real conductors on London's red double-deckers. 'Hold tight,' says the conductor as he throttles Flower Child (Dee Sadler) to death. These lines gave a resonance and menace to the character which his robot outfit was lacking. The costume, designed by Steve Bowman, may not convince, but Stephen's eerily empty, jaunty characterisation does. And the robot does explode very nicely at the end.

I had concluded that robots were better than men in rubber suits. I was partially right. But even robots can fail to convince. In *The Greatest Show in the Galaxy* we had two approaches to the challenge, and neither of them entirely worked. The bus conductor was a man in a costume. The second robot was gigantic, and was built by Jim Lancaster out of a steel framework with air rams to move it. The idea was that this giant robot was buried in the sand, an idea which added to the interest of the robot: it was like a savage animal which was trapped and it gave it a back story, making us wonder why the robot was buried in the first place. In fact the story later revealed that Bellboy built the robot and, in a clever development, he gives Ace a remote control to operate the lethal machine, and turn it against her adversaries. 'Plus, of course, by burying the damned thing in the sand we don't have to build all of it. It will save us all kinds of money.'

It was a clever idea, but it pretty much went for nought. The robot doesn't move especially well, never looks scary and never manages to menace the characters or the audience. 'It also doesn't help that it has those naff bolts coming out of its eyes,' I remarked, and it's true, the video effects are far from impressive in this strand of the story. But elsewhere there are some gorgeous and truly stunning video effects, when Sylvester is struggling through the passage between the tents – and also between the dimensions – travelling to the Dark Circus where the evil gods of Ragnarok hold sway.

Visually, *The Greatest Show in the Galaxy* generally stands up very well. The make-up and the costumes are of the highest calibre, showing imagination and flair and real feel for the story. They are elegant, convincing and expressive. We even managed to carry off one entirely successful monster. I was never entirely against monsters. But I was generally in favour of humanoid monsters that were as close to a real unadorned actor as possible (and were therefore as difficult to fuck up as possible). And a werewolf fell into this category.

John Nathan-Turner was on the phone to Stephen Wyatt, discussing the casting in Stephen's script. They were talking about the female punk werewolf. 'Do you think it's vital that she's Scottish?' asked John.

I have to say that the female punk Scottish werewolf in Stephen's script was my influence, as indeed had been the Kangs in *Paradise Towers*. John was concerned that the character might be too comedic, so she was toned down, which I felt was a bit of a shame. A punkette lycanthrope with a Scots accent might well have been funny, but it seemed to me to be the *right kind* of funny. If people laughed, they would be laughing because we wanted them to, not in response to some misfired special effect or unconvincing monster.

I felt John was worrying about the wrong thing here. But nonetheless, the character of Mags survived in a somewhat watered-down form and was played to good effect by the excellent Jessica Martin. It's a shame we ditched the Scots accent, though, since Jessica was an accomplished comedienne and could have pulled off that character nicely.

From the beginning, we had a feeling that the creative talents of the BBC might be able to carry off a werewolf successfully – there were certain cultural and mythological reference points for such beasts that would help the designers. 'They're not just another alien monster from just another inadequately imagined planet.'

It also helped that the intention was always to keep Mags as human looking as possible, with the minimum of transformation (eyes, talons, some sprouting hair). We weren't trying to change her into a wolf or even a Lon Chaney Jr-style hairy beast. She would remain obviously human, with some strategic and hopefully terrifying exaggeration and mutation.

But what helped even more than this careful tactical planning was our good fortune, and John's cunning, in getting us the crack team of Ros Ebbutt and Denise Baron. With costume and make-up talent like that we ended up with a great show indeed.

And their version of the vulpine Mags was striking, eerie and delightfully terrifying. For once we had a **Doctor Who** monster that was actually scary. John looked up at me after we'd both just watched the transformation on a preview tape. 'We are going to get complaints about this you know. Mothers with terrified children.'

He was right, too. But, to his credit, John stuck to his guns. He didn't bowdlerise it and we ended up with a great monster on the screen, all fangs, claws and glowing eyes. (This is the way the Cheetah People should have looked in *Survival*.)

There were other great monsters in the story, though, and they were all human. Ian Reddington played the Chief Clown with immense threatening panache. 'I love his mad laugh,' said Stephen.

Ian embroidered his part with laughter and gestures which reinforced all our own feelings about sinister clowns (Ace accurately describes them as 'creepy'). Ian was immeasurably assisted by the great costume and make-up which Ros and Denise had provided for him. His clown face was so sinister that they took a cast of it and used it to make masks for the robot clowns who do his bidding.

The cast for *The Greatest Show in the Galaxy* was uniformly strong, with Chris Jury making a powerful impression despite minimal dialogue as Deadbeat/Kingpin and there's an amusing moment where he gets knocked to the ground and can be heard to mutter a whispered but distinct 'Shit' on the soundtrack. Peggy Mount plays the Stall Lady (Stephen gives her a witty line where she refers to Hell's Angels as 'Infernal Extraterrestrials'), Deborah Manship plays roles within roles as Morgana, and Christopher Guard is vulnerable and burnt-out as Bellboy. Bellboy has an impressive death scene, committing suicide by commanding the robots he once created to kill him. The Chief Clown watches this nightmarish moment, his mad smile punctuating the scene.

Stephen's subtext for the story, about dead hippy ideals, gave the actors something they could latch onto and also added emotional depth to *The Greatest Show in the Galaxy*. Stephen's droll hippy names were great and I was always a little sorry that we never actually got to meet Peace Pipe or Juniper Berry. The treatment of this theme also showed Stephen's own cynically sardonic impression of the flower-power generation. 'If you hear someone going on about love and peace,' says Captain Cook, 'run a mile.'

Captain Cook was played by T. P. McKenna and both character and actor were a sheer pleasure. Developing a notion about an Indiana Jones-style explorer, Stephen created Captain Cook as a kind of villainous counterpart of the Doctor – a mysterious space traveller who wanders the galaxies with a female sidekick.

There was a suggestion in Stephen's original script of an unwholesome relationship between the Captain and his female companion. In fact, the Captain draws a parallel between himself and Mags and the Doctor and Ace which the Doctor doesn't like at all. John Nathan-Turner thought this was a bit near the knuckle, since the Doctor's relationship with his young protégés had always been vulnerable to misinterpretation.

So, at his request, Stephen soft-pedalled this aspect of Captain Cook and Mags. I still think this is a shame, though they remain great characters, with some notably sardonic dialogue from Captain Cook: 'You don't often see one like that, do you?' he remarks coolly as the giant robot springs to murderous life.

In a way, Captain Cook was another of the successful monsters in the story – a monster of a bore, egotist, coward and troublemaker. He even comes back from the dead as a zombie ('Sarcophagus face' Ace calls him) and he's *still* a crashing bore. T. P. McKenna was wonderful, taking to the character with gusto. 'T. P. can't get into his frock quickly enough,' said Ros Ebbutt, 'He loves it.'

I knew T. P. McKenna as a screen presence from his work with Sam Peckinpah on **Straw Dogs**. I asked him what it had been like working with Peckinpah on this savage and disturbing masterpiece and he told me about a riotous drunken dinner party the director had thrown, which had climaxed with T. P. falling off a table and dislocating his arm. One of the stuntmen hurried to help. 'This great fool said, "It's all right, I know what to do, let me pop it back into place."' The stuntman apparently made a grisly mess of things. So the black arm sling which T. P. sports in **Straw Dogs** was worn from necessity. 'Some female critic kept going on about what a wonderful sinister touch it was,' said T. P., 'Ha!'

T. P. was tickled by one incident that happened during the shoot. In the scene where Mags transforms into a werewolf, the Ringmaster calls for a lighting cue to trigger her transformation, 'That old devil moon effect.' As Mags metamorphoses into her lycanthropic form, the lights around the circus ring sway wildly. At one point Alan wanted a shot of a light pivoting on its pole, but with no sign of a hand moving it.

Suddenly shooting stopped while a search was made for a black glove that wouldn't be seen in the shadows. 'Let me do it,' said Ricco, who was African American, 'I don't need a glove.' Ricco duly swivelled the light for us in the shot while T. P. watched, chuckling, quoting, 'I don't need a glove!'

Besides a strong cast, *The Greatest Show in the Galaxy* also benefited immensely from some atmospheric and sympathetic lighting. Three talents were involved in providing lighting during the film. The OB footage was lit by the ever-reliable Ian Dow. Studio lighting was the work of Don Babbage and Henry Barber. Don Babbage would also work on *The Happiness Patrol*, where there was a dismaying tendency to push the lights up to full and forsake any atmosphere. This despite our every effort to achieve a moody story, by setting it in night-time streets and so on.

Henry Barber's work, on the other hand, showed a sensitivity to nuance and mood that would contribute greatly to *Ghost Light*, on which Henry did sterling work later in the season. When Don Babbage left the production, I believe due to illness, and Henry Barber took over studio lighting, Alan Wareing wasn't exactly heartbroken.

Alan did a very effective job of staging the action and he worked well with the actors, bringing out the script's irony and emotion. He succeeded in fashioning a memorable story despite considerable adversity. *The Greatest Show in the Galaxy* was a troubled production.

The trouble began when asbestos was discovered in Television Centre. This meant that the studios we were relying on to shoot the bulk of the story were suddenly unavailable. After much frustration searching for an alternative venue, John displayed his usual resourcefulness by working out a deal whereby we would film in a tent, in the car park of the BBC's studios at Elstree. In some ways this was an advantage. One of my preoccupations on **Doctor Who**, besides trying to guarantee authentically sinister-looking alien beings, was to also try and achieve authentically sinister alien settings. Luckily, the circus environment of *The Greatest Show in the Galaxy* lent itself to this. The tents were environments that could be created realistically while also providing suitable atmosphere.

I had always been a big fan of Robert Fuest, a director and designer who'd worked on **The Avengers** TV series and was later responsible for the **Dr Phibes** movies. Fuest had a great gift for creating memorable and stylish sets using limited resources. He also directed an excellent oddball science fiction film called **The Final Programme**, from the Michael Moorcock novel, which makes terrific use of tunnels formed of billowing fabric lit with coloured lights. This serves to create a moody, futuristic environment with an unsettling sense of unreality.

I decided that *The Greatest Show in the Galaxy* was an ideal story to make use of this technique. I talked to Stephen about including fabric tunnels between the tents and he was amenable. This was one of our attempts to influence the design which really turned up trumps.

The tunnels were featured in various chase and concealment scenes, as well as for mundane to-ing and fr-oing and dialogue scenes. They worked strikingly well and made a stimulating change from the usual **Doctor Who** corridor scenes.

Although *The Greatest Show in the Galaxy* gained considerably in atmosphere from being shot in a real tent, there were problems with the arrangement, notably aircraft noise and the hullabaloo of vehicles manoeuvring in the parking lot. This all interfered with the sound recording and ratcheted up the stress a notch or two.

Shooting at Elstree did have some compensations. One day an alarm went off and we all filed outside to watch fire engines roaring into the car park. Our tent had emptied and so had the various Elstree Studio buildings, so that the cast of **Doctor Who** was mingling and fraternising with the casts of other shows. It was an impromptu festive occasion and since it turned out to be a false alarm, the cast of the French resistance sitcom **'Allo 'Allo** decided to entertain the firemen. A troupe of actresses in cancan dancers outfits performed an energetic improvised dance number, to much hilarity, ending in a flourish when they threw their skirts up and offered their frilly-knickered derrières to the delighted firemen.

The Greatest Show in the Galaxy represented another phase in my campaign to rehabilitate the Doctor and make him into a formidable, mysterious entity. However, the story was conceived at a time when I was only beginning to formulate my ideas on the subject and it shows signs of the changes in thinking we had along the way.

When *The Greatest Show in the Galaxy* begins, the Doctor seems whimsical, careless even, in his insistence on taking Ace to the Psychic Circus against her will and in the face of various warnings. He seems a victim, and a none too astute one at that. But by the end of the story he has been retro-fitted with mysterious attitudes and abilities and an all-knowing air. The implication is that he got them into this scrape because he was planning to do so, as a way to engage the enemy. 'It was your show all along,' says Ace, deftly papering over cracks in the character's motivation.

7.35pm Doctor Who

starring **Sylvester McCoy**
in *The Harbinger*
by KEVIN CLARKE
It's the 25th anniversary of
Doctor Who and we give you
bows, arrows, Nazis, jazz,
Cybermen and limousines.
Imagine what you'll get for
the 50th!

Karl....................METIN YENAL
De Flores.......ANTON DIFFRING
Lady Peinforte.FIONA WALKER
Richard.........GERARD MURPHY
De Flores.......ANTON DIFFRING
Mathematician
                    LESLIE FRENCH
Jazz Quartet....COURTNEY PINE,
  ADRIAN REID, ERNEST MOTHLE
                    FRANK TONTOH
The Doctor.SYLVESTER MCCOY
Ace.................SOPHIE ALDRED
Security Man....MARTYN READ
Cyberleader.........DAVID BANKS
Stunt Arranger PAUL HEASMAN
Theme music by RON GRAINER
Theme arrangement/incidental
music KEFF MCCULLOCH
Costume designer RICHARD CROFT
Script editor ANDREW CARTMEL
Designer JOHN ASBRIDGE
Producer JOHN NATHAN-TURNER
Director CHRIS CLOUGH
●FEATURE: *page 112* and
MY KIND OF DAY: *page 118*
★ CEEFAX SUBTITLES

7.35–8.00pm Doctor Who

starring **Sylvester McCoy**
in *The Harbinger*
by KEVIN CLARKE
Second episode of the three-
part 25th anniversary special.

Andrew finds the working
environment frustrating on
location and goes home. He
returns later to continue his
darkening of the Doctor.

De Flores.......ANTON DIFFRING
Ace.................SOPHIE ALDRED
The Doctor.SYLVESTER MCCOY
Cyber Leader.......DAVID BANKS
Karl.....................METIN YENAL
Cyber Lieutenant.MARK HARDY
Lady Peinforte.FIONA WALKER
Richard.........GERARD MURPHY
First skinhead...CHRIS CHERING
Second skinhead
                    SYMOND LAWES
First Cyberman..BRIAN ORRELL
Stunt Arrangers
PAUL HEASMAN, NICK GILLARD
Incidental music KEFF MCCULLOCH
Make-up designer DORKA NIERADZIK
Script editor ANDREW CARTMEL
Designer JOHN ASBRIDGE
Producer JOHN NATHAN-TURNER
Director CHRIS CLOUGH
■ CEEFAX SUBTITLES

7.35–8.00pm Doctor Who

starring **Sylvester McCoy**
in *The Harbinger*
by KEVIN CLARKE.
The final part of this
special three-part silver
anniversary adventure.

The Cartmel Masterplan is
underway, meanwhile the
Cybermen are now so
allergic to gold that they
faint just reading the word.

The Doctor.SYLVESTER MCCOY
Ace.................SOPHIE ALDRED
Richard.........GERARD MURPHY
Lady Peinforte.FIONA WALKER
Cyber Lieutenant
                    MARK HARDY
De Flores.......ANTON DIFFRING
Karl....................METIN YENAL
Cyber leader........DAVID BANKS
Cyberman.........BRIAN ORRELL
Mrs Remington.DOLORES GRAY
Incidental music KEFF MCCULLOCH
Visual effects designer
PERRY BRAHAN
Script editor ANDREW CARTMEL
Designer JOHN ASBRIDGE
Producer JOHN NATHAN-TURNER
Director CHRIS CLOUGH
■ CEEFAX SUBTITLES

CHAPTER 10
Silver Nemesis

Such a simple bit of flying.

In February 1987, a couple months after joining the show, I discovered a terrific script by a writer called Kevin Clarke. I discovered it by letting it sit in my in-tray for about five weeks.

It was a pilot for a series called **The Score**. It was the story of a guy who obtains a van which he uses to set up a small business, moving furniture and so on. Various minor adventures ensue. It plays like a fairly light-hearted comedy drama, something in the Jack Rosenthal vein. It was well written and entertaining, right up to the stunning conclusion where the viewers (but not the protagonists) learn that there's a shipment of heroin concealed inside the van. And suddenly it's a thriller.

I set the script down thinking, 'It's dynamite. I'll ring his agent first thing Monday.'

A couple of weeks later, I met Kevin Clarke. His script had impressed me and I was impressed by him in person. He told me about his sickle cell anaemia script for **Casualty** which had been too hot to handle. I spoke to him about the possibility of his writing for **Doctor Who**. He wasn't free. At the time, he was busy writing for **The Bill**.

Kevin's scripts for **The Bill** were probably some of the best British police drama since the Troy Kennedy Martin heyday of **Z Cars**. His scripts were hard hitting, keenly observed and bitingly funny, with controversial subject matter. He also created a memorable guest character, a transvestite prostitute called Roxanne. Roxanne was great and was brought back by popular demand. Kevin ended up writing several scripts about the character for the series. (Today, with **The Bill** mutating into a long-running soap, Roxanne would probably have become part of the permanent cast.) All Kevin's **The Bill** work was exceptional, full of dark comedy and big ideas (one of his scripts featured not a car chase but a *double-decker bus* chase) and attracted considerable attention. He soon moved on to writing high-profile television drama like the ITV series **Wish Me Luck** (Kevin had a different, rather more profane name for the show), which concerned female British agents assisting the French Resistance in the Second World War. Kevin wrote the last episode of the first series and it received record-breaking viewing figures.

Kevin was a tall, slender mercurial man with close-cropped hair, a jutting Roman nose and dark, soulful eyes that could go cold with anger. He had been around a bit before becoming a writer and had a store of intriguing stories about his adventures in his bohemian days, like the time he got robbed at knifepoint in Morocco, leaving him stranded in Africa with nothing but the clothes on his back and his guitar. 'It was survival time,' said Kevin nostalgically.

Months passed before our next meeting, in October 1987, with Kevin then free to write a **Doctor Who**. Jon Hardy, a fellow script editor, came up to my office to talk about Kevin, who'd apparently had a script bounced on the police series **Rockliffe's Babies**. 'He's been shamefully treated,' said John. This made me all the more eager to commission Kevin, to treat a good writer decently.

Soon Kevin became a regular visitor to the office for story discussions and he and Ian Briggs formed a mutual admiration society in my office. Kevin said to Ian, 'I can't imagine summoning into being a fully realised fantasy world like you did. Iceworld is like this fantasy distortion of Bejam's [a freezer food chain store], the way Paradise Towers is an amplification of a tower block.' And Ian nodded happily.

Kevin Clarke and Ian Briggs were both excellent writers and both northern lads. They got along like a house on fire. Kevin even name-checked Ian in his script for *Silver Nemesis*. When Richard, the seventeenth-century villainess's henchman, sees the Cybermen for the first time he is terrified. He falls on his knees and begins to pray. 'I shall look after the sick,' he offers desperately, 'which reminds me, I'll return to Briggs his money.'

On the same day as my meeting with Kevin and Ian, I heard some alarming news about Sophie Aldred. She'd been doing a kids' TV show called **Corners**. Sophie and her co-presenter had had to go up on wires in the studio and after they did their bit they were being lowered back to the floor, and the wire wrapped itself around Sophie's neck.

She screamed for them to stop lowering her but the genius in charge (who had also reportedly rigged wires on **Doctor Who**) told them to keep lowering, to ignore the hysterical girlie. Sophie's co-presenter started screaming then and fortunately they listened to him, otherwise Sophie would have been dead. I talked to her about it on the phone, how horrible it must have been. 'And it was such a simple bit of flying,' said Sophie.

It was November, with the sun setting early and winter closing in when I next met Kevin Clarke, for a drink in a pub along Shepherd's Bush Green towards Hammersmith. We talked about a story idea and I bemoaned the fact I hadn't written anything for years. He patted me on the shoulder and said, 'Don't worry, you will.' I almost believed him.

I'd like to think I helped Kevin with his *Silver Nemesis* script and that maybe he even learned some useful craft from working with me. Certainly, I assisted in getting his head around the science fiction aspects of the show, which is something I had to do for most of the writers. But Kevin definitely helped me with my own writing.

The great American thriller writer John D. MacDonald once observed that 'Writing is the classic example of learning by doing.' Or, as I believe Hemingway said, 'Writers write.' The way Kevin put it was, 'The imagination is a muscle.' The implication being, the more you devote your imagination to writing the stronger, and better, your imagination and therefore your writing become. He was profoundly right and it is one of the best pieces of advice I've ever had.

'I like the way you talk in musical terms, jazz terms,' said Kevin as we sat in the pub on that November evening. 'You talk about writing riffs. I noticed that right away.'

I was soon having good, productive meetings with Kevin, working our way towards a storyline. I was thinking we might be onto a winner here. Kevin was a terrific writer of action and suspense, with a fondness for Second World War adventure films like Alistair MacLean's **Where Eagles Dare**, which Quentin Tarantino calls 'a bunch of guys on a mission movie' and which is also a guilty pleasure of mine. It's a very effective thriller, although it lacks the intelligence, irony and depth of Troy Kennedy Martin's **Kelly's Heroes**, another Second World War 'bunch of guys on a mission movie'.

This fondness for Second World War stories had come in useful for Kevin on **Wish Me Luck**, and it also pointed the way forward to one of the main elements of his **Doctor Who** script. We would have latter-day Nazis in *Silver Nemesis*, with an evil escaped German officer coming out of retirement from his palatial lair in South America.

But when John read early drafts of the scripts, featuring a lot of action and involving Nazis, he freaked. The notion of neo-Nazis, latter-day fascists, seemed just too political and potentially controversial. He wouldn't have it.

So I simply went through the script removing every mention of the word 'Nazi' (it never appeared in dialogue, anyway, just scene directions) and substituted the euphemism 'Paramilitary'. So, for instance, instead of a cadre of Nazi gunmen blasting away at the Doctor and Ace, we had a cadre of Paramilitary gunmen.

This did the trick, and John was happy. It was clear sailing from then on, at least as far as the Nazi – I mean Paramilitary – question was concerned.

I went into John's office and found him looking down the blackboard on the wall, running his eyes down next season's chart at the writers' column. 'And then we have that nice bloke…' He meant Kevin. I introduced John and Kevin for an informal chat on Friday to break the ice and it looked like he'd be on next season. Good.

A few days later, John was considerably less cheerful. Over the previous few weeks, a hate campaign in the **Doctor Who** fan press had been breaking through into the much wider forum of the national newspapers. **DWB** (**Doctor Who Bulletin**) had been circulating a petition for John's resignation. Now it had even got into the **Stage** and that had really got John depressed. Normally, I didn't have much sympathy for John. I felt he'd made major mistakes during his term as producer of **Doctor Who**. But now I couldn't help feeling sorry for him as he sat glumly in his office leafing through the personal attacks.

Kevin Clarke came in for a story discussion with John and me. It went well and as we wrapped up Kevin said, 'Shall we formalise this relationship?'. He meant, after all these weeks of talks and script discussions and developing a storyline, could we finally *pay him some money?* And I got a glimpse of what a precarious life it was for a freelance writer.

John responded immediately and asked Kate Easteal next door to start typing the commissioning brief.

Some time before, I had noticed that someone had written 'ITV' on the door of the BBC lifts. Just that, as if it were a blunt obscenity. (And in this context, it sort of was.) It amused me every time I looked at it. I was delighted to learn from Kevin that someone, in a symmetrical act, had written 'BBC' in the lift at the ITV offices on the South Bank. He winked as he described the graffiti.

Early in 1988, I had a long meeting with Kevin. His script had crossed the line between being a potential **Doctor Who** script and being a real one, but it still needed improvement. We'd now combined the Nazi story strand with a female sorceress from the seventeenth century and her henchman, as well as the Cybermen.

Like the Daleks, the Cybermen were familiar alien villains coming back for the 25th anniversary season. This was John's plan and I thought it was a great idea. John was reminiscing about the shooting of *Attack of the Cybermen*. 'It was so cold we had to tape Nicola Bryant's nipples down. They were obscene.' John was in good spirits. He was ringing **Debrett's** to find out the correct way to address Prince Edward in a letter. 'It's a load of old camp,' said John. Ever the astute manipulator of publicity, John wanted to enlist some royals to appear on-screen in the 25th anniversary show, which was to be *Silver Nemesis*.

The silver anniversary element of *Silver Nemesis* was obviously echoed by the choice of the 'silver' appearance of the Cybermen and the living silver metal validium, which Kevin had created and which was our McGuffin in the script. We'd also worked the anniversary theme into the story with the cunning idea of a comet which passes the Earth every 25 years. (Hereafter in this text the comet will also be referred to as a 'meteor', in a way that is guaranteed to madden any true professional astronomer.) It was John's desire to do a silver anniversary celebration for the show, but I was having fun with Kevin making it work as a story.

Kevin Clarke and I were on a train, talking about Prince Edward. John was definitely going to invite the Prince to make a guest appearance – would the Prince accept? 'Of course he'll do it,' said Kevin. 'The guy can't resist.' Kevin and I had just been to see Sylvester McCoy in a matinee of **The Pied Piper** at the National Theatre. Sylvester met us at the stage door and got us in for free, seating us with a friend of his in the director's box, which was a little cubicle at the back of the theatre with an electric window which moved up and down. An ancient staff director stared in at us, then rushed in to scoop up his belongings – a stopwatch and a **Teach Yourself Greek** book, before we could steal them. 'They can't sit in the box. You can't have people sitting in the box,' he sniffed to Sylvester, and left. 'That was the theatre ghost,' said Sylvester.

Wednesday 23 March 1988. Kevin Clarke delivered his first complete draft of episode two in a folder that had written on it 'Andrew Cartmel, Doctor Who, Urgent: The fate of the earth is in your hands'.

By this time, John Nathan-Turner had perfected a strategy for maximising the budget on the 13-episode **Doctor Who** season. In theory we had enough money for three stories each season, two four-parters and a six-parter, each story being shot half in the studio and half on location. But John had cunningly worked out that the six-parter could be split into two three-parters, providing one was shot entirely in the studio and one was shot entirely on location. Kevin's script for *Silver Nemesis* would be the all-location story for Season 25.

Both three-parters were to be handled by the same team (in terms of budgeting, they were regarded as one show), with the same director. John had chosen Chris Clough, who had done the same slot the year before, with *Delta and the Bannermen* and *Dragonfire*.

My first introduction to Chris had been Kate Easteal's description of him. 'You'll like him. Chris just laughs,' she said. 'When the pressure's on and something goes wrong or something, Chris stays cool and just laughs it off.' When we met, Chris did indeed prove immensely affable. But the pressure during the Season 25 three-parters was truly immense and eventually Chris stopped laughing. I attended the location shoot for *Silver Nemesis* and John was there too. The tension was high and it wasn't much fun. Eventually things got so bad, with so much acrimony and bad temper and general ill will in the air, that I just decided to jump on the train and go home.

I got back to London and felt an enormous relief at having escaped such a poisonous atmosphere. I returned to my basement flat in Baron's Court and the arms of my girlfriend. I was lazing around happily reading, with Kate in the kitchen mixing us cocktails made from maple syrup, lemon juice and rum. She was working from **The Esquire Cocktail Book**, which had a list of 365 special occasions in the back, an excuse for a party for every day of the year. This was National Defence Bonds Day.

Once she'd made the cocktails she set about roasting some chestnuts under the grill. A sudden powerful burnt smell emanated from the kitchen. Kate had left the chestnuts under the grill too long. 'They seem to have exploded a bit,' she said. One exploded into shrapnel as she touched it. 'They're really violent… I don't understand it. I gave them a jolly good prodding before I put them under.'

Then the telephone rang. It was John Nathan-Turner at his most friendly and charming. This was a man transformed. It was largely John's outbursts of rage that had led me to say farewell to the location shoot and return to the pleasures of London. At one point, Kevin made some remark to John that was relevant to the story and John snapped a response along the lines of 'Mind your own business.' Kevin took this incredibly well, smoothly saying 'With great pleasure' and bowing out of the confrontation with poise. John just exploded like that at times. Everybody understood it was the huge pressure he was under. Nevertheless it was always a shock, like suddenly getting a savage bite from a friendly animal. Or from a man who was more commonly amusing, affable and easygoing.

John was at his most amusing and affable on the phone, asking why I had departed the unit. I explained about the poisonous atmosphere and how **Doctor Who** had ceased to be fun. Naturally it didn't *have* to be fun, it could just be a job. So I was perfectly happy to get on with my work back at the office in London, instead of wasting time down in Arundel on location. I tried to stand my ground as John invited me back to the shoot. But, as I said, he was at his most amusing and affable and he soon charmed me into it.

The next day, I returned to location and everyone seemed pleased to see me. Kevin said that my departure had cued a change in the emotional weather of the unit. The poisonous atmosphere had gone. 'You did a good thing by leaving,' said Kevin. 'Welcome back.'

The *Silver Nemesis* shoot was fun again, though often tense fun. Kevin had been delighted to learn that his Nazi officer was going to be played by Anton Diffring. Kevin said it was great having him in a show he'd written. Indeed, it was the first time he'd ever done anything that had impressed his father.

Kevin's dad knew who Anton Diffring was. Everybody knew who Anton Diffring was. He'd established a classy speciality of playing senior Nazi officers in war dramas like our motion picture favourite **Where Eagles Dare**.

Kevin and I were amused to see *the* Anton Diffring sitting with the actors who played the young Nazi troopers, sunning themselves, discussing who was the most handsome man any of them had ever seen. One of the Nazi troopers tentatively suggested Robert Redford. Anton leant back in his deckchair in the sunlight. 'Ach, Redford? Redford's nothing. The most handsome man *I* ever saw was…' I never did hear Anton's conclusion on this subject.

The character he played was called de Flores. A pseudonym, of course, adopted by the evil Nazi renegade during his South American exile. But the name was also a clever reference by Kevin. De Flores is the murderous servant in a Jacobean play called **The Changeling** by Thomas Middleton. And the other main strand of *Silver Nemesis* (besides the rather boring Cybermen) is the adventures of the Jacobean duo Lady Peinforte and Richard Maynard, played with aplomb by Fiona Walker and Gerard Murphy.

Kevin's fondness for literature of this period, specifically Shakespeare and **The Winter's Tale**, cropped up in the gag in the story where Richard is afraid of being attacked by a (purely hypothetical) bear. 'The bear will not pursue us,' Lady Peinforte assures him, 'Such things happen only in the theatre.'

Silver Nemesis is by no means perfect, but it turned out well. Chris Clough evokes the diverse mix of traditional action, Jacobean sorcery, 1980s jazz and Cyberman-style science fiction with a good measure of coherence. The audience has a chance to get engrossed in the story and have some kind of emotional response to it. It doesn't fall apart into confusion and embarrassment the way that, say, *Battlefield* does. It also has some of the best source music in any **Doctor Who** adventure, thanks to the presence of a genuine jazz virtuoso, Courtney Pine.

The story begins strongly. The opening sequences in South America are intriguing and well handled. In the event, absolutely no bones are made about de Flores's 'Paramilitary' background, with a swastika paperweight on his desk, Wagner blaring from a gramophone on the balcony and a toast being proposed to the 'Fourth Reich'.

Then, with our interest piqued by this contemporary, neo-Nazi story, we're suddenly plunged into an equally engrossing plotline about seventeenth-century sorcery. It's Windsor in 1638 and, as always, the BBC does a splendid job recreating historical detail. The inside of Lady Peinforte's cottage is beautifully equipped with necromantic paraphernalia of the period, and it's tastefully and moodily lit by the reliable Ian Dow.

Kevin's characterisation is excellent here, with Lady Peinforte, Richard and the ill-fated mathematician, played by Leslie French, who is found busily doing their calculations for them. Leslie French interpolated some delightful business here, murmuring over his sums. He also has the mathematician sound amusingly sad when he announces that the meteor's orbit is decaying. Decay is clearly a sad thing, even for the orbit of a meteor.

I encouraged Kevin to make the mathematician an unknown genius, on a par with Leonardo da Vinci. We've never heard of him because, unlike Leonardo, his life is cut short just as he's having his great revelation. 'I shall build a flying machine. Why, I can change the world,' says the mathematician. But Lady Peinforte and Richard have just realised that they need human blood for their time travel potion. So the mathematician's world-altering genius is snuffed out before it can achieve anything, in an irony which gives the character's demise some dramatic weight despite his brief tenure in the story.

From the murder and sorcery of 1638, we jump 350 years forward to the present day, using rather a nifty cut into the shadowed bell of a saxophone. More precisely, Courtney Pine's tenor saxophone. Courtney Pine is a living jazz hero. Inspired by John Coltrane and Sonny Rollins, he is one of the few British players of genuine international stature, having played with George Russell and Art Blakey. His haunting playing adds immeasurably to the Trevor Jones film score for the supernatural thriller **Angel Heart**.

Kevin and I were both jazz fans. Kevin and Kevin's girlfriend and Kate and I sat through the entire bum-numbing length of Clint Eastwood's Charlie Parker biopic **Bird** at the Lumiere cinema in St Martin's Lane and got tickets to see Nina Simone sing at the Royal Festival Hall.

When the question arose of who to cast for the jazz musician in Kevin's script, Kevin had immediately suggested Courtney Pine. What the hell, we thought, we might as well start at the top. And work our way down. John shrugged amiably. Jazz wasn't his field, but he'd try to make the writer and the script editor happy by trying to get this Courtney Pine guy.

To our amazement, the lights all went green. Everyone said yes. And Courtney did it. So, on a sunny day, in front of Black Jack's Mill Restaurant in the idyllic green of the Harefield countryside, we found ourselves listening to Courtney and his band playing for us, for the cameras, and for the audience at the outdoor tables – more black people than ever seen on-screen in a **Doctor Who** episode.

After the shooting, Courtney Pine and his band went into the studio to record the music for the show. It was a Sunday afternoon in Shepherd's Bush and Kevin and I were in attendance. It was a blissful little interlude, one of the blessings brought my way by **Doctor Who**. Courtney played beautiful, fluent tenor sax and we listened. I might have been smoking something besides tobacco.

Kevin's fondness for jazz even transmitted itself to the Doctor. Suddenly he was an aficionado. Listening to Courtney Pine play outside Black Jack's, the Doctor has the line, 'My favourite kind of jazz – straight blowing.' This scene also features some other mischievously good writing by Kevin.

'Have you seen this?' says Ace, lifting up a newspaper with the glaring headline 'Meteor Approaches England'. 'Charlton have picked up three points,' she continues, blithely reading the sports page and ignoring the headline.

As they leave, Ace buys a tape of Courtney's music, which she'll later play in the tape deck that the Doctor has built for her. Actually, the tape deck was the handiwork of Mike Tucker, who gave it a lovely retro look, with its art deco Bakelite sunrise façade. This 'ghetto blaster' is later used in the story to jam the communications of the Cyber space fleet. Courtney's jazz echoes out across a beautiful deep-space vista, and blares from the Cybermen's receiver on Earth, where they all stand around dumbfounded, looking like the most un-hip sentient beings ever.

After a skirmish with the Cybermen's brainwashed human assassins, Sylvester and Sophie go on to pay a visit to Windsor (actually Arundel) Castle. The Doctor breezily breaks in, wanting to enlist the aid of the Queen. 'It's probably treason,' says Ace, 'I'm too young to go the tower.' Cue a close encounter with the Queen ('I know that woman from somewhere,' says the Doctor, not immediately recognising her) and her corgis. Sadly the woman was just an actress, or professional celebrity-impersonator, rather than our actual monarch. Unfortunately, there were no real royals available. Prince Edward declined our offer of a part, though John read between the lines of the royal response and remained convinced that Edward would have loved to do it if his mother hadn't put the kibosh on things.

As the Doctor and Ace blunder around the castle looking for royal assistance, the Doctor utters the line, 'There is no alternative.' During rehearsals one of the other actors greeted the line with a vague sense of recognition. 'That's a quote from someone. Who said that? Hitler?' 'Close,' replied Sylvester with a fiendish grin. It was, of course, a catchphrase of Prime Minister Thatcher.

Among the extras playing tourists at Windsor is a trio of **Doctor Who** writers making a cameo appearance. Graeme Curry, Stephen Wyatt, and Kevin. You can see them at the back of the line outside the castle. Graeme is tall and broad, Kevin is tall and slender, and Stephen is the small guy in a cap standing between them (Stephen had gone on record complaining that we had too many tall writers on **Doctor Who**). I was invited to join them on camera in the scene, but by this time I was firmly convinced that public exposure, at least in the strange intense and incestuous world of **Doctor Who** fandom, was a bad idea. I declined all interviews and avoided being photographed. I quite enjoyed pursuing this J. D. Salinger/Thomas Pynchon/B. Traven-style approach to literary fame.

Kevin also features in another brief Hitchcock-style walk-on in *Silver Nemesis*. He can be glimpsed as the pedestrian in the street who glances back in puzzlement at Lady Peinforte and Richard in their seventeenth-century garb, as they make their way towards an encounter with a hapless pair of skinheads. Kevin was highly amused by one of the shops in the street, a photographer's establishment called Apertures of Arundel. 'Joe Orton would have loved it,' he said.

Silver Nemesis is notable for doing a generally successful job of ushering in the new, more mysterious, powerful and shadowy Doctor that I was aiming towards. It presents the Doctor as a calculating chess player, manipulating events in an intricate strategy that cuts across centuries. I was tired of the notion of the Doctor as a mere Time Lord amongst other Time Lords. He had started off in 1963 in the shape of William Hartnell as a scary enigma, a being of unlimited mystery. He could have remained a total enigma. This strategy certainly worked for **Sapphire and Steel**, P J Hammond's classic dark fantasy drama. But if **Sapphire and Steel** had run for as many years as **Doctor Who** did, explanations might well have begun to creep in. These kinds of explanations had ruined the Doctor. The trajectory of his mysterious character had been one of steady decline. First we had no idea who or what he was. Then we learned he was a Time Lord. Then we learned he was a Time Lord among other Time Lords. And, the next thing you know, he was the kind of chump who could be put on trial by the other Time Lords, and generally be pushed around with impunity.

So I set about restoring the awe, mystery and strength to the character. With the help of Marc Platt and Ben Aaronovitch, the two writers I was working with who were interested in the **Doctor Who** mythos and had a knowledge of it, I set about making the Doctor once again more than a mere chump of a Time Lord.

Kevin Clarke, like Stephen and Graeme and Malcolm, knew little of the mythology that had encrusted itself around **Doctor Who** over the years. So he was probably baffled, though entirely good natured, about the inclusion of certain dialogue. For example, Ace senses that there is plenty that the Doctor isn't telling her. And she's beginning to get a scent of his secret. They are talking about the living metal validium, a kind of ultimate weapon developed on the Doctor's home planet of Gallifrey. Ace is quizzing him about the stuff. 'It was created by Omega,' says the Doctor. 'And...' says Ace meaningfully. 'And Rassilon,' says the Doctor. 'And...' says Ace again, with persistent insinuation.

All this was deeply meaningful to hardcore fans. The point was that Omega and Rassilon were the founding fathers of Gallifrey. They towered above the Time Lords who followed. They were demigods. And Ace's nifty dialogue 'And...' coupled with the Doctor's neatly evasive response, are a subtle attempt to say that there was a third presence there in the shadowy days of Gallifrey's creation.

In other words, the Doctor was also there. So he's more than a Time Lord. He's one of these half-glimpsed demigods. Marc Platt was going to work this idea into his story 'Lungbarrow', which was eventually set aside in favour of *Ghost Light*.

But the Doctor's secret did become part of the plot of *Silver Nemesis*. Lady Peinforte threatens to expose him. But the Cybermen simply aren't interested in any of it. 'The secrets of the Time Lords mean nothing to us,' says the Cyber Leader, speaking for just about everyone, it has to be said.

All of this went over the heads of most of the production team and most of the writers, and certainly most of the viewers. But it was a good first move towards making the Doctor darker and more enigmatic and powerful, which was exactly what the character needed.

When we had finished shooting and I saw *Silver Nemesis* in the editing rooms, I thought that it generally worked. Admittedly, some scenes just don't come off. Why does Lady Peinforte suddenly smash her way through a window with a chair? In the script, our intention had been that the sixteenth-century sorceress was thwarted by a mundane twentieth-century lock, so she resorted to direct action. In the version on-screen she just seems to erupt into violence for the hell of it.

There are other occasional infelicities. We have Richard nonplussed to encounter his own tombstone. 'If the dogs would not eat thee I ordered you put out here to attend me in the next world,' says Lady Peinforte happily. It's a good scene but it would have been a great scene if it had been shot in a sufficiently moody fashion, at night, say.

But given our budget and resources the notion of night shooting, even for such an amusingly chilly little gem of a scene, was just a pipe dream.

Silver Nemesis also features plenty of other classic dialogue from Kevin. One day, before we started filming, Ben Aaronovitch was to be found in the **Doctor Who** office snorting and shrieking with laughter at such an embarrassing volume that I was sure that the production team was going to start staring. Ben was laughing because I'd just shown him my favourite page from Kevin's episode two:

The Doctor
I don't suppose you've completely disobeyed my instructions and secretly prepared any Nitro-9 explosive, have you?

Ace
What if I had?

The Doctor
You naturally wouldn't do anything so insanely dangerous as carry it around with you, would you?

Ace
Of course not. I'm a good girl and I do what I'm told.

The Doctor
Excellent. Blow up that vehicle.

In the years that have elapsed since *Silver Nemesis*, Kevin Clarke and I seem to have fallen out. Our friendship came to grief in some stupid conflict, now forgotten — possibly over a pretty girl who lived in a witch's spire overlooking Clapham Common. In any case, it's an abiding regret of mine that I've lost touch with Kevin.

7.35pm Doctor Who

starring **Sylvester McCoy**
in *The Crooked Smile*
First of a three-part
adventure by GRAEME CURRY
Bertie Bassett helps
overthrow the Thatcher
government while the Doctor
and Ace play in a go-cart.

Killjoy.................MARY HEALY
Silas P............JONATHAN BURN
Daisy K.........GEORGINA HALE
Ace.................SOPHIE ALDRED
The Doctor.SYLVESTER MCCOY
Helen A.........SHEILA HANCOCK
Trevor Sigma
          JOHN NORMINGTON
Joseph C.........RONALD FRASER
Harold V..............TIM BARKER
Priscilla P............RACHEL BELL
Gilbert M....HAROLD INNOCENT
Kandyman.....DAVID JOHN POPE
Earl Sigma....RICHARD D.SHARP
Susan Q...........LESLIE DUNLOP
Theme music composed by
RON GRAINER
Incidental music DOMINIC GLYNN
Costume designer RICHARD CROFT
Script editor ANDREW CARTMEL
Designer JOHN ASBRIDGE
Producer JOHN NATHAN-TURNER
Director CHRIS CLOUGH

★ CEEFAX SUBTITLES

7.35–8.00pm Doctor Who

starring **Sylvester McCoy**
The Crooked Smile
Second of a three-part
adventure by GRAEME CURRY
Fruit machines make their
first appearance in the
Cartmel era. Like honey,
they're not seen anywhere
else in *Doctor Who*'s prior
history.

The Doctor.SYLVESTER MCCOY
Earl Sigma....RICHARD D.SHARP
Kandyman.....DAVID JOHN POPE
Gilbert M....HAROLD INNOCENT
Ace.................SOPHIE ALDRED
Daisy K.........GEORGINA HALE
Priscilla P............RACHEL BELL
Susan Q...........LESLIE DUNLOP
Wences................PHILIP NEVE
Wulfric..........RYAN FREEDMAN
Helen A.........SHEILA HANCOCK
Trevor.......JOHN NORMINGTON
David S............STEVE SWINCOE
Alex S...........MARK CARROLL
Joseph C.........RONALD FRASER
Doorman................TIM SCOTT
Incidental music DOMINIC GLYNN
Make-up designer DORKA NIERADZIK
Script editor ANDREW CARTMEL
Designer JOHN ASBRIDGE
Producer JOHN NATHAN-TURNER
Director CHRIS CLOUGH

★ CEEFAX SUBTITLES

7.35–8.00pm Doctor Who

starring **Sylvester McCoy**
in *The Crooked Smile*
Last of a three-part
adventure by GRAEME CURRY
The Doctor defeats Margaret
Thatcher and teaches Terra
Alpha the blues. Next...
teaching jazz to Mondasians.

The Doctor.SYLVESTER MCCOY
Forum doorman......TIM SCOTT
Ace.................SOPHIE ALDRED
Susan Q...........LESLIE DUNLOP
Daisy K.........GEORGINA HALE
Helen A.........SHEILA HANCOCK
Trevor Sigma
          JOHN NORMINGTON
Newscaster.......ANNIE HULLEY
Priscilla P............RACHEL BELL
Gilbert M....HAROLD INNOCENT
Earl Sigma....RICHARD D.SHARP
Joseph C.........RONALD FRASER
Wulfric..........RYAN FREEDMAN
Wences................PHILIP NEVE
Kandyman.....DAVID JOHN POPE
Incidental music DOMINIC GLYNN
Visual effects designer
PERRY BRAHAM
Script editor ANDREW CARTMEL
Designer JOHN ASBRIDGE
Producer JOHN NATHAN-TURNER
Director CHRIS CLOUGH

★ CEEFAX SUBTITLES

CHAPTER 11
The Happiness Patrol

I'll get out my Doctor Who pen.

Sunday 6 March 1988. Graeme Curry had a smear of jam on his chin from the doughnut Kate Easteal had brought him from the BBC canteen. Graeme played with the Sellotape dispenser on my desk while we discussed ideas. I was impressed with Graeme. He was a big, tall, amiable man who looked rather like the result of a Kodiak bear attempting to disguise himself as a literate young Englishman. Or maybe the other way round. He was an interesting writer. He was **Cosmopolitan**'s young journalist of the year before he wrote an award-winning radio play called **Over the Moon**. It's about football or, more accurately, about football supporters and their love of the game.

Graeme was encouraged to get in touch with me by Tony Dinner at the BBC Script Unit. Tony Dinner was a kind of mentor for me, so when he recommended Graeme I paid attention.

A script about football may not immediately sound like the most obvious recommendation for writing **Doctor Who**, but I was immediately struck by Graeme's witty dialogue and skilful characterisation. His new script about yuppies and greyhounds also sounded wonderful as he described it to me.

I lent him the **Halo Jones** books which I was handing out to all the writers as an example of what I thought a good science fiction story should be, and also a collection of Ray Bradbury stories. (Returning the books to me, Graeme would say he'd been particularly struck by Bradbury's time travel masterpiece 'A Sound of Thunder'.) I then explained the pitfalls of **Doctor Who** stories set on other planets (we ended up shooting in quarries) and monsters (potentially dodgy special effects). As usual, I suggested that something Earth based or involving humanoid aliens, or both, was the best bet.

Three weeks later, after numerous meetings and discussions, Graeme came into my office wearing a suit. He'd just been to a BBC 'board' (ie job interview) and it hadn't gone well. I knew what it was like to have a shitty job interview, so I took him out for a drink.

When we got back to my office, he returned the **Halo Jones** books I'd lent him and launched into a **Doctor Who** idea. I listened with a certain degree of resignation because I'd already made up my mind that, after all our attempts, Graeme wouldn't be able to come up with anything suitable for **Doctor Who**. I was depressed about this, but not for long, because after a moment I was paying close attention to what Graeme was saying.

This new idea was great. It was set on a planet ('I know you don't like planets,' said Graeme) where it's a crime to be unhappy.

A writer's visit to location for *Silver Nemesis*: Kevin Clarke, Sophie Aldred, Stephen Wyatt, Sylvester McCoy and Graeme Curry. Sylv is deliberately holding his question-mark umbrella over Stephen's head, to give a cartoon effect

Sylvester, Sophie, Anne Reid, Tomek Bork (standing), Dinsdale Landen
(seated) and Alfred Lynch in costume on set for *The Curse of Fenric*

Sylvester on location for *The Curse of Fenric*. Note the
new "darker Doctor" jacket

Non-speaking haemovores take a break on *The Curse of Fenric*

Marc Platt, Claire Kinmont who succeeded Kate Easteal as our production secretary, riding the rocking horse on the set of *Ghost Light*, with production assistant Gary Downie and myself

Me with some impressive *Ghost Light* props

*Sophie looking spiffy cross-dressing for *Ghost Light*.
Me in a jacket and tie for a change

Sophie and I on the staircase, part of the main *Ghost Light* set

Me on the same staircase. It was a truly fantastic set.
The BBC excelled itself on this story

Marc Platt and I examining the laboratory set on *Ghost Light*

On the set of *Ghost Light*, posing with some of
those magnificent Victorian props

Sylvester and JN-T's dog Pepsi resting between
takes on location for *Survival*

'Great,' I said. 'You're on.'

Over the next couple of months, we discussed and developed the idea whenever I had a free moment between working on Season 24's shows. If Graeme were to write for us it would be for Season 25 the next year.

One morning, I went up to see Carrie in the stationery office and get a new hole puncher. In the box with it was a slip in German and in English that read, 'Please don't forget to grease regularly all friction possibilities of your perforator. It will be rewarded by full activity and long endurance.' I made a point of showing it to Graeme. He came in for a talk about his possible **Doctor Who** story – the Happiness Patrol one (Graeme was still calling this outline *The Crooked Smile*, a title which would survive into early drafts of the script. But John Nathan-Turner and I never referred to it as anything but *The Happiness Patrol*). For some weeks, Kate Easteal and I had been conducting a study of what the writers played with on the script editor's desk while they were discussing their stories. For instance, Stephen tore pieces of tape off the Sellotape dispenser and Malcolm bent paperclips into perfect triangles and taped the ends together. Graeme also favoured the Sellotape dispenser.

While we were trying to create a story, Graeme and his wife were busy having a baby. On 26 May, while I was occupied trying to track down a promising writer called Ben Aaronovitch, I got a phone call from Graeme to say Tessa had had the baby. Had an epidural and caesarean section, in fact. 'We spent 17 hours having contractions,' said Graeme.

Friday 7 August 1987. I took Graeme to lunch. We sat in Sulgrave House, eating vegetarian moussaka and chips and Graeme told me about his university thesis (I believe Graeme went to Cambridge) which was on the grotesque in literature. I thought that was a pretty damned good qualification for writing **Doctor Who**.

It had been an excellent day. We'd had a fruitful discussion about his *Happiness Patrol* script. John Nathan-Turner had read his outline and liked it. 'Graeme is like Stephen,' he said, 'he's created his own unique world.' 'With a lot of prodding,' said Graeme.

'What would you like to do?' asked John. 'Would you like to commission Graeme for an episode?' For a second I was speechless, then I said yes.

Three days later, John and I had a meeting with Jonathan Powell and John got approval to renew my contract and for us to commission a script from Graeme Curry for the next season. I finally got to tell Graeme that he was definitely going to be commissioned. I could have told him on the phone, but I wanted to give him the good news in person. I wish I'd bought some champagne.

I spent all morning talking to Graeme, working through his storyline. 'A lot of Cartmel touches in that,' said Ben, as he read it. The meeting with Graeme went very well. I was laughing out loud. Graeme was great. There was a whole new feel in his script. A whole new feel for the whole show, for **Doctor Who**. I loved the way the Doctor was plunged into an entire weird world and casually took it all in his stride. This might be a keynote for the entire series.

After reading Graeme's script, I had a sudden glimpse of what was really going on. I could see clearly, fleetingly, that we had some of the great writers of tomorrow working on these crazy **Doctor Who** scripts.

We worked on *The Happiness Patrol* throughout August 1987. In early September, I was depressed because *Time and the Rani* was transmitting and I was getting a lot of flak from people about how dreadful the show was. One good thing – we signed Graeme's commissioning brief. He was officially writing for the show.

By November, we were deep into writing the script. 'This is the trumpet-throwing episode,' said Graeme. Graeme, Lindsay MacGowan, and Ben Aaronovitch, Sophie Aldred, Kate Easteal and I had a lunch arranged, a **Doctor Who** bun-fight, and we went out for pizza. It was very nice and it was a chance for the writers to get the measure of Sophie. But as we walked back to the office, all in a group, we passed John Nathan-Turner and I could see he was pissed off as he snapped a curt hello. He'd got it into his head that it was a conspiracy. Either that or he was upset because he'd been left out. I went into his office and talked him out of his moodiness – but what a pain it was to have to deal with this.

'He's just like a kid. He's probably pissed off because he didn't think of it himself. Forget it,' Kate Easteal said to me on the phone that night. She rang me up after work as I was lying in bed running the events through my mind. I appreciated the call. She must have known I was a brooder. I went back into our bedroom and my girlfriend Kate was suddenly attentive to me, just because another woman had rung me up. It was quite nice.

The following day, I was off work, under the blue duvet, feeling snotty and pleasantly at-home-from-school-with-a-cold. John rang to give me the audience figures (and to make friends again). The figure was 5.3 million for the first episode of *Delta and the Bannermen*. The highest so far for that season.

By February 1988, the scripts were still being written but *The Happiness Patrol* was already rolling into production. It was the season's all-studio three-parter and like *Silver Nemesis, The Happiness Patrol* was to be directed by Chris Clough.

'Now we're in business,' said Graeme Curry as we finally found our way out of the maze of one-way streets in North Acton. Graeme was driving a battered yellow Renault with a 'Baby on Board' sticker in the back window. I had an old London *A–Z* in my lap. We were looking for the BBC Rehearsal Rooms, where we were going to have lunch with Mike Tucker and Lindsay MacGowan and discuss the special effects for Graeme's script. It was marvellous to see Graeme again. I was feeling very good about his script.

Sophie Aldred joined Graeme and Lindsay and Mike and me at our table. She was rehearsing **Corners** downstairs. She was wearing earrings made of twisted bits of copper which were very Ace-ish. Lindsay took us down into the visual effects workshops and showed Graeme his maquettes (small clay models) of the Pipe People. Graeme decided the Pipe People needed a Pipe Ferret to chase them – and so Fifi was conceived. Lindsay suggested putting a Pipe Person in Ace's rucksack (à la **Gremlins**).

A couple of weeks later, we were still in the thick of the *Happiness Patrol* scripts. Graeme said, 'Tessa's taking our baby to see a new baby. You do that sort of thing when you have babies.' I spent a good part of my script conference with Graeme trying not to double over with pain. I was falling ill fast. My brother dropped in at the office with some curry spices for me and I got him to walk me home. It was just like when I was a little kid at school in Canada: when I fell sick they got another little kid to walk me home. Only I didn't throw up in a snowdrift this time. Back at the flat I shared with Kate, I crawled into bed shivering. It was four days before I was anything like recovered, stepping gingerly out onto the street. Cool air, tall houses. Still feeling frail and a little dislocated from reality, but good. All the people on the street looked beautiful, the shortest, fattest, ugliest people were beautiful through the sheer fact of being alive.

Once I was back at work, Graeme came in with a splendid draft of his script. He'd sort of been away on a sabbatical, writing an episode of **The Bill** between episodes one and two of *The Happiness Patrol*. I didn't know if it was the increase in confidence and experience as a result of writing something else, but suddenly Graeme's ability had shot up. He was turning into a terrific writer.

Graeme was also a voracious reader. 'My hands start to shake if I'm not reading a novel,' he said. It was late afternoon and we were concluding a very successful script meeting. Graeme's work was really becoming superb.

The next day, I met Dominic Glynn for lunch. Dominic was one of the composers on the show and I thought his music was exceptional. He was going to score *The Happiness Patrol* for us. He was a thin young guy, who looked slightly exhausted and chronically overworked. I think he was probably a child prodigy. Dominic had done the music for *Dragonfire*, a splendidly moody orchestral-sounding score (of course Dominic did it all on synthesiser and electronics; we could never afford an orchestra for the show). He brought me a tape of *Dragonfire* and in exchange I gave him a cassette with a couple of Jerry Goldsmith soundtracks on it. We sat having lunch at Sulgrave House, talking about film and TV music. Like Keff McCulloch, Dominic basically came from a pop music background and was interested in learning more about instrumental soundtracks by non-pop composers. This was a subject I loved. We talked about Goldsmith, James Horner, Jerry Fielding, Johnny Mandel, Michael Small, Toru Takemitsu. Dominic was approachable and he seemed happy to have somebody to talk to about soundtracks. I liked his music, and thought that maybe if we kept swapping cassettes we could work out a common ground. That would be very useful indeed.

British TV needed someone like Dominic in 1988 and they still need him now. He has a talent which encompasses both the cutting edge of contemporary club music and classic-style orchestral film soundtracks. His score for *The Happiness Patrol* was a real asset to the show, providing mood to establish the nocturnal sorrow and menace of the city and suspense when the Doctor is defusing a bomb (he won't let Ace do it; 'I never get to have any fun,' she says). Dominic's music incorporates the mournful harmonica blues which is the calling card of the character Earl Sigma (played by Richard D. Sharp).

Richard took a stab at playing his own harmonica, but he wasn't a virtuoso. The script required Earl Sigma to play melancholy tunes at some points and jaunty tunes at others. Graeme said to Sophie, 'Andrew rather cruelly said he couldn't tell the difference.' It was true, I couldn't. Richard's solos were later replaced by Dominic's score, which worked beautifully.

The blues harmonica was part of the world we were evolving in the scripts for *The Happiness Patrol*. I had seen how unrelentingly unsympathetic the lighting had been on some of the previous year's **Doctor Who** stories that were shot in the studio. It was possible to get interested and imaginative people doing the lighting, but it was also possible to get someone who would light the soliloquy from **Hamlet** and a game of snooker in exactly the same way. Or, as Mike Tucker put it, 'They would come in, set up a pole in the middle of the studio floor, and arrange the lights so that whatever angle you shot from, the pole wouldn't cast a shadow. That was how they were trained.' Not exactly conducive to creating mood or atmosphere.

When we were working on the scripts for *The Happiness Patrol*, we had no idea who would do the lighting. But I knew that it was an all-studio story and I wanted to make it bullet proof.

So we set about building moody atmosphere into the script. It would all take place during the course of one night, and it would be largely set on the streets of a city. Nocturnal city streets, we felt, would require shadows and atmosphere. So when Graeme and I discussed the setting of the story we were talking in terms of **One from the Heart**, Francis Coppola's nocturnal Las Vegas love story that was entirely shot in the studio, and also New Orleans. And therefore the blues.

Our attempt to bullet-proof the script was partially successful. The street sets in the studio were for the most part suitably shadowy and sinister. But all the interiors were lit in the usual unrelenting artificial glare. Nonetheless, all the sets benefited from John Asbridge's brilliant design. Last seen painting roses black for *Delta and the Bannermen*, John Asbridge was back on the team for this season's three-parters. The sets he created for *The Happiness Patrol* were another great asset to the production, along with Dominic's moody, suspenseful music.

In fact, the design on *The Happiness Patrol* was uniformly strong, with memorable work by Richard Croft on costumes and Dorka Nieradzik on make-up. Sheila Hancock, who played our chief villain, the tyrant Helen A, looked unearthly and yet entirely appropriate with her white face, scarlet hair and red velvet suit. **Doctor Who** had frequently had camp or bizarre costumes and make-up, but here the look was deliberate and sinister and made sense in the lethally saccharine world of the story.

We'd finished the writing of the first two episodes of *The Happiness Patrol* and needed to start thinking about the third. Graeme came into my office, sat down and got ready to take notes. 'I'll get out my **Doctor Who** pen and my **Doctor Who** book,' he said. Graeme seemed uncomfortable in the chair opposite my desk so I suggested he use the chair by the table with my (chronically non-functional) computer on it. 'That's more sensible,' said Graeme, 'but tradition demands that that chair lives over there.'

Now that Graeme had finished his script for **The Bill** ('Finished it except for the endless rewrites to make it both longer and shorter'), we could concentrate on his **Doctor Who**. His episode two was pretty much done and we were going to finish his episode three as fast as possible and then go back to revise, improve and unify the other two. That was the plan.

At that point, Graeme had been having trouble plotting his episode three. I went through it with him, suggesting the general structure, which scenes could go where and so on. Graeme was soon a lot happier. 'This is great – all of my problems falling away,' he said. 'It's good isn't? It's great. I like this.' Graeme was a good guy. He suddenly stared down at my desk. 'Oh God,' he said, 'I haven't eaten my Kit Kat.'

My girlfriend Kate and I went to see Oliver Stone's **Salvador** again, at the BBC Film Club. After the film, I helped her on with her coat. 'Let's go and kill some fascists,' she said.

On April Fool's Day 1988, a Friday, Graeme and I were talking about the world he'd created, the world of the Happiness Patrol. We decide that there should be some sort of running slogan throughout the story, something like 'Confidence is high', which they used in the War Room scenes in the film **WarGames**. Graeme had cleared the decks for the weekend and was taking a crack at episode three. That night, he rang me at home in Kent to give me a progress report. 'I've got rid of the baby; now I'm just tied to the word processor. Confidence is high.'

We ended up with an assortment of catchphrases. 'Happiness will prevail' was one. But my favourite was the dual, call-and-response 'I'm glad you're happy' / 'I'm happy you're glad', which I still think is marvellous. It always reminds me of Lewis Carroll, or maybe I mean Edward Lear.

Another decision we made was to give the characters distinctively alien, futuristic names which were nonetheless still recognisable. I've always had an aversion for science fiction where characters are called things like Zargon or Axbor; those kinds of names tend to go hand in hand with silver jumpsuits for costumes. The approach we hit on for *The Happiness Patrol* was simple: everyone had normal first names, followed by an initial. And the initial reflected their place in the rigid hierarchy of the planet. So Helen A, the tyrant, is at the top of the heap. Amusingly, her husband is no better than Joseph C (Ronald Fraser). Helen A's chief lieutenant is Daisy K (played by Georgina Hale, a member of Ken Russell's repertory company, who drilled her *Happiness Patrol* extras into a crack troop). Others near the bottom of the food chain like Susan Q (Lesley Dunlop) are so far from the elite of the planet that they are headed for execution.

We also used Sigma as a surname, as the designation for off-world visitors, like Earl Sigma, our wandering blues trumpet player. (For boring practical reasons, the trumpet would turn into a harmonica as we moved into production.)

Back in the office between two days of Dalek location shooting in April, I worked madly with Kevin Clarke and Graeme to finish their scripts. With Kevin's we basically needed to just finish it but with Graeme we wanted to finish it then go back over the earlier episodes and improve them because we had started his script so long ago and my thinking about **Doctor Who** had changed so much, clarified so much since then.

It was a race against time, but we managed it, with seconds to spare. Things became particularly interesting when we suddenly learned that we'd lost a major set from the story. I ended up sitting around on location at the school on Macbeth Street while we shot the Dalek story madly rewriting – often on the back of Dalek scripts – to compensate for this setback.

We'd lost the prison set where the Doctor and Ace are incarcerated and meet other victims of the totalitarian regime. Necessity and adrenaline brought out a high level of inventiveness. Graeme, Ben Aaronovitch and I all threw ourselves into an emergency salvage job, collaborating on the rewrite. That's how we ended up with the Waiting Zone instead of a prison.

The Waiting Zone is just an area with a line painted on the floor. You have to wait inside the Zone, and if you step over the line a Happiness Patrol guard shoots you dead. This led to some useful dialogue about how 'There are no prisons on Terra Alpha' – a characteristic piece of totalitarian mendacity since the Waiting Zone is just a prison by another name. Although much cheaper to build.

The Waiting Zone would be equipped with a one-armed bandit machine for the prisoners to play, a holdover from the original concept of the prison as a kind of sinister amusement arcade.

We got the script revisions finished just before *The Happiness Patrol* went in front of the cameras on Wednesday 10 August 1988.

Doctor Who stories are at their most vulnerable when they involve monsters or strange creatures and, despite my caveats, we had plenty of them in *The Happiness Patrol*. First and foremost was the Kandy Man, a synthetic creature who is the chief torturer and executioner for Helen A.

We had conceived the Kandy Man as an imposing humanoid figure made out of candy, possibly fat and curved and pink. It was always an open question who would do creature design on **Doctor Who**. It could be argued with equal justice that it was the job of the special effects crew, the costume team, or the make-up people. I generally kept my fingers crossed that it would go to special effects. In the case of the Kandy Man, the job was handed to make-up designer Dorka Nieradzik. It turned out to be a very good decision in my opinion.

Graeme's reaction was rather different. 'I always thought the Kandy Man was a bit of a disaster,' he says now. 'I thought the story always needed to be harder edged and I think the Kandy Man could have been more vicious and terrifying. Once you've invoked the spirit of liquorice allsorts you can't be frightening. We were at one point thinking labs and white coats and Nazi doctors. More subtly sinister, rather than in primary colours, which is what we ended up with. The Kandy Man should have been in a sinisterly stained white coat and glasses. We had him wearing glasses and eating the stems of the glasses, which like him were made of candy. He was someone who experimented on people in a completely dispassionate way.

What we got was utterly different from our original concept but, unlike Graeme, I thought it worked well: a robotic figure made out of sweets who was blatantly modelled on Bertie Bassett, a trademark character belonging to a sweet manufacturer. I thought this version of the Kandy Man was marvellous, but I was worried that he would get us enmeshed in litigation – which he damned nearly did. But, legal worries aside, the Kandy Man was highly effective, with his swirling spiral discs for eyes and his menacing, croaking artificial voice. (Robert Allsopp assisted Dorka in the creation of the Kandy Man and those spinning eyes were provided by the special effects company Artem.)

Another successful monster was Fifi, the vicious predatory wolf-like creature, called a Stigorax, who is Helen A's pet and only true love. Fifi had arisen from Graeme's decision to create something to chase the Pipe People – a Pipe Ferret. She was a puppet, the handiwork of Sue Moore and Stephen Mansfield. Sue and Stephen were skilful, experienced sculptors who'd also worked on the wonderful political caricature puppets brought to life every week in **Spitting Image**, the topical comedy sketch show. Sue and Stephen would later do exemplary work in Season 27, on *Battlefield*.

Fifi was terrific, proving quite convincing when fawning in Helen A's lap – helped no end, it has to be said, by Sheila Hancock's performance. She played the role absolutely straight, but with a lethal edge of satire. However, once Fifi goes down into the system of pipes beneath the city, to hunt the Doctor and Ace and the Pipe People, the illusion of a living creature is soon lost. There's only one sequence in which Fifi really looks like she's scuttling along those pipes.

The pipes are also the scene, early on, of the Doctor and Ace discovering a mysterious footprint. John Nathan-Turner rolled his eyes when he saw this scene. 'Don't you love design people?' he said. 'Just one footprint!'

The Pipe People themselves, friendly indigenous aliens, were also less than successful. Steve and Sue designed their masks, which worked well enough, but there was something ultimately unconvincing about their eyes. And, crucially, the voices of the Pipe People were all wrong (in contrast to the wonderful Kandy Man).

The Happiness Patrol was always intended, on some level, to be a satire of Thatcher's Britain. Helen A was obviously modelled on Prime Minister Thatcher and Joseph C on her husband Dennis. I realised that if we were too explicit about this it could get the show into trouble, so I asked Graeme to soft-pedal any mention of the parallels in interviews. He did this faithfully, but there wasn't a lot of point. Sheila Hancock saw what we were getting at as soon as she read the part of Helen A, and she latched on to a note-perfect Mrs Thatcher piss-take. And she never hesitated to boldly say as much in public.

Despite the occasional failures of lighting (John Asbridge's brilliant sets occasionally look like sets instead of real environments); special effects (the death of Fifi in a welter of lightweight rubble wouldn't fool anyone), and the clumsy staging of odd scenes (Earl Sigma knocking the Happiness Patrol undercover guy unconscious is just a joke and the Kandy Man's death in the pipes was such a failure it didn't make it into the final cut), the Happiness Patrol generally works.

It is a genuinely sinister story, with memorable villains in the shape of both Helen A and the Kandy Man. It also gains immeasurable strength from being *about* something. The world it depicts makes references to Argentina under the Junta ('He will disappear') and South Africa during Apartheid (references to massacres in the townships) without ever being too specific or heavy handed. And throughout, Graeme Curry's dialogue is brilliant: 'Depressives – manic, reactive, endogenous, we've got them,' says the guard in the Waiting Zone. 'A man after my own soft centre,' says the Kandy Man and the Doctor warns him, 'That red-hot poker will cut through you like a knife through butterscotch.' As the Doctor flees the Kandy Kitchen with Ace she asks, 'What about the Kandy Man?' 'He'll keep,' says the Doctor, 'He's full of colouring, flavouring and preservative.'

And of course, Helen A's line at the end, 'I always thought love was overrated.' And then she sees Fifi's corpse and breaks down into the kind of overwhelming grief that was punishable by death under her own regime.

Graeme was happy with the way his story turned out, and I was glad he was happy.

7.35pm
Doctor Who

starring **Sylvester McCoy.**
Storm over Avallion
Part 1 of a four-part
adventure by
Ben Aaronovitch.
Ben's back, the Brigadier is
back, Bessie's back.
Meanwhile Benton suffers
alliterative disappointment.

Doris...........ANGELA DOUGLAS
Brigadier Lethbridge-Stewart
NICHOLAS COURTNEY
Sgt Zbrigniev......ROBERT JEZEK
Brig Bambera....ANGELA BRUCE
Morgaine.............JEAN MARSH
Ace.................SOPHIE ALDRED
Peter Warmsley......JAMES ELLIS
Ancelyn........MARCUS GILBERT
Mordred..CHRISTOPHER BOWEN
Shou Yuing...............LING TAI
Elizabeth Rowlinson
JUNE BLAND
Pat Rowlinson...NOEL COLLINS
Theme music composed by
RON GRAINER
Theme arrangement/incidental
music KEFF MCCULLOCH
Stunt arranger ALF JOINT
Costume designer
ANUSHIA NIERADZIK
Script editor ANDREW CARTMEL
Designer MARTIN COLLINS
Producer JOHN NATHAN-TURNER
Director MICHAEL KERRIGAN
•CEEFAX SUBTITLES
•S

7.35pm
Doctor Who

starring **Sylvester McCoy.**
Storm over Avallion
Part 3 of a four-part
adventure by
Ben Aaronovitch.
Sophie has a near-miss
during a stunt with a water
tank, and both Ben and
Andrew are having second
thoughts about killing the
Brigadier.
Ace.................SOPHIE ALDRED
Peter Warmsley......JAMES ELLIS
Ancelyn........MARCUS GILBERT
Brig Bambera...ANGELA BRUCE
Brig Lethbridge-Stewart
NICHOLAS COURTNEY
Shou Yuing...............LING TAI
Elizabeth.............JUNE BLAND
Mordred..CHRISTOPHER BOWEN
Morgaine.............JEAN MARSH
Knight commander
STEFAN SCHWARTZ
Pat Rowlinson...NOEL COLLINS
Flight Lt Lavel.....DOROTA ROE
Major Husak......PAUL TOMANY
Incidental music KEFF MCCULLOCH
Stunt arranger ALF JOINT
Visual effects designer
DAVE BEZKOROWAJNY
Script editor ANDREW CARTMEL
Designer MARTIN COLLINS
Producer JOHN NATHAN-TURNER
Director MICHAEL KERRIGAN
•CEEFAX SUBTITLES

7.35pm
Doctor Who

starring **Sylvester McCoy.**
Storm over Avallion
Part 2 of a four-part
adventure by
Ben Aaronovitch.
Andrew is frustrated with
seeing good ideas realised
badly on screen.
Ancelyn.........MARCUS GILBERT
Ace.................SOPHIE ALDRED
Shou Yuing...............LING TAI
Brigadier Bambera
ANGELA BRUCE
Mordred..CHRISTOPHER BOWEN
Flight Lt Lavel.....DOROTA ROE
Brigadier Lethbridge-Stewart
NICHOLAS COURTNEY
Elizabeth Rowlinson
JUNE BLAND
Pat Rowlinson...NOEL COLLINS
Peter Warmsley......JAMES ELLIS
Morgaine.............JEAN MARSH
Knight commander
STEFAN SCHWARTZ
Incidental music by
KEFF MCCULLOCH
Make-up designer JULIETTE MAYER
Script editor ANDREW CARTMEL
Designer MARTIN COLLINS
Producer JOHN NATHAN-TURNER
Director MICHAEL KERRIGAN
•CEEFAX SUBTITLES

7.35pm
Doctor Who

starring **Sylvester McCoy.**
Storm over Avallion
Part 4 of a four-part
adventure by
Ben Aaronovitch.
The Destroyer makes an
impressive entrance, but
Andrew is again
disappointed with how
things are being translated
on screen.
Ace.................SOPHIE ALDRED
Shou Yuing...............LING TAI
Morgaine.............JEAN MARSH
The Destroyer....MAREK ANTON
Mordred..CHRISTOPHER BOWEN
Brigadier Lethbridge-Stewart
NICHOLAS COURTNEY
Knight commander
STEFAN SCHWARTZ
Ancelyn........MARCUS GILBERT
Brig Bambera...ANGELA BRUCE
Doris...........ANGELA DOUGLAS
Incidental music KEFF MCCULLOCH
Stunt arranger ALF JOINT
Studio lighting DAVID LOCK
Script editor ANDREW CARTMEL
Designer MARTIN COLLINS
Producer JOHN NATHAN-TURNER
Director MICHAEL KERRIGAN
•CEEFAX SUBTITLES

CHAPTER 12
Battlefield

The situation is normal, and it doesn't get much worse than that.

Early in Ben Aaronovitch's involvement with **Doctor Who**, a couple of months before he was officially commissioned to write *Remembrance of the Daleks*, Ben came in for a story discussion. We spent all afternoon talking about it. As we concluded our discussion, Ben took a copy of **Starburst** magazine out of his bag. (Over a decade later, by an odd piece of synchronicity, I would briefly become editor of **Starburst**, Britain's most interesting science fiction magazine, before moving back into television.)

'It's the script editor's turn for a bit of ego massage,' said Ben, and he proceeded to read from an article which referred to things like 'the Cartmel Factor' in the upcoming new season of **Doctor Who**. I was duly gratified.

But, more importantly, I had spent the afternoon talking to Ben about one of his **Doctor Who** ideas, a space-age Arthurian story. The story was coming along nicely and now, crucially, it had found its missing element. We had decided that the ancient crashed spaceship required by the story would now be under water. *Quatermass and the Lake*, as it were. 'We've buried the reference to **Quatermass and the Pit**,' I told Ben, and he laughed.

Nigel Kneale, who wrote the **Quatermass** television serials, and subsequently two of Hammer's film adaptations of them, specialised in blending the futuristic, the alien, and the frighteningly primordial. 'The story first came to me when we were shooting *Dragonfire*,' says Ben. 'I was sitting in the Red Assembly smoking cigarettes and drinking coffee and thinking about it. I wanted the story to be Nigel Kneale-y. You know, the past comes back to bite you in the arse. So I was thinking about the past, in England, and I started to think about King Arthur. What if the Arthurian legend was based on aliens from another dimension, a place where magic actually worked?'

You could argue that in *Battlefield* we are dealing with advanced science, not magic. Or, as Ben put it in the script, 'Clarke's Law', referring to Arthur C. Clarke's assertion that any sufficiently advanced technology is indistinguishable from magic. 'And vice versa,' as the Doctor says. (The great thing about this scene is that, when the Doctor cites Clarke's Law, Ace immediately knows what he's talking about. This not only makes the point that Ace is no dummy, it also spares us giving the Doctor all the exposition.)

At this early stage, the story was still called *Storm Over Avallion*, a title for which both Ben and I have some residual affection. John Nathan-Turner asked us to change it to something less obscure and more punchy. We perhaps lost something by changing the title, because the original, with its strange echo of Avalon, hinted at a moody neo-Arthurian piece, which is precisely what we were aiming at.

And then of course, since it was a **Doctor Who** story, we had to think about how the Doctor would fit in. 'If you're going to do an Arthurian story,' says Ben, 'then the Doctor just has to be Merlin. And it couldn't be a story about the Doctor's past, because we were already doing that with *Remembrance of the Daleks*. So it had to be the Doctor's future – his *future* comes back to bite him in the arse. After all, it is a time travel show. This fitted nicely with the fact that it was set in the near future, just the way the Dalek story was set in the near past. I saw them as a pair, a philosophical pair, if that's not too pretentious a way of putting it.'

Although our discussions about this neo-Arthurian adventure pre-dated the commissioning of Ben's Dalek script, *Battlefield* wouldn't see the light of day until the 26th season of **Doctor Who**, two years later. In some ways, 'Battle Fatigue' might have been a more appropriate title for the story, because by the time we mounted the production we were all beginning to succumb to something akin to that.

Personally, I wasn't exhausted by script editing the show, although that was certainly exhausting enough. I was simply getting worn down by the constant struggle to try and make an intelligent science fiction drama in an environment which simply didn't understand science fiction. They *just didn't get it*. We were up against a culture of incomprehension. No matter how hard we tried or how good the scripts were, what ended up on the screen was all too often a travesty of our intentions.

Battlefield was the classic example of that. Despite it being a brilliant script, a fact which I keep reminding him of, to this day the writer can't bear to watch the show. While I was working on this book, I borrowed Ben's VHS tape of the story. When I put it into my machine, the tape was wound a few minutes into the first episode. 'Did you see where that tape was wound to?' says Ben. 'That was as far as I got. That was as much as I could bear to watch. As soon as I saw the knights…' He falls silent. 'The performers were good, though,' he adds.

Battlefield was directed by Michael Kerrigan who, like Andrew Morgan, had worked on the series **The Knights of God**. Michael was a nice guy and a very intelligent director who elicited good performances from the actors and worked hard on the logistics of the action scenes. But like the rest of us he was up against problems that seemed insurmountable. Specifically, the design.

The design of *Battlefield* pretty much guaranteed the story wouldn't work. That was what Ben means about the knights. 'They were supposed to be futuristic knights in powered armour which had a vague resemblance to medieval armour,' says Ben. Hence Ace's line when they find Ancelyn lying in the brewery: 'Is it an android?' This piece of dialogue ended up seeming a bit baffling, since it's clearly a conventional knight in armour lying there.

'It should have been powered armour,' says Ben, 'like the armour in Heinlein's **Starship Troopers** – the book, not the movie. But they just didn't get it. The designers just didn't get it. That was inexperience on my part. I didn't realise they just couldn't think outside the box.' Instead of this futuristic powered armour we got standard medieval chain mail. 'And it wasn't even stock armour,' says Ben. 'I wouldn't have minded if it was stock armour. But they made it especially. They *especially made* the wrong kind of armour. Instead of using the word *android*, I should have said *robot*, in the hope that the designer might read it.'

Indeed, by the time we were starting work on *Battlefield*, the writers and I had evolved the trick of specifically putting important design details into dialogue, on the assumption that if we put them in the scene directions (where they traditionally belonged) they would simply be ignored. In contrast, it's hard to ignore a piece of dialogue which is spoken aloud repeatedly in every read-through and rehearsal.

But this approach backfired, or at least failed spectacularly, in *Battlefield*. The spaceship at the bottom of the lake was supposed to be an organic style of technology, akin to H. R. Giger's 'bio-mechanoid' designs for **Alien**, and Ben's script makes this point repeatedly, but the design team failed to take the hint. Thus we have Ace saying to the Doctor, 'It's like being in some huge animal,' when in fact all we get is the two of them trotting up a spiral staircase with some Christmas tree lights on it.

This sort of design debacle didn't just affect the mood and stature of the piece, it frequently interfered with the clarity of the story. For instance, the miniature model of the underwater spaceship is a sadly inadequate piece of hardware. But one could live with it if it managed to get the plot points across in an any kind of effective way. It doesn't, though. Consequently we have the scene where our heroes are exploring the spaceship and Ace, who is clutching Excalibur, finds herself trapped in a chamber which fills with water while the Doctor watches helplessly.

What should happen then is that we see Ace being ejected from the ship, shooting up through the lake water towards the surface. But the model shot doesn't offer us any clue to this. All we see is a frail stream of bubbles gush up from the patently artificial, miniature model. We have no idea what they signify and there is no sign of a tiny Ace being shot from the ship. So the viewer is perplexed when Ace, who was desperately trapped a few moments earlier, suddenly appears without explanation on the surface of the water, clutching Excalibur, in a funky late 1980s version of the Lady of the Lake.

This is a cheeky and clever scene with some excellent dialogue. The Tennyson quotations were suggested on location by James Ellis, who plays the archaeologist Peter Warmsly, and they fitted in beautifully. 'What are you doing in the lake?' they ask Ace as they pull her out. 'Drowning,' says Ace. But there's a dark aspect to it when you realise that Sophie Aldred did damned nearly drown, or at least came close to serious injury, when the scene was shot in the studio. The transparent tank full of water in which Sophie was 'trapped' nearly became a real death trap when it began to crack ominously under the weight of the water — while she was still inside it.

Sophie had actually spotted some water leaking out of the tank earlier, soaking into towels which had been thoughtfully placed on the floor for that purpose. But she decided, as she puts it, 'to keep my nose out of other people's business' and went ahead with the stunt. She was always utterly fearless, possessing by nature some of the gutsiness of the character she played. Here's how she described what followed (in the book she wrote with Mike Tucker): 'There was now a lot of water in the tank and I was bobbing slightly, my jacket filling with air and acting as a buoyancy aid. I spread my hands across the glass in front of me to steady myself and a few seconds later heard a loud cracking sound.'

Sylvester's powerful voice thundered across the studio, 'Get her out of there!' and the crew rushed to drag Sophie out of the water, just as the tank broke up, flooding water onto the studio floor. Sylvester had alerted everyone to the situation and saved her. Sophie was picking splinters of glass out of her hands as she was rushed to safety, along with everyone else. We were fleeing the studio floor where gallons of water was sluicing across electrical cables...

Sylvester's concern for Sophie in real life exactly mirrored the Doctor's concern for Ace when she was under fictional threat in the show. They were a unique team.

Battlefield was originally conceived as an all-OB three-parter, to be shot entirely on location, like *Delta and the Bannermen*, *Silver Nemesis* or *Survival*. When it transformed into a four-parter shot both OB and in the studio, it also changed into a UNIT story. 'When it became a four-parter there was suddenly room to put UNIT in,' says Ben. 'I'd always wanted to do a UNIT story. It was my era of **Doctor Who**. I grew up watching Pertwee and Tom Baker.'

There was no problem getting John Nathan-Turner to agree to the UNIT concept. 'John thought it was a fabulous idea to have UNIT in it,' recalls Ben. 'It made sense to find out what had happened to UNIT in the last 20 years. I also wanted to rehabilitate the Brigadier, who had tended to be presented as a bit of a buffoon at times. I felt there was potential in the character which hadn't been explored and I wanted to make UNIT credible.'

The UNIT material, and the near-future aspect of the story are some of the most successful things about *Battlefield*. Small details like the reference to the King of England, the mention of using the phone in a car (years before car phones came into use) and the exorbitant cost of a round of drinks in the local pub all served to effortlessly establish a futuristic milieu, and for the most part proved to be highly accurate predictions (although we haven't got the King yet).

Tellingly, though, these points were all made through dialogue. The design was another matter. 'Couldn't they have researched the missile control room?' laments Ben. 'In *Remembrance of the Daleks* they researched every little detail, right down to the cap badges. But no one ever researches the *future*. All they needed to do was look at the current state of the art for technology and use that for what would be run-of-the-mill in the near future.'

Ben's re-imagining of UNIT as a multicultural force also seems prescient now, with a black female Brigadier, Polish sidekick, and Czech reinforcements (led by a Major Husak). 'Although Zbrigniev was supposed to be American,' says Ben. 'They just could never wrap their heads around the idea that someone with a name like that could be from the Bronx. That dates back to the original concept for the story when it was a three-parter and UNIT wasn't involved. It was the US Air Force and Bambera was a USAF captain. The story involved a stranded missile and who would be driving missiles around in England except the American Air Force? But the switch to a four-parter and the involvement of UNIT changed all that.'

When we decided to do a UNIT story, the obvious first question was what to do about the Brigadier. Should we bring the marvellous Nicholas Courtney out retirement, or should we recast with a new actor in the role? In the event, we did both, having our cake and eating it too. The new Brigadier was Winifred Bambera, played by Angela Bruce, who acquits herself well, although she doesn't know what to make of the epithet 'shame', which the script requires her to repeat as a sort of all-purpose exclamation. '"Shame" is something a West Indian would say,' says Ben. 'But she was a Geordie. I like her a lot. She's a good actress. But if I'd known she was from Newcastle I would have written her as a Geordie with great pleasure. It's another case of perverse casting. Why did they chose someone who wouldn't make sense of "shame"?' Incidentally, the character's name Winifred is a variant of Guinevere, just as Ancelyn is a version of Lancelot. More power to Ben's battered paperback copy of **The Oxford Dictionary of English Christian Names**.

In fact, the slowly growing romance between 'Lancelot' and 'Guinevere' is one of the many nice character touches in the story. The special effects and the design in *Battlefield* may not work, but the characters definitely do. In fact they're terrific. Marcus Gilbert does a marvellous job as Ancelyn and through his performance brings a reality to the story which the effects and design signally failed to convey. When Ancelyn says, 'She's coming,' signalling the arrival of Morgaine, he succeeds in lending an eerie anticipation to the arrival of the chief villain which a great deal of flashing lights and sinister laughter have failed to give it. And the moment where Ancelyn first sees the Doctor and says 'Merlin – against all hope' sends shivers down the spine.

This first encounter between the two is altogether an excellent little scene – and funny – with the Doctor echoing Ancelyn and saying 'Yes, remember my mighty arts' when clearly he doesn't know what the hell the guy is talking about.

Another excellent, though minor, character is the Brigadier's helicopter pilot Lavel, played by Dorota Rae. The scene where she stumbles into the pub and confronts Mordred is one of the best things in the story. Mordred, who has been swilling the local real ale and terrorising the blind barmaid, is somewhat drunk and immediately becomes lustful, fancying this strong, kick-ass woman. Then his mother, the evil Morgaine turns up and confronts the gun-toting Lavel. Lavel fires at her and Morgaine catches the bullet in her hand, crushing it to dust. This outstanding and entirely successful sequence works without the involvement of any special effect more sophisticated than a handful of powder.

Then Morgaine uses her sorcery to suck the thoughts from Lavel's mind and leaves her dead on the floor. Just to top it all, Morgaine pauses as she goes and pays for the beer her son has consumed – by restoring the barmaid's sight. Then we have a rather fake-looking video effects sequence of Lavel's body disappearing.

Video effects, like physical effects, were always unpredictable on **Doctor Who**. There were some brilliant video sequences in *Remembrance of the Daleks*, like the fleeting shot of the Dalek's interior. But the green serpent that attacks the Doctor in the sunken spaceship in *Battlefield* is just risible, with Sylvester tumbling and dodging a feeble visual artefact that was added weeks later in post-production. And then there was the lamentable sparkly effect that was supposed to be the 'interstitial vortex', a portal between dimensions, but which looks more like a twinkly bead curtain in a Shanghai knocking shop.

The physical effects weren't much better. There's a gag in the first episode where the Doctor has to pay for drinks in the pub and he empties out a purse full of strange coinage, one of which the script described as crawling away like a living thing. But the clockwork spider-type device we ended up with was disappointing – at least the way it's shot is disappointing – and the gag falls flat. 'It was supposed to be a jelly thing,' recalls Ben, 'a little blob.' In fact,

John Nathan-Turner cut the line about it which said, 'It's a mutated Jelly Baby.'

But while the effects were busy letting *Battlefield* down, the actors were doing a stalwart job of bringing to life the script's excellent and diverse characters. Nick Courtney is effortlessly engaging as the Brigadier, striking up a rapport with his pilot Lavel ('The situation, Lavel, is normal, and it doesn't get much worse than that. You know, I'm rather enjoying this'); sending figurative sparks flying in his confrontation with Morgaine; alienating both Bambera ('Yes sir. Perhaps I should make some tea, too') and Ace, who refers to him as 'Colonel Blimp'. Best of all, though, is his interaction with the Doctor: 'This whole area is crawling with armed extraterrestrials and they're hostile.' 'Same as ever, eh Brigadier?'

The crucial question concerning the Brigadier was whether he should survive the story or if we should use this opportunity to kill him off in a suitably dramatic and noble fashion, giving the character a fitting end. Again, we chose to have our cake and eat it by deceiving the audience into thinking the Brigadier is dead, then revealing that he's survived his encounter with the Destroyer, the story's big monster. I'm glad we did this. I've far too much affection for the character, and for Nick, to be the one responsible for putting an end to the Brigadier.

Again, though, the success of the UNIT concept in the script was hindered by design decisions on-screen. 'They gave UNIT the wrong guns,' observes Ben. 'Uzis! A serious military force would never use Uzis. Not for fighting in the open. Uzis are for use in an urban environment, at close quarters. They're good for drug dealers, I suppose. What they really needed were assault rifles, ironically just like the ones that were used in **The Knights of God**.'

Besides Nigel Kneale, the other writer whose work influenced us on *Battlefield* was Richard Matheson, specifically his brilliant script for **The Devil Rides Out**, another Hammer film, which adapted a classic novel of black magic by Dennis Wheatley. **The Devil Rides Out** climaxes with a scene in which satanic forces assault the heroes who are sheltering in a pentagram drawn on the floor. I suggested Ben should think about **The Devil Rides Out** and come up with a similarly creepy sequence for *Battlefield* and he devised a memorable scene for Ace and Shou Yuing (played by Ling Tai).

In **The Devil Rides Out**, the attack takes the form of a torrent of special effects (including a rather dodgy giant spider). Luckily, our homage involved a purely mental attack (which is somewhat reminiscent of Nigel Kneale again, particularly **The Creature**). This psychological warfare is one of the more successful sequences in the script. 'Someone's playing games with our minds,' says Ace.

Another moment that works because it's purely performance is the scene where the Doctor hypnotises the locals to convince them to evacuate what is about to become a war zone. This helped pave the way for the powerful, mysterious Doctor we were developing throughout Seasons 25 and 26. I'd begun to frequently refer to this more potent, shadowy Doctor as a chess player and Ben had decided to freshen up this notion in a confrontation between the Doctor and Morgaine. 'I could always defeat you at chess,' says Morgaine. 'Who said anything about chess?' replies the Doctor, 'I'm playing poker – and I have an Ace up my sleeve.' At which exact moment Ace pops up and helps save the day.

The first climax of *Battlefield* involves the summoning of a monster called the Destroyer. This spike-faced blue brute was an exceptional piece of design, beautifully executed by Sue Moore and Stephen Mansfield, who elaborated from a Plasticine devil's head they had shown John earlier in the season.

The original intention in the script was for the Destroyer to arrive, after much diabolical fanfare, and turn out to be, against all expectations, an inoffensive and meek-looking little nebbish of a guy in a pinstriped business suit, like a timid Civil Service clerk inexplicably bound with chains. *Then*, when his chains were removed he would transform into a hideous towering demon, with talons bursting through his skin and so on. This was a lovely idea, but budgetary constraints prevented any attempt at a transformation and we ended up with a Destroyer that looked demonic throughout.

The Destroyer was about as good as a man in a rubber suit can get, aided by the fact he was largely shot from a low angle, taking advantage of the raised set. Unfortunately, the effect is somewhat undermined by an establishing shot that doesn't do justice to the Destroyer and manages, in our first glimpse of the creature, to make it look as phoney as possible. *And* these shots are preceded by glimpses of the Destroyer's shadow on a wall, which unfortunately look about as frightening as one of those shadow-bunnies you make with your hands. Later shots, however, reveal just how good Sue and Stephen's prosthetic is, and go some way towards compensating for this.

In the early days of BBC science fiction, for example the aforementioned **The Creature** by Nigel Kneale from 1955, frequent skilful use was made of sound. The programme-makers were aware that visual effects could never live up to the demands of the script, so they employed sound to get their message across, to chilling effect.

So it's sad to report that, some 30 years later, the sound design on *Battlefield* was completely ineffectual. There are numerous occasions throughout the story where the actors are responding to what are supposed to be powerful, weird or disturbing sounds, and these sounds just aren't realised. At the beginning of episode one, the Doctor and Ace are supposed to be responding to an extraordinary, eerie audio signal in the TARDIS, but the appropriate effect simply isn't there. What *is* there is disappointing in the extreme. Ben shakes his head in despair when he discusses it. 'And you wonder why I can't watch the show?'

This problem of inadequate sound effects runs right through the four episodes. When, near the end of the story, the Destroyer shouts 'At last!' it's supposed to be an apocalyptic eruption. 'What's that?' exclaim our astonished characters. 'It's nothing,' would be the appropriate answer, since the sound effect has completely let us down again.

The second, and final, climax of *Battlefield* comes when Morgaine teleports into the control room of the nuclear missile convoy which has become bogged down by the lake. The implied threat of this missile never really comes across to the viewer, because the shot of the bogged-down convoy simply looks like a bunch of vehicles casually parked by a body of water, perhaps so the drivers can go for a swim.

More crucially, we don't ever *see* the missile in question. It's theoretically inside one of the trucks instead of being on display in all its evil glory (the Doctor refers to nuclear weapons as having a 'graveyard stench'). This is probably factually accurate, but this was a time for dramatic licence, not factual accuracy. Anyway for reasons of authenticity, limited budget, or simply because no one thought it was important, the missile doesn't exist on-screen. Unfortunately this also means it never exists in the minds or emotions of the audience. Hence the threat never exists, or at best is extremely abstract.

Nonetheless this scene features some chilling performances and cracking dialogue provided by Ben. Morgaine demands to know the incantations which will unleash this dreadful weapon – 'The failsafe release code' she spits out, adapting swiftly to the language of this modern world, and bringing magic and technology together in a deadly synthesis.

The Doctor has to stop Morgaine detonating the missile and he does this by the unusual expedient of *talking* to her. He delivers what came to be known, rather irreverently, as 'the CND speech', a tirade against nuclear weapons which I have to confess that I wrote. I showed Ben the first draft of this dialogue for the Doctor and his response was succinct. 'It's too long,' he said. 'It's way too long.'

I dismissed his reaction. I loved the speech. I loved every heartfelt word of it. The sequence was duly shot and eventually I saw the rushes and when I did, it was immediately clear. It was too long. It was way too long.

I sat with John in his office, playing the scene over and over again, finding little moments to trim here and there until finally it had been reduced to a reasonable length. In the process, I learned a crucial lesson. It's very simple to spot when someone else's writing is overlong. It's not so easy when it's your own stuff. The writer becomes attached to his own words. If the writer is also the script editor he has to learn to approach his own work with the same cold-eyed ruthlessness he'd apply to anyone else's. It's a lesson I never forgot.

The end result was very good, though. The fragments that were left of the long speech proved powerful and entirely effective, with its description of a child's eyes burned out by the flash of nuclear detonation: 'No more tears, only ashes.' (An image which was inspired, incidentally, by Peter Watkins' unforgettable BBC film **The War Game**.) We'd managed to cut a long, self indulgent, unwieldy speech down to a terse, sharp, forceful one. But the place for such cutting is on the script page before you start shooting, not on videotape in post-production.

After the CND speech, Ben's dialogue resumes as the Doctor tells Morgaine that King Arthur is dead and gone, he's been dust for centuries. And, brilliantly, it turns out that Morgaine loved Arthur. Jean Marsh is superb here, showing tenderness and vulnerability and profound depths of regret as she remembers her lost love. 'When we were together, the air was like honey,' she says. It's another scene that sends a shiver down the spine. (Rather embarrassingly, Ben tells me that I actually wrote that bit of dialogue, too. Oh well.)

But for all the excellent material that lurks in the depths of the four episodes of *Battlefield*, it's difficult to get past the terribly shaky opening few minutes of the show, with Bambera's uncomprehending delivery of her catchphrase 'Shame', the pathetically battered prop which is supposed to be the TARDIS, the impotent sound effects, the inappropriate and overbearing music (uncharacteristic of Keff, who elsewhere delivers deft and effective themes and who saved *Paradise Towers*) and the utterly silly looking knights with their phoney, sparking gun blasts.

It's easy to see why Ben's tape was ejected just a couple of minutes into the episode and one can only speculate on how many other viewers bailed out almost before *Battlefield* begins, missing out on the flashes of genius that are still scattered through the show.

7.35pm
Doctor Who

starring **Sylvester McCoy**.
Wolf-Time
First in a four-part adventure by Ian Briggs.
Once again, Ace is at the forefront of the plot and again we have a period setting which the BBC recreates superbly.

Sgt Prozorov
................................PETER CZAJKOWSKI
Captain Sorin.......TOMEK BORK
Ace.................SOPHIE ALDRED
Petrossian.........MARK CONRAD
Vershinin...........MAREK ANTON
Sgt Leigh........MARCUS HUTTON
Perkins........CHRISTIEN ANHOLT
Dr Judson....DINSDALE LANDEN
Nurse Crane............ANNE REID
Captain Bates
...........................STEVAN RIMKAS
The Rev Mr Wainwright
.................NICHOLAS PARSONS
Miss Hardaker..JANET HENFREY
Jean..................JOANN KENNY
Phyllis................JOANNE BELL
Commander Millington
........................ALFRED LYNCH
Kathleen...........CORY PULMAN
Baby................AARON HENLEY
Theme music composed by
RON GRAINER
Incidental music MARK AYRES
Costume designer KEN TREW
Script editor ANDREW CARTMEL
Designer DAVID LASKEY
Producer JOHN NATHAN-TURNER
Director NICHOLAS MALLETT
•CE

7.35pm
Doctor Who

starring **Sylvester McCoy**.
Wolf-Time
by Ian Briggs.
It's not a Super Ted toy. It's clearly not a Super Ted toy. The design is completely different. Stop looking for things to complain about.

Ace.................SOPHIE ALDRED
Prozorov.....PETER CZAJKOWSKI
Vershinin...........MAREK ANTON
Dr Judson....DINSDALE LANDEN
Captain Sorin.......TOMEK BORK
Nurse Crane...........ANNE REID
Jean..................JOANN KENNY
Phyllis................JOANNE BELL
Millington........ALFRED LYNCH
Rev Mr Wainwright
.................NICHOLAS PARSONS
Miss Hardaker..JANET HENFREY
Leigh............MARCUS HUTTON
Perkins........CHRISTIEN ANHOLT
Captain Bates..STEVAN RIMKAS
Kathleen...........CORY PULMAN
Baby................AARON HENLEY
Incidental music MARK AYRES
Stunt arranger TIP TIPPING
Make-up designer DENISE BARONS
Script editor ANDREW CARTMEL
Designer DAVID LASKEY
Producer JOHN NATHAN-TURNER
Director NICHOLAS MALLETT
•CEEFAX SUBTITLES

7.35pm
Doctor Who

starring **Sylvester McCoy**.
Wolf-Time
A four-part adventure by Ian Briggs.
3: The Doctor knows what's going on and isn't telling Ace. The Cartmel Masterplan is on fire now.

Commander Millington
........................ALFRED LYNCH
Dr Judson....DINSDALE LANDEN
Ace.................SOPHIE ALDRED
Rev Mr Wainwright
.................NICHOLAS PARSONS
Nurse Crane...........ANNE REID
Captain Bates..STEVAN RIMKAS
Perkins........CHRISTIEN ANHOLT
Captain Sorin.......TOMEK BORK
Vershinin...........MAREK ANTON
Sgt Prozorov
.................PETER CZAJKOWSKI
Kathleen Dudman
..............................CORY PULMAN
Baby................AARON HENLEY
Jean..................JOANN KENNY
Phyllis................JOANNE BELL
Sgt Leigh......MARCUS HUTTON
Incidental music MARK AYRES
Stunt arranger TIP TIPPING
Producer JOHN NATHAN-TURNER
Director NICHOLAS MALLETT
•CEEFAX SUBTITLES

7.35pm
Doctor Who

starring **Sylvester McCoy**.
Wolf-Time
Last in a four-part adventure by Ian Briggs.
Ace nearly ruins things by giving the game away to Fenric, but the Doctor manages to resolve her issues with her mum. Nicholas Parsons dies.

Nurse Crane...........ANNE REID
Dr Judson....DINSDALE LANDEN
Commander Millington
........................ALFRED LYNCH
Ace.................SOPHIE ALDRED
Captain Sorin.......TOMEK BORK
Kathleen Dudman
..............................CORY PULMAN
Baby................AARON HENLEY
Captain Bates
...........................STEVAN RIMKAS
Sgt Leigh......MARCUS HUTTON
Jean..................JOANN KENNY
Phyllis................JOANNE BELL
Vershinin...........MAREK ANTON
Ancient haemovore
.................RAYMOND PRICKETT
Incidental music MARK AYRES
Stunt arranger TIP TIPPING
Producer JOHN NATHAN-TURNER
Director NICHOLAS MALLETT
(Next week a new story: 'Catflap')
•CEEFAX SUBTITLES

CHAPTER 13
The Curse of Fenric

Aquatic vampires?

Tuesday 8 September 1987. *Time and the Rani* Part One had been broadcast the previous night, and I think even John Nathan-Turner had clocked that Pip and Jane's script was not a complete masterpiece. He told me that we wouldn't be using them again. Great. However, he was playing with the idea of using Malcolm Kohll again: 'I think Malcolm blossomed.'

Personally, I liked Malcolm very much, but I had other plans. Specifically, another Ian Briggs script. I reminded John of when we were looking for a new companion for the Doctor and we were comparing Malcolm's character Ray and Ian's character Ace, and how John himself had said there was no contest.

Thus began a long and demanding process that was both political and artistic. The political aspect was shepherding a new Ian Briggs script to the commissioning stage, and then into production, under the approval of John. The artistic aspect was the evolution of a new story which would satisfy Ian and me as a creative piece of work, as an adventure story, as science fiction, and as a **Doctor Who** story. It was the usual demanding combination but the script that would become *The Curse of Fenric* fulfilled it uniquely well.

When Ian first started coming up with ideas for **Doctor Who**, in the process that eventually gave us *Dragonfire*, it rapidly became clear that my judgement had been accurate. He wrote brilliantly and his scripts had real thematic depth. And his particular strength was coming up with fascinating three-dimensional characters. On the other hand, he knew little or nothing about science fiction at that stage and the early, pre-*Dragonfire* ideas he came up with had science fiction trappings which were merely that, tacked onto the plot and characters which were what really interested him.

All that had changed by the time we began to work on *The Curse of Fenric*. Ian hadn't exactly become a science fiction fan. But then, that wasn't what was required of him. He simply needed to have enough of an understanding of the possibilities of science fiction to build it into his story at a foundation level and to take advantage of its possibilities rather than just suffering it as something imposed on the 'real' drama of his script ideas. And by the time we started *The Curse of Fenric* Ian had reached this point and gone beyond it. He was emerging as an ideal **Doctor Who** writer.

In an odd way, Ian's work on **Doctor Who** was always intertwined with the writing of Alan Moore. Alan Moore was the British comics writer whose work (at that time, chiefly his **Swamp Thing** stories) had been my main inspiration when I was first approached by John and when I joined the show. Eventually, other influences would come to dominate (William Gibson's cyberpunk novels) but they would never supplant Moore entirely. It was Alan Moore's work that inspired my first ever attempt at a **Doctor Who** story – the eco-parable I had pitched to Jonathan Powell in my crucial job interview.

And, of course, it was Alan Moore who had inspired the 'crazy paving' monologue which had ended up being inserted into the conclusion of Ian's *Dragonfire*, much to Ian's chagrin and my own. Moore would also be a crucial influence on the first germ of an idea which eventually gave rise to *The Curse of Fenric*. So, who is Alan Moore and what was his connection with **Doctor Who**?

It's hard to describe the impact of Alan Moore's work on anyone who, like myself, was a fan of comic books in their childhood and then repudiated the whole medium as soon as they were old enough to appreciate what crap comics are. Not that comics are badly drawn. They are often beautifully drawn. But they are also often badly written. During the 1970s, at least, they were so invariably badly written that no adult could approach them as anything other than kitsch. There were a few honourable exceptions, of course, but these were mostly newspaper strips such as Peter O'Donnell's brilliant **Modesty Blaise** or Hal Foster's **Prince Valiant**. By and large, comic books were written with what seemed like a deliberate intent to produce ephemeral mediocrity.

Until Alan Moore came along. Moore took the extraordinary view that comics could be an art form, and an adult one at that. And he had the talent to prove that this was possible. When I read his stuff I was immediately converted, though when I tried to tell other people about it I met with a certain amount of resistance. I remember the appalled look of a young flame haired film executive when I tried to explain to her how great **Swamp Thing** was. The fact that it was a comic and it was called **Swamp Thing** was enough for her. (Though a year or two later she had **Watchmen** and **V for Vendetta** jutting from her trendy shoulder bag. It had become okay to read comics by then, thanks to Alan Moore.)

I always thought that Moore would be an ideal writer for **Doctor Who** and when I joined the show it was one of my first priorities to try and track him down. But fate decided that I should bump into him by accident.

On a bright Saturday in February 1987, I breathed the cold winter air of Westminster as I approached a building called the Methodist Hall. Here at the seat of British government I was going to a Comic Mart. And here among those other early risers perusing the back issues, I recognised Alan Moore. He was a distinctive figure with his long hair and beard. I froze on the spot. Pathetic, I know. But only the night before I had been reading the latest **Swamp Thing** that he'd scripted and on my desk at the BBC was a yellow Post-it note that read 'Write to Alan Moore.' He he was, a tall man in a black suit with long flowing hair and a long beard. I forced myself to go over to him and introduce myself. We shook hands. I told him I wanted him to do a script for **Doctor Who**. He looked at me with his level grey eyes. A man with a steady gaze, thin black tie.

'I don't write for Marvel,' he said. I explained it was the TV show, not the comic.

He gave me his address and phone number and I exited the Comic Mart, grinning with triumph.

Monday 9 March 1987. I phoned Alan in Northampton. His wife was covering the mouthpiece. 'It's the script editor of **Doctor Who**.' Alan came on the line. 'Hello, Andrew.' Very open, friendly Northern voice. He told me he was busy. 'I'm finishing off **Watchmen** and the **Swamp Thing**.'

So I waited then rang him again. He was still snowed under by commitments writing for comics but was quite into the idea of doing a **Doctor Who**. We talked for about 40 minutes. He said he remembered *The Celestial Toymaker* and wouldn't mind doing something like that. I explained to him my fascination with that particularly English kind of fantasy. 'Poking into dark nursery corners,' said Alan. We arranged to meet in July to talk about the possibility of him doing a **Doctor Who** TV script. 'Then you can tell me what the scam is,' Alan said, alluding to the financial and contractual side of things.

Alan Moore never did write for the show, sadly, but his influence remains, most obviously in the two scripts by another one of my favourite writers, Ian Briggs. As I said, *Dragonfire* contained the monologue which I'd written under the influence of **The Watchmen**. (Colin Brake, the script editor of **EastEnders** and a **Doctor Who** and comic book fan had been unkind enough to refer to it as 'that *Doctor Manhattan* rip off'.)

And *The Curse of Fenric* also began with a conversation about Alan Moore…

Aquatic vampires?' said Ian Briggs. He was gamely trying to conceal any dismay or amusement he might have felt. We were sitting in my office trying to work out the basis for his second **Doctor Who** script and I was suggesting ideas for potential villains and monsters. I'd read Alan Moore's **Swamp Thing** story 'Still Waters', which featured an underwater colony of vampires in a flooded Midwestern American town and I thought that aquatic vampires might be just the thing to provide a new monster for **Doctor Who**. Ian smiled tolerantly, took the concept on board, and began dreaming up the story that would become *The Curse of Fenric*.

The Curse of Fenric is rich and complex and it's all thanks to Ian Briggs. He took the notion of vampires from the sea and promptly made the connection with Dracula, and the Count's first landfall in England. The ocean association also suggested Vikings to Ian, who'd just returned from a holiday in Sweden. From here, Ian and I began to elaborate the details.

The key aspect to the story was a Second World War setting. I'd already determined that Earth-based historical stories had the strongest chance of working on-screen. *Delta and the Bannermen*, *Remembrance of the Daleks* and the Elizabethan sections of *Silver Nemesis* had established that.

Here we were going to do World War Two, but we wanted to get away from the standard Allies versus Germans dynamics, so we introduced Russian soldiers into the plot.

Ian's story for *The Curse of Fenric* was amazingly prescient. The incorporation of an Alan Turing-style scientist and an Enigma-type code-breaking machine were brilliant ideas, and decades ahead of the revival of interest in Turing which would come with Robert Harris's excellent novel **Enigma** and the intelligent film version of it.

We also decided, despite the cold war aspects of the story, that the apocalyptic threat in it would not be nuclear weapons but chemical ones. 'I want to call the poisonous substance dioxin,' said Ian, 'Because dioxin really is a threat to the environment and if some little kid picks up on the name and registers that it's dangerous, then that's a good thing.'

So the elements of Fenric came together, Vikings, Russian soldiers, chemical warfare, computers, logic games, chess, the Second World War, and of course aquatic vampires. John was enthusiastic about the story but he had some legitimate concerns. The idea was complex and in danger of becoming confusing to the average viewer. It was a story that reached deep into the past and far into the future We needed some strong, simple concept to thread it all together. One day, I walked into John's office and said, 'Why don't we make it a curse? Call it *The Curse of Fenric* so right up front people understand that it's something ancient which is having an effect in the present.' John slowly began to smile.

The Curse of Fenric begins confidently, with its moody underwater shots, the Russian troops paddling to shore, and the Doctor and Ace arriving on a secret naval base in full 1940s regalia. It also kicks off with some great Ian Briggs dialogue ('If this is a secret naval base, I'm Lord Nelson,' says Ace).

The superior script and authentic period setting make for a particularly strong story. And a strong cast does it justice. Even in the relatively minor role of Miss Hardaker we had a superlative actress, Janet Henfrey. Janet had played the unforgettable schoolteacher in Dennis Potter's **The Singing Detective** and I made a point of seeking her out during rehearsals and telling how great she'd been. She seized my wrist, beaming with gratitude. Mark Ayres' music is also an asset, ranging from contemporary boogie-woogie quotations to eerie pulsing synth moments. And Nicholas Mallett, who was above all an actor's director, thrived on the detailed and in-depth characterisation that Ian provided, even for the most minor characters. At one point one of the Russian soldiers begins to regret all the killing that surrounds him. 'If you need to explain why he's having a change of heart,' said Ian, 'It's because his wife has just had their first child and he's beginning to see things differently, to see the preciousness of life.' Nick Mallett nodded and scribbled notes.

But *The Curse of Fenric* has its flaws, too, particularly as a vampire story. For example, the Russian soldiers' fear of nightfall is irrelevant since we can't *afford* nightfall in the story.

As Mike Tucker said, 'How can you do a vampire story without night shooting? And we can't shoot at night as we can't afford the overtime.' Ian and I were aware that this was likely to be the case and Ian had cunningly come up with a solution. The vampires would emerge from a sinister black mist. 'The black fog turned day into night,' reads the Viking inscription in the local church. 'Dead men coming out of a black fog,' says the Russian officer, quoting from a report about supernatural doings on the Eastern Front.

Both quotes were evocative, but rather optimistic as it turned out. 'Black smoke is toxic,' Mike Tucker told us, 'We have to go with white fog.'

Mike was a key influence on the design of *The Curse of Fenric* and we were lucky to have him on our team again. He was working for the visual effects designer Graham Brown. But Graham was that rare thing, a man who encouraged other talent and didn't feel threatened by it. He realised that Mike had a better grasp of vampire stories and horror films than he did; 'he relied on me to bring everyone up to speed,' said Mike. Mike showed the design team films and TV shows from his VHS collection: **Fright Night**, **Dracula**, **Salem's Lot** and John Carpenter's **The Fog**.

As usual, the demarcation line between visual effects, costume and make-up was vague and it was Ken Trew, our costume designer, who came up with the design for the aquatic vampires. He showed me a sketch of an extraordinary-looking half-melted creature. It had a definite marine organism look to it, with the suggestion of gills and suckers and was a distinctive lavender blue colour. I didn't know what to make of it. It was unlike any vampire I'd ever seen, with a flaccid sucking maw rather than sharp fangs. But the suit and mask that resulted from Ken's drawings were very impressive. Once again, Stephen Mansfield and Sue Moore were hired to execute the masks. The look was complex, distinctive and horrible and, best of all that lavender blue colour gave it a unique look that was both beautiful and repellent.

The whole vampire thing had by now begun to worry John Nathan-Turner. He was concerned that the show would be too horrific, particularly for small children. He decided he didn't really want to do a vampire story.

At one time, this would have been cause for panic. But by now I'd learned to be resourceful to get things to work on **Doctor Who**. So Ian and I simply pulled the same trick that Kevin and I had worked on *Silver Nemesis*. In that case we had merely changed every reference to 'Nazis' to 'Paramilitaries'; now Ian and I went through *The Curse of Fenric* scripts and removed every reference to vampires, replacing it with a word Ian had coined, 'Haemovores' – or 'blood-eaters'. *Plus ça change*. This global substitution did the trick. ('Those vampires – I mean Haemovores,' says Ace, rather cheekily, at one point.) John was mollified and the vampires, I mean Haemovores, stayed in the script.

Unfortunately, as so often happened, the rubber Haemovore masks that looked awe inspiring at rest became almost comical once attempts were made to animate them. In particular, the chief monster, the Ancient Haemovore, was risible. He stood in a tunnel, his gills pulsing and his eyes moving convincingly enough, but his jaw flapped haplessly and comically during this, his big speech. Various bits of padding and sticky tape were applied to try and remedy it. I sighed and resigned myself to another near miss in the special effects.

There is plenty that does succeed in *The Curse of Fenric*, though. The conflict between the Russians and the British is a definite bonus, making the story feel relevant and modern, looking ahead to the cold war and the global tensions that were still dominating the world when we were filming. And the choice of chemical weapons makes the story seem painfully relevant even now, in a new century.

Above all though, is the stature of Ian Briggs's writing, with its depth and wit and edge. 'Thinking machines,' says Dr Judson (Dinsdale Landen). 'Yes, but whose thoughts will they think?' asks Commander Millington (Alfred Lynch). Even the simplest moments are transformed by the atmospheric accuracy of Ian's dialogue. Jean and Phyllis (Joann Kenny and Joanne Bell) are two teenagers evacuated from London. When they walk along the beach they find a Haemovore artefact, a futuristic scrap of metal. 'It feels all funny and tingly,' they exclaim. 'It's like electric!'

One particularly resonant and telling scene involves Kathleen Dudman (Cory Pulman) and her baby. Ace asks, quite innocently, if Kathleen is married. Kathleen is offended and her icy response causes Ace to realise her blunder and the vast gulf in the social attitude towards unmarried mothers between the 1940s and the 1980s.

There are also moments of wild humour, even at the centre of a cyclone of action and terror: 'Don't interrupt me when I'm eulogising,' says Dr Judson, now transformed into the demonic Fenric.

Along with these internal dynamics, *The Curse of Fenric* offers plenty of external action. Action sequences weren't Nick Mallett's forte. Scenes like the girl vampires' confrontation with Reverend Wainwright (Nicholas Parsons) in the graveyard could have worked, despite being shot in broad daylight, but they just aren't shot properly. They needed to be staged by someone who understood the visual possibilities of the suspense and action – the way that Alan Wareing handled *Survival*. The girl vampires certainly look suitably scary, with their fangs and talons (although this may have become one of John Nathan-Turner's reasons for not wanting to go this route later with the Cheetah People in *Survival*; maybe he just didn't want to repeat himself). The various Haemovore attack sequences, obviously based on **The Night of the Living Dead**, are equally unconvincing and the siege on the church, which should have been a highpoint of suspense, action and horror just falls flat as the floppy costumes of the creatures try to thrust in through the doors and windows.

But the Doctor is suitably powerful and resourceful. When he and Ace first arrive at the base, guards are soon swarming over them, so the Doctor deals with this by the simple expedient of preparing his own letter of authorisation from the War Office. He hammers it out on a typewriter then signs and countersigns it himself, using two different pens in both hands simultaneously. A moment later, the ink barely dry, he proffers it to the guards who are pouring in to arrest him and they immediately lower their guns and apologise – they didn't realise such an important figure was coming to visit.

I loved this scene and I felt it was a key moment in the rehabilitation of the Doctor. It shows him as powerful, resourceful and witty. He's no longer the fall guy. He's in charge, and in a quirky alien way, too. Plus Sylvester looks great in a duffel coat.

And of course, since this is an Ian Briggs script, there's a powerful erotic element. The scene where Ace seduces a guard (Marcus Hutton) to distract him has some fascinating dialogue, which is almost blank verse: 'Is he making the right moves or just going through the motions?' In fact, Ian and I had to hastily adjust the dialogue in this scene to account for unseasonable weather conditions on location (snow in April). It originally featured lines like 'Too hot. Clothes sticking to me.' These lines were greeted with howls of cynical laughter by the freezing crew, so Ian came up with 'There's a wind whipping up. I can feel it through my clothes.'

There's also a persistent subtext in the story, with deep water and swimming as metaphors for sexual experience. 'Come into the water with us,' say the evacuee girls, who are now vampire sirens, 'Deep down everybody wants to come into the water.'

But the depths of Lulworth Cove (chosen because they had acceptable conditions for diving and underwater shooting) stand not just for sexuality but also for maturity. 'Don't be afraid of the water,' says the Doctor, encouraging Ace. And Sophie responds by executing a beautiful dive into the cold, dangerous, problematical waves.

7.35pm
Doctor Who

starring **Sylvester McCoy**.

The Bestiary
Part one of a three-part adventure by Marc Platt. Andrew and Marc create a story which plays to the BBC's strengths. A period setting in studio sets hopes high for next year.

Mrs Pritchard.......SYLVIA SYMS
Mrs Grose....BRENDA KEMPNER
Rev Ernest Matthews
    JOHN NETTLETON
Ace.................SOPHIE ALDRED
Gwendoline
   KATHERINE SCHLESINGER
Josiah......................IAN HOGG
Redvers....MICHAEL COCHRANE
Nimrod..........CARL FORGIONE
Control.............SHARON DUCE

Theme music composed by
RON GRAINER
Incidental music MARK AYRES
Costume designer KEN TREW
Script editor ANDREW CARTMEL
Designer NICK SOMERVILLE
Producer JOHN NATHAN-TURNER
Director ALAN WAREING
●CEEFAX SUBTITLES

7.35pm
Doctor Who

starring **Sylvester McCoy**.

The Bestiary: part two of a three-part adventure by Marc Platt.

While the viewers are confused, the cast and crew are having a great time. Ace is at the forefront of the storytelling.

Ace.................SOPHIE ALDRED
Nimrod..........CARL FORGIONE
Control.............SHARON DUCE
Gwendoline
   KATHERINE SCHLESINGER
MacKenzie.....FRANK WINDSOR
Josiah......................IAN HOGG
Mrs Pritchard.......SYLVIA SYMS
Rev Matthews
    JOHN NETTLETON
Mrs Grose....BRENDA KEMPNER
Redvers Fenn-Cooper
    MICHAEL COCHRANE
Incidental music MARK AYRES
Make-up designer JOAN STRIBLING
Script editor ANDREW CARTMEL
Designer NICK SOMERVILLE
Producer JOHN NATHAN-TURNER
Director ALAN WAREING
●CEEFAX SUBTITLES

7.35pm
Doctor Who

starring **Sylvester McCoy**.

The Bestiary
Final part of a three-part adventure by Marc Platt. Burnt toast, primordial soup, husks and damned tsetse flies.

Control..............SHARON DUCE
Josiah.......................IAN HOGG
Nimrod...........CARL FORGIONE
Gwendoline
   KATHERINE SCHLESINGER
Ace.................SOPHIE ALDRED
Mrs Pritchard.......SYLVIA SYMS
Light...............JOHN HALLAM
MacKenzie.....FRANK WINDSOR
Redvers Fenn-Cooper
    MICHAEL COCHRANE
Incidental music MARK AYRES
Visual effects designer
MALCOLM JAMES
Script editor ANDREW CARTMEL
Designer NICK SOMERVILLE
Producer JOHN NATHAN-TURNER
Director ALAN WAREING
●MUSIC: *the theme from 'Doctor Who is performed by Keff McCulloch and included on 'The World of BBC TV Themes , available from record shops on LP, cassette and CD*
●CEEFAX SUBTITLES

CHAPTER 14
Ghost Light

A very big explosion. Very soon.

Although (in the chapter on *Battlefield*) I've discussed my exhaustion with fighting a system that just didn't understand science fiction, *Ghost Light* showed a way forward out of the trap. It suggested an approach to **Doctor Who** which would have allowed us to spin proper science fiction stories yet guarantee they were well executed on-screen.

The crucial point was that while BBC design teams were frequently baffled by science fiction – anything set in outer space or the distant future – they were the best in the world at doing *historical* drama. The Victorian setting for *Ghost Light* would prove wonderfully successful and I would begin to think about doing a season of all historical stories.

Ghost Light was the brainchild of Marc Platt. When I first sat down at my desk as script editor, I was besieged by would-be **Doctor Who** writers, many of them hardcore fans. Some of them were fellow BBC workers. Marc fell into both these categories.

He loved **Doctor Who** and knew the show intimately; and he worked at the BBC, in a bureaucratic niche entitled Radio Programme Index where his labours, endlessly cataloguing radio transmissions, were worthy of a story by Borges. But Marc immediately distinguished himself from the usual writers who were submitting unsolicited material. He scored a lot of points because, while his writing might have been informed by a deep love and knowledge of the show, it wasn't constricted or crippled by it like most fan offerings. It displayed real talent. So much so that I invited Marc in for a chat.

And it was only when he sat down in the office that Marc revealed that he was a fellow worker in the BBC hive. This scored him even more points, because most aspiring **Doctor Who** writers would have assumed that being in the Corporation would put them on an inside track. Some had even sent me scripts in the internal post, thinking this added to their cachet. Marc had taken the opposite tack, concealing his affiliation until his work had earned him an invitation to talk to us. I thought this was classy behaviour and was duly impressed.

The story Marc had sent in was called 'Shrine'. It was set in Russia in the early nineteenth century, after the time of Napoleon, and showed the influence of Tolstoy, Chekhov and Pushkin ('That's pretentious for you,' said Marc). Marc was an opera lover, so he'd been particularly inspired by **Eugene Onegin**, which was by Tchaikovsky from Pushkin – the Russian Shakespeare. '**Onegin** set the Russian theme off because I just loved it.'

Pushkin or no Pushkin, 'Shrine' was sufficiently impressive to draw the following letter from me:

(Addressed to Marc's flat in Aubert Park, North London)

11 February 1988

Dear Marc,

I'm sorry for the ridiculous length of time it's taken me to respond to your script *Shrine*. First, I'll give you the bad news. The script is too short of incident, lacks development of story and is extremely under-length. On top of that, the 1988 season of **Doctor Who** is fully commissioned.

However, I was very impressed with *Shrine*. When I read your storyline *Cat's Cradle*, I was aware of a powerful imagination and a gift for imagery. Now you've demonstrated that you can write dialogue and do the other basics involved in constructing a television script.

There is no guarantee that there will be another season of **Doctor Who** after 1988 and there is certainly no guarantee I will continue as Script Editor. But if, despite all these reservations, you are still interested in coming in for an informal chat, why don't you ring the **Doctor Who** office on 01-576-7366. The secretary you'll speak to will be Kate Easteal. Explain that I asked you to ring and she will either put you through to me if I'm in the office or make an appointment if I'm not.

Looking forward to hearing from you.

Yours sincerely,

Andrew Cartmel

I wasn't the first script editor to sense that Marc had talent, and the peculiar knack that might make for a really good **Doctor Who** writer. The first piece of writing he'd ever sent in to the show had elicited a letter from the legendary **Doctor Who** script editor (and writer) Robert Holmes, who had said, 'Of the many unsolicited scripts I receive every year, yours was the only one of any merit whatsoever.' Holmes gave him a list of things to read but moved on from the job before he could get any further with commissioning Marc. Several such near misses ensued.

Then Marc approached me.

Wednesday 2 March 1988. This was the day Ben and I went on the Dalek recce at the school in Macbeth Street. Two hours later, we were back in Union House meeting a prospective new writer, who was Marc Platt. Marc said he didn't like *Dragonfire* much. *Dragonfire* was Ian Briggs' script, which was transmitted as the last story of last season. Marc was a pleasant-faced, bald young man. The slightly predatory jut of his ears made me think of an amiable Caliban. He sat in my office at the BBC building in Shepherd's Bush, beaming at Ben and I. Marc was a bizarrely talented writer and we were auditioning him as a possible for the next season – assuming that there would be a next season, and that I would have anything to do with it (that eternal television mantra).

'Let me be more specific about that,' said Marc. 'I didn't like *Dragonfire* except for that wonderful final scene of Sylvester's, with lines like "days like crazy paving".'

'You've said the right thing,' said Ben glancing at me, his eyebrows at a sardonic angle, 'He wrote that.'

I immediately got Marc to come up with ideas for the show. His next effort was *Cat's Cradle*, a story which featured the TARDIS turned inside out and a monster called the Process – which was rather ill-defined for a **Doctor Who** villain. I told Marc gently, 'Just the first episode of *Cat's Cradle* would use up the entire year's budget,' and he indefatigably set to work on another idea.

This proved to be *Lungbarrow*, which is in some ways a lost classic of **Doctor Who** to be set beside Douglas Adams' *Shada* (though none of 'Lungbarrow' was actually filmed; Marc eventually turned it into a novel). Coming on like an unholy hybrid of Mervyn Peake and Agatha Christie, it featured the Doctor's return to his ancestral home on Gallifrey, the titular Lungbarrow, which was no ordinary house. One of Marc's notes accompanying a revised draft of the story read, 'The furniture is getting more aggressive.' More aggressive furniture was just what we needed, because

Marc's early work tended to be long on mood, philosophy and wit and short on action sequences.

Lungbarrow would have been another plank in our campaign to reinvest the Doctor with stature and mystery, and redeem him from being merely a flunky of the Time Lord hierarchy. Marc had the ideal imagination to be set loose on this theme and he was soon dreaming up a cobwebbed blend of suspense and mystery.

But, despite our best efforts, *Lungbarrow* remained somewhat abstract and esoteric, and John Nathan-Turner was right when he persuaded us to set it aside. By this time, I wanted very much to get Marc writing for the show, so I had an alternative ready to offer John. 'Let's take all the best elements from *Lungbarrow* and put them in a Victorian setting.' This was the genesis of *Ghost Light* and it was an inspired notion because, when given the familiar reference points of an historical Earth setting, all the weirdness of *Lungbarrow* suddenly became focused and gained power.

And the Victorian era was ideal because it also inspired some of Marc's finest writing.

The resulting script, which was brilliant, did however inspire a certain amount of awe and bafflement though. In fact, it was considered positively hallucinatory compared to your average television drama, or even your average **Doctor Who**.

When we sat down for the first read-through in North Acton, Sylvia Sims smiled and leaned over to Marc and said, 'What have you been sprinkling on your cornflakes, then?' Marc blushed at the ensuing general laughter and said, 'Nothing, nothing, really. It all just came into my head quite naturally.' Which was absolutely true. Marc wasn't even a drinker. He just possessed an innate visionary quality.

We had Alan Wareing as our director again for *Ghost Light*, which was a real stroke of luck, or synchronicity. Alan would do a superb job for us, aided by an exceptionally able team. Ken Trew's costumes were first rate and Nick Somerville's sets were staggeringly good – in both cases, our strategy to go Victorian came up trumps. But, for my money, the real hero of the crew was lighting director Henry Barber. Henry had saved *The Greatest Show in the Galaxy*, and on *Ghost Light* he showed what he was capable of, which was brilliance – expressed in murk, gloom and shadows.

Alan's tenacity and intelligence and continuous striving for quality was brought to bear on *Ghost Light* immediately. As we went into rehearsals he was on the phone to Marc frequently. Marc grins, remembering it. 'I don't think he understood the script fully, but who did? He was striving hard to do it justice and was always asking if he was getting it right.' In fact, Alan was a dream director for a writer to work with. One day, he called me into the office and told me about his plans for the maids in the house. The script called for them to emerge at nightfall, just as the clock in the hallway strikes six, appearing from alcoves and cupboards in the wall. Alan said that instead of simply making their entrance by walking, he wanted to have the maids slide out from their recesses in an unearthly fashion, using a kind of skateboard device (he had just been watching **The Blues Brothers** where there's a similar scene).

Ghost Light is the jewel in the crown of the Seventh Doctor's adventures. It begins in a moody, convincing fashion and seldom sets a foot wrong. Marc immediately stakes out the territory of the story, weird menace and witty Victorian tropes. The housekeeper, Mrs Pritchard (Sylvia Syms), presents a tray to an unseen captive creature behind a sliding panel. 'I've brought your dinner – and your copy of **The Times**.' The TARDIS appears and the Doctor and Ace step out into one of the creepiest, funniest and most effective **Doctor Who** stories ever.

Sylvester never looked better than he does in this story, dressed in 'dark Doctor' mode in his chocolate brown jacket. And the same is true of Sophie. Ken Trew continued the trend with her costumes he began on *Survival* and her outfit reveals just how lovely she is, instead of concealing her in the shapeless swathes of a bomber jacket. Sophie seems to be reaching a new maturity, along with Ace. As they look around the room where the TARDIS has materialised, the Doctor and Ace are under observation, although this is staged too subtly, with just the glowing eye of the rocking horse to clue the audience in.

By now, Sylvester and Sophie had both evolved into their roles. The Doctor had his humour and mystery and core of immense strength. Ace was gutsy, had her own street-level wit and humour and, above all, was intelligent. Unlike other companions, she didn't need to receive constant words-of-one-syllable explanations. Instead, she's always guessing, anticipating, meeting the Doctor halfway. 'He's a Neanderthal, isn't he?' she says. 'Is it a race memory?' Or, elsewhere, 'This is a stone spaceship.' And in the opening scenes, when they find a snuff box lying on the floor and the Doctor points a device at it, provoking a sinister clicking, she immediately gets the point. 'It's radioactive!' Then she asks a highly sensible question, 'Is it safe?' And the Doctor's response was one of my own public safety warnings. 'There is no safe level,' he says bluntly.

As the Doctor and Ace prowl the house, we're treated to Mark Ayres' best score for the show. The theme for Redvers Fenn-Cooper is a particular delight, with its hint of the darkest jungles, or rather of the Victorian fantasy of the darkest jungles. Redvers is a fantastic character, beautifully played by

Michael Cochrane. Like all the actors in this notable cast, he could relate to the script and his performance is grounded in familiar reference points (plucky explorers, the Empire, etc). This was the great joy of our Victorian setting. 'Damn tsetse flies,' mutters Redvers as the radiation counter buzzes at his back. Then he brandishes a gun at the Doctor who coolly asks, 'Is that a Chinese fowling piece?' – a line I asked Marc to put in as a reference to *The Talons of Weng-Chiang*.

After they have disarmed him, Redvers is taken away by the denizens of the house, crying 'I don't want to go back to the interior' – an especially poignant plea from a man who is a prisoner in his own mind.

The sets for *Ghost Light* are faultless and they are moodily lit and beautifully shot. The rich darkness and powerful atmosphere make me wonder how *The Happiness Patrol* might have turned out if Henry Barber had been involved.

And inhabiting this shadowy world is a wonderful cast of characters brought to life by a dream cast. Katharine Schlesinger's Gwendoline is a beautiful young woman with an unsettling hint of something strange about her. She's a foil for Ace and when they both dress for dinner in gentlemen's suits the whole story moves into another gear. We're not in Kansas anymore, nor even in the usual West London mindset of a **Doctor Who** story.

Katharine Schlesinger also perches at a piano and does a marvellous performance of a song, 'That's the way to the zoo. The monkey house is nearly full but there's room enough for you.' She sings beautifully but the lyrics are chilling in view of what is about to happen to the dogmatic clerical bigot, Reverend Matthews (John Nettleton). He ends up de-evolved into a hairy simian brute, then killed, stuffed and mounted in a glass case with a label reading 'Homo Victorianus Ineptus'. ('I think I'm going to throw up,' says Ace when she sees this nasty piece of taxidermy.)

But the song Katharine sings is also a remarkable piece of synchronicity in other ways, capturing the evolutionary theme of *Ghost Light* in exactly the peculiar Victorian manner the story requires. And it's a genuine period song, provided for Marc by the BBC Gramophone Library, who took pains to provide the perfect piece.

Other stalwarts in the cast include Ian Hogg's Josiah, master of the house and Gwendoline's guardian; there's a suggestion of a wonderfully unwholesome relationship between her and her 'uncle'. Frank Windsor plays the obtuse Inspector Mackenzie, who is the occasion for a lot of terrific dialogue. 'Now, Inspector, perhaps you can help us with our enquiries,' says the Doctor. Or the terrifically gruesome wisecrack where he's referred to as 'The cream of Scotland Yard' after Light has reduced him to primordial soup.

Light is played in a suitably eerie and mad fashion by John Hallam, in a spectacularly operatic costume courtesy of Ken Trew. (Ken's work is so good on this story that one can only wonder what the Haemovores in *The Curse of Fenric* might have looked like with sympathetic lighting and proper movement.)

Throughout the story Marc's dialogue is a delight and a marvel. Josiah tells the Doctor, 'I'm as human as you are.' And the Doctor says, 'Yes,' with deep, laconic irony. Similar witty double meanings ripple under the scene where Josiah exclaims 'I must change' and Ace observes 'He sounded a little husky' as Josiah flees upstairs to change into a new form and abandon the husk of his old body. When Josiah tries to bribe him into becoming his hired executioner, the Doctor says 'I'm not interested in money… How much?' When Josiah says 'Five thousand pounds,' the Doctor whistles and says, 'That's what I call Victorian value…'

It's like the Marx Brothers meet **Alice in Wonderland** with a hefty dose of satirical science fiction. Indeed Marc tips his hat to Douglas Adams when the Doctor remarks, 'Who said Earthmen never invite their ancestors around to dinner?' But I think it's Douglas Adams fans who should be doffing their caps to Marc. Who else could come up with lines like, 'He knows as much about [that spaceship] as a hamburger does about the Amazon desert,' a densely packed philosophical joke with real bite. And a line that Sylvester was delighted to deliver. Sylv loved it, and he got it. Marc had written a great role for him and the Doctor comes across as powerful and strange. 'Doctor, where have you been?' 'Where haven't I been?' Nimrod the Neanderthal (Carl Forgione) immediately recognises the stature of this stranger when the Doctor hands him a cave bear's tooth, a potent totem.

Other dialogue highlights include 'Gone to see a man about a god' and 'It's very, very old. Maybe even older' and 'There go the rungs in his evolutionary ladder.' Marc also has a gift for terse plot summary: 'A very big explosion. Very soon.'

Ghost Light isn't perfect. Now and then the special effects fall a little short of the mark. The video effects that pass for lightning on a stormy night remain as unconvincing as ever, though there is some good video work later, such as when the character of Light zaps one of the maids and she turns blue. The only traditional monsters in the stories, inserted largely at John's insistence, are the ambulatory husks in the basement. They lurch around unconvincingly, despite one of them having an excellent insect head sculpted by Mike Tucker (which now resides in Mike's kitchen). The husks are redeemed though, by the fact that they are dressed, surreally, in Victorian gentlemen's evening garb.

But these are minor flaws. *Ghost Light* was the closest we came to a perfect story. As our final night in the studio drew towards a close, Kate Easteal came to find me in the control room. She gestured for silence as she led me through a shadowy labyrinth above the studio floor. We came to an observation gallery. There in the dark, glass walled room were crouched dozens of figures. Young men and women, intently watching the goings on down below, studio lights reflected on their faces.

'Fans,' whispered Kate.

7.35pm
Doctor Who

starring **Sylvester McCoy**.
Catflap
Part one of a three-part adventure by Rona Monro. A contemporary Earth setting is again much easier for the BBC designers to achieve on the programme's budget. We do still end up in a quarry though.

Woman.....KATHLEEN BIDMEAD
Ace.................SOPHIE ALDRED
The Master...ANTHONY AINLEY
Paterson.......JULIAN HOLLOWAY
Stuart...................SEAN OLIVER
Harvey.............NORMAN PACE
Len....................GARETH HALE
Ange....................KATE EATON
Karra.............LISA BOWERMAN
Shreela...SAKUNTALA RAMANEE
Midge................WILL BARTON
Derek...................DAVID JOHN
Theme music composed by
RON GRAINER
Incidental music DOMINIC GLYNN
Costume designer KEN TREW
Script editor ANDREW CARTMEL
Designer NICK SOMERVILLE
Producer JOHN NATHAN-TURNER
Director ALAN WAREING
•CEEFAX SUBTITLES

7.35pm
Doctor Who

starring **Sylvester McCoy**.
Catflap
Part two of a three-part adventure by Rona Munro.

Like all the other new writers during the Cartmel era, Rona Munro brings a fresh new approach to *Doctor Who*.

Paterson......JULIAN HOLLOWAY
The Master....ANTHONY AINLEY
Ace.................SOPHIE ALDRED
Shreela...SAKUNTALA RAMANEE
Midge................WILL BARTON
Derek...................DAVID JOHN
Karra.............LISA BOWERMAN
Incidental music DOMINIC GLYNN
Stunt arranger PAUL HEASMAN
Make-up designer JOAN STRIBLING
Script editor ANDREW CARTMEL
Designer NICK SOMERVILLE
Producer JOHN NATHAN-TURNER
Director ALAN WAREING
•CEEFAX SUBTITLES

7.35pm
Doctor Who

starring **Sylvester McCoy**.
Catflap
Final part of an three-part adventure by Rona Munro.

Somewhere the tea's getting cold.

The Master....ANTHONY AINLEY
Midge................WILL BARTON
Paterson......JULIAN HOLLOWAY
Derek...................DAVID JOHN
Ace.................SOPHIE ALDRED
Shreela...SAKUNTALA RAMANEE
Karra.............LISA BOWERMAN
Squeak................ADELE SILVA
Neighbour....MICHELLE MARTIN
Incidental music DOMINIC GLYNN
Visual effects designer
MALCOLM JAMES
Script editor ANDREW CARTMEL
Designer NICK SOMERVILLE
Producer JOHN NATHAN-TURNER
Director ALAN WAREING
•CEEFAX SUBTITLES

CHAPTER 15
Survival

Down the plughole without a paddle.

Although *Survival* was made before *Ghost Light*, it was to be the last story transmitted and we were well aware of this when we were shooting it. And we were also keenly aware that *Survival* might be the last **Doctor Who** for a long time. Perhaps even forever.

This gave the story an elegiac quality. But it also had a further edge of poignant finality for me. I felt that *Survival* was of the highest calibre in its script, it was well directed and it had a strong and talented cast. If we couldn't make a wholly successful **Doctor Who** story with these ingredients, then I was beginning to feel we never would.

And, to be candid, the version of *Survival* that ended up on our screens was not wholly successful. The old problems of costumes and special effects were knocking at our door again.

Friday 14 August 1987. The day after we finished shooting *Dragonfire*, I attended a lunch thrown by the BBC for the writers on this year's writers' workshop (the course I tried to get Ben Aaronovitch on). I was introduced to Winsome Pinnock, one of the writers, a woman with regal features. She smiled as the introductions were made until she heard that I was the script editor on **Doctor Who**. Then she got away pronto and swept off with the guy from Special Features.

Next I was introduced to Mina Parisella (from Liverpool) and Rona Munro (from Edinburgh) who, in contrast to the previous writer, simultaneously screamed with delight when **Doctor Who** was mentioned. That was more like it.

Wednesday 9 October 1987. Rona, a brilliant and very funny young Scots playwright came into my office for a chat. If we'd had more time and more slots I'd have asked her to do a **Doctor Who** then and there. As I showed her out of the building we talked about her play, **Baby Minder**. Rona was wearing a rucksack.

Meanwhile, back in the office, I discovered there was a move afoot to make a **Doctor Who** feature film. John Nathan-Turner was on the phone to Chris Clough, talking about the people who were going to make the film. 'They've done horror stuff. 'April the 13th' or something. They sent me a cassette. Not my kind of thing. People getting their stomachs cut open. But well done.'

Tuesday 15 December 1987. I went to the Theatre Upstairs at the Royal Court to see Rona Munro's play **The Way to Go Home**, inspired by disturbing true events she experienced as a woman travelling alone in Turkey. The Theatre Upstairs is a small space and when the lights went up I immediately spotted in the audience a Turkish ex-girlfriend of mine. We said hello, what a coincidence, and it's nice to talk to her, but my girlfriend and her boyfriend couldn't get us separated quickly enough. Both the jealous type, I guess. My Turkish ex-girlfriend is beautiful, intelligent, funny and we were together for a year or two. And yet the sight of her left me strangely unmoved. Maybe I wanted to forget the person I was when I was with her.

The Way to Go Home was a further hint of Rona's considerable talent. She would go on to write award-winning plays and be commissioned to write movies, the summit of achievement for a screenwriter. She wrote **Ladybird Ladybird** for Ken Loach and a German film called **Aimée & Jaguar**.

Rona is a brilliant writer and her script for *Survival* was full of wit and intelligence but it was also good strong **Doctor Who**. Along with Ben and Marc Platt, Rona was the only writer with any real affinity or fondness for science fiction. She was science fiction literate and although her early work had tended to imagery and impressionism (magic realism, I suppose), she quickly developed a formidable facility for telling an effective adventure story.

In discussing the kind of storytelling we needed, I suggested she look at Tintin. I believe that Hergé's comic strip is a model of clear, concise and gripping storytelling, with rich plot, adroit characterisation and plenty of humour.

Rona just laughed. 'I never could take Tintin seriously. With that haircut and those trousers. He's such a wimp.'

Rona and I became good friends when my girlfriend Kate Druce and I went up to the Edinburgh festival and stayed with her and her boyfriend Sandy Draper (nicknamed Cindy Dripper at school). We hit it off and there was a crew of us who spent the next two Hogmanays (New Years) together in an assortment of freezing cottages. I remember sitting in the lounge of one such on the Isle of Skye, seeing in 1989, when I found myself taking a solo stand, arguing against an entire troupe of fast-witted, acerbic Scottish feminist comedians about censorship.

Survival was 1989's all-location three-parter, the Yin to the Yang of *Ghost Light*'s all-studio three-parter. John was still ingeniously turning what was officially the budget for a single six-parter into two three-part stories. He wanted to do this because six-part stories were unwieldy, and it was also enormously beneficial to me, since it allowed me the diversity of four writers a year instead of just three.

It also allowed me to commission Rona. The script that developed in discussions with her was called, at one point, *Cat Flap*, a title which would have been brilliant, though it would inevitably have been much misunderstood by fans. What Rona was getting at was a phenomenon known to anyone who's ever had a cat flap. You get all sorts of things coming in through it, unwanted, uninvited creatures…

And the notion was that someone has created a cat flap that opens onto the Earth, allowing unpleasant alien predators access.

John was open, as ever, to giving new talent a chance and, after meeting with Rona and watching her story evolve, he agreed to commission her. However, as a kind of insurance policy on an unproven writer, he wanted to involve a tried and tested **Doctor Who** villain. So we had to incorporate into the story the Master (Anthony Ainley), an evil renegade Time Lord – unlike Sylvester's benign renegade Time Lord. Being a realist, Rona didn't object to having an established **Doctor Who** villain grafted onto her story and would actually make good use of the character of the Master.

Survival would begin and end in an Earth setting, a very mundane setting. In fact, Ace's old stomping ground of Perivale, a suburb of west London. Ian Briggs had established Perivale as a kind of hell of boredom from which Ace had been eager to escape. In fact, it's a perfectly agreeable place, leafy and green, and I felt a bit bad for the abuse it receives in *Survival*. Here in Perivale, Ace and the Doctor would discover that Ace's old friends were the victims of alien aggressors. The intelligent, savage Cheetah People had found access to our world through the assistance of animals who looked just like domestic cats. These 'Kitlings' (a great name coined by Rona) manifested telepathic powers. They were the biological equivalent of the matter transmitters in *Remembrance of the Daleks* or *The Greatest Show in the Galaxy*.

The Cheetah People and the Kitlings and their chosen prey (human beings and the odd Time Lord or two) had a rather complex, symbiotic relationship which also involved the Cheetah People's unstable volcanic planet. This all seemed clear enough to Rona and me as we evolved the script, stage by stage, but it aroused a certain amount of bafflement from the production crew and I ended up writing a long memo to Alan's team giving the natural history of the Cheetah People, the Kitlings and their world.

In the script itself, some of the more complex issues are made clear in some pithy, evocative dialogue. The Cheetah People, the Doctor and the Master are among those who have been teleported by the Kitlings and find themselves trapped on an alien planet. But the Kitlings can't take them away again, it's a one-way teleportation. The Doctor grasps why: 'They can only return home with their prey,' he says.

Rona then shapes the solution with neat ingenuity. 'We need an animal whose home is Earth,' says the Doctor. The Master overhears him and promptly captures Midge, a teenager who is indeed turning into an animal under the influence of the planet, and uses him to return to Earth.

Survival has a lot going for it. For one thing, Sylvester was never better. Perhaps responding to a script by a Scots writer (and a brilliant Scots writer at that) and a story that is rooted more in real emotions than in science fiction abstractions, he gives a faultless performance.

We were also lucky enough to have Alan Wareing directing. Alan had earned my respect with the good work he'd done on *The Greatest Show in the Galaxy* and it was a relief to know he was going to be responsible for two stories this season. Alan used the word 'achieve' a lot; he was always seeking to achieve more in the stories he directed for us, and it showed. When he first read the *Survival* scripts, he actually went to the zoo to look at cheetahs, which is rather more than Rona or I ever did.

Episode one of *Survival* begins strongly with adroit, atmospheric music from Dominic Glynn and a deceptively peaceful, normal urban setting as a man washing his car is attacked. The fact that we don't see the assailant is very effective. Alan Wareing stages the sequence extremely well, with the car wash bucket being knocked over as visual counterpoint to the violent abduction.

Then the Doctor and Ace appear and we immediately know that this innocent, mundane environment is going to be the setting for some kind of unearthly adventure. These opening scenes are full of promise. There is a suspenseful undercurrent of anticipation, Sylvester and Sophie have never been better, and the characterisation and dialogue are superb.

Things go off the rails rather soon, though, when the first Kitling appears. The Kitlings are supposed to look just like ordinary black cats. Rona and I had imagined when the script was being written that real cats would be used. But cats, unlike dogs, are considered hard to train and unreliable for filming. So the fatal decision was made to create an animatronic cat for the show.

'The reason they went for the animatronic cat,' said Mike Tucker, 'was because of a show starring Norman Lovett called **I, Lovett**. That show featured an animatronic dog that everybody was very impressed by. That's why Malcolm James got the gig on *Survival*. He'd done **I, Lovett**. But the problem is that a dog is at least twice the size of a cat. An animatronic cat is way too small. You can't get your hand into the head to operate it or even do the movements of the body properly by hand. With hindsight we could have built a cat that was twice life size and used it for the close-up shots, where there's nothing to give reference to the distortion in scale. But that's with hindsight.'

If the animatronic cat failed to convince, and it definitely did, it was not for lack of trying. I know that Paul McGuiness, one of the visual effects assistants and a highly talented designer, worked furiously all night trying to get the damned thing to work, to make it look good. But he never really stood a chance. A cat is one of the most difficult things to render animatronically. Even today you can see in shows like **Sabrina the Teenage Witch** that it still hasn't been remotely achieved.

The surrealist comedian Harry Hill has a cat sidekick called Stufa. The whole point about Stufa is that it is the phoniest-looking hand puppet possible. And when I see the animatronic black cat in *Survival* I am irresistibly reminded of Stufa. On the first day of shooting, we had so much trouble with this animatronic cat that we ended up in desperation asking some local kids for a real black cat, and they found us one, too, though I don't think any of the footage of it survived into the show.

Even worse than the animatronic cat are the two cat corpses the show calls for – the dead 'Tiger' in the grocery shop in episode one and the equally dead kitten who belonged to Squeak in episode three. Not the slightest feeling of realism is achieved with these cat cadavers. They just look like discarded fluffy toys and inspire not shock or sadness but simply gales of laughter. In fact, Mike Tucker had put a lot of work into coming up with a convincing dead version of Tiger using real butcher's shop offal and a corpse fashioned from the same mould used to create the animatronic cat. He apparently succeeded too well because the result was deemed too grisly to use.

Despite all the special effects problems, *Survival* was still a classic story, added to immeasurably by Dominic's masterful music score. But for me the mainstay of the show's strength is Rona's writing. The script is full of humour ('Down the plughole without a paddle') and good, subtle, elliptical dialogue: 'They're always fixed anyway, those machines,' says Ace as she produces a handful of coins – implying, in fact, that's she's just robbed the gambling machine in the pub. Or when Ange (Kate Eaton), an old friend of Ace's, is bemused by the Doctor's cryptic mutterings and says simply, 'Is he…?' and Ace quickly shakes her head no. The unspoken question being, is this guy in fact insane?

It wasn't surprising that Rona wrote strong, vivid female characters. But she also wrote very knowingly about the rigidly masculine, desperately rationalistic Sergeant Paterson (Julian Holloway) who teaches self-defence at the youth club. 'Ever heard of survival of the fittest?' says Paterson, introducing the theme of the story.

Of course, all this brilliance goes swirling down the drain when the Cheetah People actually turn up, looking like giant teddy bears.

It helps a little that they're on horseback (Rona was thinking of how powerful **Planet of the Apes** had been, with the apes on horseback, hunting down humans) and there are some good sound effects and there's a well-staged

I felt these costumes were a complete failure because they were cute and cuddly instead of menacing. They should have been more like Mags in full werewolf mode in *The Greatest Show in the Galaxy*

Photograph courtesy of Ian Briggs

Sophie with two 'haemovores' (vampires by any other name…)

Photograph courtesy of Mike Tucker

Myself, Sophie in costume, writer Marc Platt and special effects
wizard Mike Tucker on the *Ghost Light* set

Outside the 'Acton Hilton', the BBC Rehearsal Rooms: Susie Brazier and Ian Briggs in the rear, Sophie Aldred and special effects genius Lindsay MacGowan in the front, and me

Above, left: On location for *The Greatest Show in the Galaxy* with the hippie bus in a quarry

Above, right: Me wearing a very silly Dalek hat in the **Doctor Who** production office. This garish red painted inner sanctum was JN-T's lair and was decorated with **Doctor Who** paraphernalia

John Nathan-Turner, myself and Stephen Wyatt in the TARDIS control room during *Paradise Towers*

A fetching Sophie Aldred on location for *Silver Nemesis*, reclining beside the beautiful retro ghetto-blaster built for her by Mike Tucker

Sylvester and Sophie on location for *The Curse of Fenric*

Early publicity shot of Sophie in costume as Ace

Alan Wareing and JN-T keep a watchful eye on the monitor
during the shooting of *Survival*

Sylvester and Sophie on location for *Siver Nemesis*

Stephen Mansfield and Ken Trew help Raymond Trickett into his Ancient Haemovore costume.

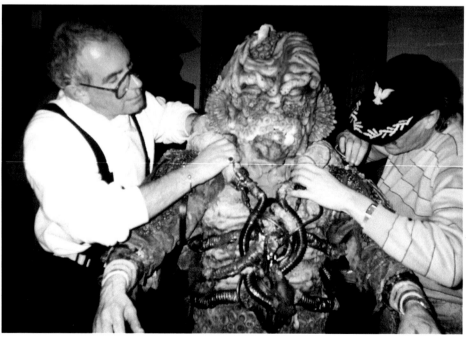

The mask was designed by Susan Moore and Stephen Mansfield

chase in the playground with Ace dodging around slides and swings. But none of it is enough to compensate for those fatally cuddly costumes. As soon as I saw them, my heart sank and I knew we'd had it. The worst parts of the costumes were the hands, or paws. Where they should have been lean, skinny, menacing talons they were instead chubby cumbersome and rather endearing. In fact Mike Tucker told me the hands were built around gardening gloves, 'And the feet are Wellington boots.'

Rona and I had originally intended the Cheetah People to be very humanoid, with the minimum of make-up. They would have had fangs, talons, contact lenses, possibly pointed ears and whiskers and perhaps some trace of fur on their bodies. This was all part of my policy to have the monsters in our stories as near to ordinary humans as possible, because we couldn't rely on costumes, make-up or special effects to deliver the goods on anything more emphatically alien. But John was onto me, and he insisted that we should have 'proper monsters'. The Cheetah People would be full-blown creature costumes instead of sparingly applied prosthetics. And as soon as that decision was made, we were dead in the water.

If only the Cheetah People had looked like Mags in *The Greatest Show in the Galaxy*. If only the animatronic cat had been replaced with footage of a real one…

Or, if it had been ten years later, we could have used CGI. This is one area where computer effects could have saved the day. If the Cheetah People had been imaginatively evoked as a computer-generated effect they would have allowed *Survival* to develop from a brilliant script to a brilliant show. As it is, we had a brilliant script but an uneven show.

So, at the end of episode one, Ace is captured by a teddy bear on horseback and spirited off to another planet.

In the early stages of discussions with Rona, I'd been hoping for an Earth-based story, for all the usual reasons of wanting to avoid a phoney alien environment. John insisted on another planet, just as he'd insisted on full-on monster suits for the Cheetah People. But unlike the Cheetah suits, the planet location wasn't a complete debacle.

Thanks to Alan Wareing's knack for strong visuals, Warmwell Quarry in Dorset manages to look interesting and passably alien. The video-processed pink sky, actually something I'd lobbied for, is never especially convincing though. And the highly artificial trickling of video smoke which are supposed to signify volcanoes could hardly look any more fake. There is, however, a great scene where the Doctor and Sergeant Paterson ride along through this desert landscape on horseback and Dominic Glynn provides some splendid

Spaghetti Western music to accompany them. Indeed, Dominic's music goes a long way to providing the menace the Cheetah People don't provide. The score is a real asset.

Rona had imagined the planet as a world that corrupts, seduces and entraps: 'This place bewitches you.' Anyone who stays there long enough begins to manifest the beast within. The descent into animal nature affects all the characters, and it's one of the strengths of the story. The Doctor, Ace, Midge and the Master all look terrific as they descend into savagery. The fangs and contact lenses are fine. There should have been a convergence between this make-up and a more extreme version of it for the Cheetah people.

As it is, the Master is all majestic fangs and yellow eyes... but then Stufa the animatronic cat pops up again and the spell is broken.

But the script and the acting frequently rise above the limitations of the special effects. There's a touching, disturbing scene where Ace gives water to one of the Cheetah People and the creature says, 'I'm Karra. I'm your sister.' Ace begins to be seduced by the planet. 'This is good. I like feeling like this,' she says. 'I feel like I belong here.' Her slow-motion return to the wild is abetted by some fine music from Dominic Glynn and the sequence would be entirely cool, if not for the laughable Cheetah Person, who has a ruff around the neck of her fur costume that looks positively Elizabethan.

Finally the Doctor reclaims Ace, taking her back to Earth and humanity. As they leave, he shoots a marvellously cold look at Karra (Lisa Bowerman), the corruptor of Ace. This is Sylvester at his most effective.

There's a memorable scene where the Doctor gets Sergeant Paterson, Shreela (Sakuntala Ramanee) and Derek (David John) to link hands and uses Ace to teleport them from the savage volcanic world back to Perivale (she is now the 'animal whose home is Earth'). And the moment they find themselves back on those mundane urban streets Paterson looks at Derek, who is holding his hand, and shouts 'What's your game!' Paterson drops the lad's hand like a hot potato and immediately begins rationalising – 'I had a blackout' – and within seconds his old world-view is intact again.

The script for *Survival* plays a neat trick with the plotting. Just when you think the story is over, and everyone is safely returned to Earth, a whole new threat kicks in with the Master behind it and Midge as his cat's-paw (pun definitely intended). Rona's audacious climax involves the Doctor against Midge in a duel on motorcycles on Horsenden Hill.

The two bikes roar towards each other and collide in an explosion which was one of the most well-staged stunts I'd ever seen. It was achieved in post-production by Dave Chapman, our laid-back, long-haired video effects genius. 'The bikes were recorded separately. One was going one way and one was going the other. There was a predetermined spot for the explosion and that was recorded as a third element. Simple.' The trick works perfectly.

After the explosion the Doctor is apparently dead and Ace is at the mercy of a menacing all-male gang. They close in on her, threatening death and other torments and Ace cries out for help. It arrives in the shape of her sister – Karra – who drives off the men. It's an outstanding scene by Rona, ending with the death of Karra and her striking and unexpected return to human form.

After a final battle between the Doctor and the Master, the story has run its course. It's a story about the bestial nature we all share and our ambivalent feelings towards it. Rona wraps it up with brilliant double-edged dialogue. A woman (Michelle Martin) protests to the Doctor about cats running wild in the neighbourhood. 'They want the animal,' she complains, 'But do they keep it under control?'

The Doctor, who has just overcome his own animal nature says, 'Well, we try.'

As we finished our final season of **Doctor Who**, John Nathan-Turner and I were keenly aware that the show was drawing to a close. We had no idea for how long. If we'd known it would be over 15 years, we would have been shocked. But also relieved, because we were afraid it might have been forever.

For the final scene of the final story John wanted me to write some appropriate dialogue, a kind of eulogy or affectionate farewell. I came up with a voiceover, a monologue from the Doctor. I read it to Rona over the phone and she was kind enough to okay it.

As he leads Ace back to the TARDIS the Doctor says:

'There are worlds out there where the sky is burning, the sea's asleep and the rivers dream. People made of smoke and cities made of song. Somewhere there is danger and somewhere there's injustice and somewhere else the tea is getting cold...

'Come on Ace, we've got work to do.'

AFTERWORD
by Sophie Aldred

My first memory of Andrew Cartmel is of a tall lanky guy loping across the BBC North Acton rehearsal studio towards me at the end of the read through for my first **Doctor Who** story, *Dragonfire*.

'Cool outfit,' he said, passing an approving glance over my army surplus shorts, charity shop blue and white stripy T-shirt and black Doc Marten lace ups. 'Do you think that would be a good look for Ace?'

So began a truly collaborative relationship which resulted in a 'good look' and a character who, twenty six years on, I am still immensely proud to have played. Ace would simply not have happened without Andrew Cartmel.

And although he and JN-T were like chalk and cheese — one the bespectacled intellectual, his softly modulated tones talking politics and popular underground culture, the other flamboyant, Hawaiian-shirted, all eyes and teeth, fags and vodka — somehow this strange partnership engendered mutual respect and understanding.

JN-T seemed to give Andrew *carte blanche* when it came to the characterisation details, possibly because he recognised that Ace's character was one that was outside his world of show biz and glitz and very much in Andrew's of student politics and punk.

Andrew and I would keep a weather eye open for what the kids on the street were saying and doing. Andrew owned a (then) state of the art Sinclair portable computer which he carried everywhere with him and would input the latest Ace phrases we (and the writers) came up with: 'Gordon Bennet, what a bunch of spots.' 'You toe rag.' And of course the universal 'wicked!' Some had to be translated, diluted or adjusted. We couldn't fall foul of the BBC policies on swearing or religion, of course, which often proved tricky.

As a complete television newbie, I found Andrew's presence on set reassuring as he was totally supportive and appreciative of my performance. I was reminded of this recently when recording Andrew's **Big Finish** audio stories at Moat Studios. At one point I looked over to the gallery and saw Andrew leaning politely towards the director, obviously making a suggestion, giving a note, in his quiet polite way.

Suddenly I was transported back half a century: the quarry in Warmwell, Dorset, the playground in Perivale, the army camp in Crowborough. Great memories of a great collaborative few years in **Doctor Who**'s history in which, as you have just read, Andrew Cartmel played a large, creative and enduring part.

Sophie Aldred
On a train to Norwich
8 September 2013

EPILOGUE
by Andrew Cartmel

It's a brilliant summer's day in February 2001 and I've just stepped off a plane in Wellington, New Zealand. I've spent the last 25 hours literally flying halfway around the world to end up here, to script edit a new television show.

I'm working on **Dark Knight**, a sword and sorcery re-telling of the Ivanhoe legend. A taxi is taking me to my hotel and I'm staring out the window of the car, blinking in the brilliant sunlight. I ask the driver what that eerie noise is. It takes him a moment to work out what I'm talking about because he's so accustomed to it, then he tells me it's the local insects. Ten minutes later I'm stumbling into my hotel room. After all those long hours on the plane I find that the concrete floor of the hotel is heaving and swaying under my legs as if I'm still in midair. I haven't slept a wink and all I want to do is crash in bed. But there's a message from the studios. They need me out there right now, to help salvage a script.

I splash some water on my face and go down to the lobby where Keith Claxton is waiting. Keith is one of the directors on the show. He drives me out to Avalon Studios in Lower Hutt. The drive along the freeway takes us past a beautiful bay of blue water on our right, tiered green hills on our left. I'm half asleep in a car driving through paradise, thinking of a day almost 13 years ago when I was driving through west London, on the way to a location for the Dalek story. Then I was talking to Ben Aaronovitch. Now I'm talking to Keith Claxton. New collaborators, new allies.

Soon we're at the studios and I'm unlocking my office. From the window there is a gorgeous vista of blue sky and distant green headlands. I switch on my computer and open the window to breathe the clean, fresh air. Immediately some beautiful white doves land on the window sill and come into my office to make friends. Soon the office is full of birds, there's dove shit on my computer, and I'm in the thick of script conferences and rewrites.

Dark Knight will prove to be an invigorating, frustrating, challenging blend of occasionally dodgy special effects and sometimes brilliant writing… Why do I have this sense of déjà vu?

Terry Marcel, the producer, takes me down to the edit suite to watch some material. There's a blonde goddess in the lift and a dwarf in the canteen. We sit in air conditioned darkness in front of a bank of screens and watch some footage together.

The witch needs new dialogue, the werewolves are making the wrong noises and the winged monster's prosthetic hands look silly in the close ups.

Never mind, we'll get it right next season.

Assuming that there is a next season, and that I have anything to do with it (that eternal television mantra).

Andrew Cartmel
London 31 January 2005

CODA
by Andrew Cartmel

It's an unseasonably sunny autumn day here in south London. I'm listening to jazz (on vinyl, naturally) and making plans for a cruise of the Caribbean which I'll be embarking on next week.

Of course, it's a **Doctor Who** cruise.

Doctor Who never really goes away. When I first wrote an end-piece for this book, the show was just about to return to our screens after a lay-off of decades. Since then it's become an established hit again under the aegis of first Russell T. Davies and then Steven Moffat. And now **Script Doctor** is back in print and we're in the 50th year since the show first hit our screens.

So I've been invited as a guest on a tropical cruise catering to the fans of **Doctor Who** and, as soon as I get back, I've been invited to attend the BBC's official 50th anniversary celebrations. It's all happening…

When I penned the previous afterword I concentrated on describing a new TV series I'd been involved with. That's all over now, but another one is gathering on the horizon and once again my services as a writer and script editor may be called upon. We're gearing up to launch a television adaptation of **Rivers of London**, based on the bestselling series of novels by my old friend Ben Aaronovitch, concerning the division of the Metropolitan Police that deals with supernatural threats.

That's right, Ben is a now hugely successful novelist. More power to him. And my other allies and collaborators? Graeme Curry is living near Cambridge and is writing for the theatre. Ian Briggs is also working in the theatre and is contemplating a move to the countryside, possibly close to Graeme (watch out, Graeme!). Marc Platt is the mainstay of Big Finish's **Doctor Who** audio adventures, his wild imagination still fizzing away as marvellously as ever. Stephen Wyatt is an award winning radio writer and his recent brilliant plays about Raymond Chandler's experiences in Hollywood (**Double Jeopardy** and **Strangers on a Film**) are classics. Malcolm Kohll is a film and television producer currently working in South Africa on an adaptation of Deon Meyer's highly successful crime novels. Rona Munro is a leading screenwriter on acclaimed international feature films by directors like Ken Loach. Kevin Clarke has been writing for the cream of British television drama such as **Wycliffe**, **Inspector Lynley** and **The Last Detective**. Pip and Jane are reportedly still bad-mouthing me in interviews…

Long may they all thrive.

And, meanwhile, it seems **Doctor Who** will go on forever.

I certainly hope so.

Andrew Cartmel
London, 12th October 2013

DOCTOR WHO AUDITION PIECE #1
by Andrew Cartmel

(The DOCTOR is busy. MEL comes in.)

MEL	Well, I suppose it's time.
DOCTOR	Time? Strange old business time. You'd think I'd know something about it by now. A time traveller. A Time Lord. Sailing here and there on the sea of time. Swimming in it, diving in it. Sometimes almost drowning in it. But I don't know anything about it… time.
MEL	No, I meant it's time I should be going.
DOCTOR	Oh.
MEL	Time I left.
DOCTOR	Yes, you could be right. Time for you to go.
MEL	I just wanted to say…
DOCTOR	Funny old business time.
MEL	Doctor, I…
DOCTOR	Yes, well if you must go, you must go.
MEL	Before I go, I just wanted to say…
DOCTOR	No point, Mel. No point in hanging about. Wasting time.
MEL	No, before I go I wanted to say my piece…
DOCTOR	No, Mel. You wanted to say 'What a strange and exciting journey', I know, Mel. Quite right! Goodbye, Mel.
MEL	Aren't you going to at least let me say it?
DOCTOR	No, Mel
MEL	Why?
DOCTOR	No time.
MEL	Alright, you win.

DOCTOR	I do? I usually do.
MEL	Oh, shut up!
DOCTOR	In the end. Given enough time.
MEL	Leave me alone. I'm going. It's over. I've already gone.
DOCTOR	Yes, right. You have already gone. You've been gone for ages. You're still here.
MEL	Not for long
DOCTOR	But you've only just arrived. I haven't even met you yet.
MEL	Goodbye!
DOCTOR	Oh it all depends on how you look at it and who you are. Funny business time. I remember one time when you laughed. Do you remember, Mel?
MEL	Not many laughs with you. Not much fun at all.
DOCTOR	Another time you cried.
MEL	I never cried
DOCTOR	Do you remember, Mel?
MEL	I never cried.
DOCTOR	You're crying now.
MEL	I'm sorry.
DOCTOR	I'm sorry too, Mel. Think about me when you're living your life, day after day, all in a neat pattern. Think of the old man in his old phone box. His days like crazy paving.
MEL	I think I'd better be going.
DOCTOR	Going? But you've only just arrived.
MEL	I must.
DOCTOR	Must you?
MEL	It's time.
DOCTOR	I suppose it is.
MEL	Funny business time.

DOCTOR WHO AUDITION PIECE #2
by Andrew Cartmel

(The IRON WOMAN, a formidable dictator, is busy at her desk in her office. The DOCTOR enters.)

DOCTOR	Hello. I've come for a little chat
IRON WOMAN	How did you get in here? Who are you?
DOCTOR	To answer the second question first, I'm the Doctor
IRON WOMAN	Leave at once. I am the Iron Woman, dictator of ten galaxies…
DOCTOR	Oh yes. I know all that. And believe me, you need a Doctor.
IRON WOMAN	I need no-one. I have iron and I have fire. I am the great dictator.
DOCTOR	And you intend to save the universe?
IRON WOMAN	Through iron and fire I'll save it. Crush it with iron, scorch it with fire. Slaughter all living things and save it.
DOCTOR	Oh yes. Well I must say the logic of that eludes me for the minute.
IRON WOMAN	Logic would always elude you, I can see that. I can see what you are now. You're a clown, you're dressed like a clown.
DOCTOR	Actually, in my experience, the biggest clowns are the ones in uniforms.
IRON WOMAN	You've got the clown's gleam in the eye. The gleam of tears. You're a pitiful sentimental clown who cries over spilt milk
DOCTOR	And spilt blood. Right, let's get on with the consultation. How are you sleeping? Any dreams?
IRON WOMAN	I never dream when I sleep.
DOCTOR	That's because you're dreaming all the time you're awake. You know, the strange thing about you is that you're not

	really evil. Wrestling with smoke. That's what it's like. I have spent seven lifetimes wrestling with evil and just when I feel I've got my hands on it – puff! You know, wrestling with smoke.
IRON WOMAN	I don't wrestle with smoke.
DOCTOR	You do nothing else. Smoke and illusion.
IRON WOMAN	I have no illusions.
DOCTOR	That's the biggest illusion of them all. Now what exactly is it that you are scared of?
IRON WOMAN	I am scared of nothing.
DOCTOR	Oh yes. Nothing. Very terrifying, nothing.
IRON WOMAN	I mean nothing scares me.
DOCTOR	Oh! Yes, ah I see, yes. I get the drift. Nothing scares you. That's why you are the great dictator, because you are scared of nothing. That's why we have to put up with all this nonsense about blood and iron.
IRON WOMAN	Nonsense?
DOCTOR	Sit down. Right, I'll write you a prescription, so keep quiet. Now, you're badly ill. But there's still time. You've killed, but nothing compared to the killing you're planning to do. My diagnosis is this. A very bad case of the fear of nothingness. Listen to me. In the beginning there was some dust. And the dust formed a star. And the star caught fire and the fire was reflected in an ocean and out of that ocean crawled life and out of that life came you. And me. And everyone. But we are still just dust. Out of the great black nothing we came and into the great black nothing we will go. But in the meantime we have our moments. Precious moments. Few moments. No time to waste on all this blood and iron nonsense. No time for killing. No time for war. Only time for this.

DOCTOR hands IRON WOMAN her prescription

IRON WOMAN	I can't read your writing.
DOCTOR	Life. That's all it says. Life. You do understand it?
IRON WOMAN	I think so.
DOCTOR	Good. I don't like making house calls.

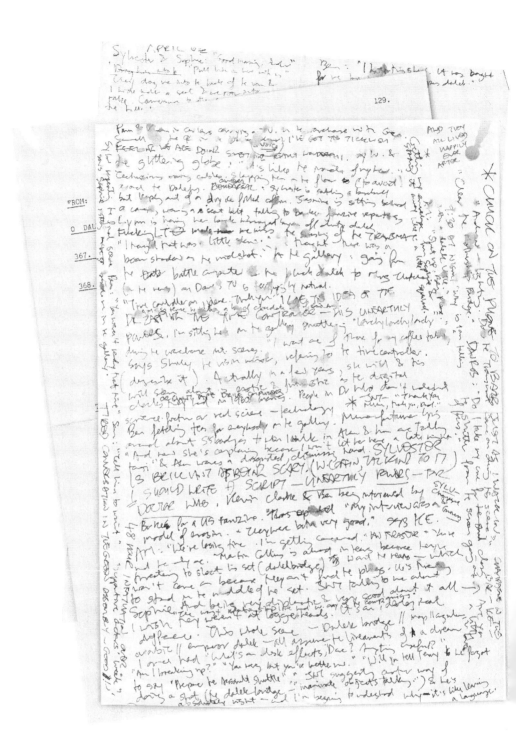